# THE O'LEARY SERIES

# Microsoft® Excel 2000

## Brief Version

**Timothy J. O'Leary**
*Arizona State University*

**Linda I. O'Leary**

**Irwin**
**McGraw-Hill**

Boston   Burr Ridge, IL   Dubuque, IA   Madison, WI   New York
San Francisco   St. Louis   Bangkok   Bogotá   Caracas   Lisbon
London   Madrid   Mexico City   Milan   New Delhi   Seoul
Singapore   Sydney   Taipei   Toronto

## McGraw-Hill Higher Education

*A Division of The McGraw-Hill Companies*

MICROSOFT® EXCEL 2000, BRIEF EDITION

Copyright © 2000 by The McGraw-Hill Companies, Inc. All rights reserved. Printed in the United States of America. Except as permitted under the United States Copyright Act of 1976, no part of this publication may be reproduced or distributed in any form or by any means, or stored in a database or retrieval system, without the prior written permission of the publisher.

This book is printed on acid-free paper.

1 2 3 4 5 6 7 8 9 0 BAN/BAN 9 0 9 8 7 6 5 4 3 2 1 0 9

ISBN 0-07-233750-8

Vice president/Editor-in-chief:   *Michael W. Junior*
Sponsoring editor:   *Trisha O'Shea*
Developmental editor:   *Stephen Fahringer*
Senior marketing manager:   *Jodi McPherson*
Senior project manager:   *Beth Cigler*
Manager, new book production:   *Melonie Salvati*
Freelance design coordinator:   *Gino Cieslik*
Cover design:   *Francis Owens*
Supplement coordinator:   *Marc Mattson*
Compositor:   *Rogondino & Associates*
Typeface:   *11/13 Century Book*
Printer:   *The Banta Book Group*

Library of Congress Catalog Card Number 99-62022

http://www.mhhe.com

THE O'LEARY SERIES

# Microsoft® Excel 2000

## *Brief Version*

**Timothy J. O'Leary**
*Arizona State University*

**Linda I. O'Leary**

**Irwin**
**McGraw-Hill**

Boston   Burr Ridge, IL   Dubuque, IA   Madison, WI   New York
San Francisco   St. Louis   Bangkok   Bogotá   Caracas   Lisbon
London   Madrid   Mexico City   Milan   New Delhi   Seoul
Singapore   Sydney   Taipei   Toronto

At McGraw-Hill Higher Education, we publish instructional materials targeted at the higher education market. In an effort to expand the tools of higher learning, we publish texts, lab manuals, study guides, testing materials, software, and multimedia products.

At **Irwin/McGraw-Hill** (a division of McGraw-Hill Higher Education), we realize that technology has created and will continue to create new mediums for professors and students to use in managing resources and communicating information with one another. We strive to provide the most flexible and complete teaching and learning tools available as well as offer solutions to the changing world of teaching and learning.

**Irwin/McGraw-Hill is dedicated to providing the tools for
today's instructors and students to successfully
navigate the world of Information Technology.**

■ **Seminar series**—Irwin/McGraw-Hill's Technology Connection seminar series offered across the country every year demonstrates the latest technology products and encourages collaboration among teaching professionals.

■ **Osborne/McGraw-Hill**—This division of The McGraw-Hill Companies is known for its best-selling Internet titles *Harley Hahn's Internet & Web Yellow Pages* and the *Internet Complete Reference*. Osborne offers an additional resource for certification and has strategic publishing relationships with corporations such as Corel Corporation and America Online. For more information visit Osborne at **www.osborne.com**.

■ **Digital solutions**—Irwin/McGraw-Hill is committed to publishing digital solutions. Taking your course online doesn't have to be a solitary venture, nor does it have to be a difficult one. We offer several solutions that will allow you to enjoy all the benefits of having course material online. For more information visit **www.mhhe.com/solutions/index.mhtml**.

■ **Packaging options**—For more about our discount options, contact your local Irwin/McGraw-Hill Sales representative at 1-800-338-3987 or visit our Web site at **www.mhhe.com/it**.

# Preface

## Goals/Philosophy

The goal of *The O'Leary Series* is to give students a basic understanding of computing concepts and to build the skills necessary to ensure that information technology is an advantage in whatever path they choose in life. Because we believe that students learn better and retain more information when concepts are reinforced visually, we feature a unique visual orientation coupled with our trademark "learn by doing" approach.

## Approach

*The O'Leary Series* is the true *step-by-step way to develop computer application skills*. The new Microsoft Office 2000 design emphasizes the step-by-step instructions with full screen captures that illustrate the results of each step performed. Each Tutorial (chapter) follows the "learn by doing" approach in combining conceptual coverage with detailed, software-specific instructions. A running case study that is featured in each tutorial highlights the real-world capabilities of each of the software applications and leads students step by step from problem to solution.

## About the Book

*The O'Leary Series* offers 2 *levels* of instruction: Brief and Introductory. Each level builds upon the previous level.

- **Brief**–This level covers the basics of an application and contains two to three chapters.

- **Introductory**–This level includes the material in the Brief text-book plus two to three additional chapters. The Introductory text prepares students for the *Microsoft Office User Specialist Exam (MOUS Certification)*.

Each tutorial features:

- **Common Office 2000 Features**–This section provides a review of several basic procedures and Windows features. Students will also learn about many of the features that are common to all Microsoft Office 2000 applications.

- **Overview**–The Overview contains a "Before You Begin" section which presents both students and professors with all the information they need to know before starting the tutorials, including hardware and software settings. The Overview appears at the beginning of each lab manual and describes (1) what the program is,

(2) what the program can do, (3) generic terms the program uses, and (4) the Case Study to be presented.

- **Working Together sections**—These sections provide the same hands-on visual approach found in the tutorials to the integration and new collaboration features of Office 2000.

- **Glossary**—The Glossary appears at the end of each text and defines all key terms that appear in boldface type throughout the tutorials and in the end-of-tutorial Key Terms lists.

- **Index**—The Index appears at the end of each text and provides a quick reference to find specific concepts or terms in the text.

## Brief Version

The Brief Version is divided into three tutorials, followed by Working Together, which shows the integration of Excel 2000 with Word 2000.

**Tutorial 1:** Your first project is to develop a forecast for the Café for the first quarter. You will learn to enter numbers, perform calculations, copy data, label rows and columns, and format entries in a spreadsheet using Excel 2000.

**Tutorial 2**: After creating the first quarter forecast for the Downtown Internet Café, you have decided to chart the sales data to make it easier to see the trends and growth patterns. You also want to see what effect a strong advertising promotion of the new Café features will have on the forecast sales data.

**Tutorial 3:** You have been asked to revise the workbook to include forecasts for the second, third, and fourth quarters. Additionally, the owner wants you to create a composite worksheet that shows the entire year's forecast and to change the data to achieve a 5 percent profit margin in the second quarter.

**Working Together:** Your analysis of sales data for the first quarter has shown a steady increase in total sales. Evan, the Café owner, has asked you for a copy of the forecast that shows the growth in Internet sales if a strong sales promotion is mounted. You will include the worksheet and chart data in a memo to the owner.

Each tutorial features:

- **Step-by-step instructions**—Each tutorial consists of step-by-step instructions along with accompanying screen captures. The screen captures represent how the student's screen should appear after completing a specific step.

- **Competencies**—Listed at the beginning of each tutorial, the Competencies describe what skills will be mastered upon completion of the tutorial.

■ **Concept Overview**–Located at the start of each tutorial, the Concept Overviews provide a brief introduction to the concepts to be presented.

■ **Concept boxes**–Tied into the Concept Overviews, the Concept boxes appear throughout the tutorial and provide clear, concise explanations of the concepts under discussion, which makes them a valuable study aid.

■ **Marginal notes**–Appearing throughout the tutorial, marginal notes provide helpful hints, suggestions, troubleshooting advice, and alternative methods of completing tasks.

■ **Case study**–The running case study carried throughout each tutorial and is based on real use of software in a business setting.

■ **End-of-tutorial material**–At the end of each tutorial the following is provided:

**Concept Summary**–This two-page spread presents a visual summary of the concepts presented in the tutorial and can be used as a study aid for students.

**Key Terms**–This page-referenced list is a useful study aid for students.

**Matching/Multiple Choice/True False Questions**

**Command Summary**–The Command Summary includes keyboard and toolbar shortcuts.

**Screen Identifications**–These exercises ask students to demonstrate their understanding of the applications by identifying screen features.

**Discussion Questions**–These questions are designed to stimulate in-class discussion.

**Hands-On Practice Exercises**–These detailed exercises of increasing difficulty ask students to create Office documents based on the skills learned in the tutorial.

**On Your Own**–These problems of increasing difficulty ask students to employ more creativity and independence in creating Office documents based on new case scenarios.

# Acknowledgments

The new edition of the Microsoft Office 2000 has been made possible only through the enthusiasm and dedication of a great team of people. Because the team spans the country, literally from coast to coast, we have utilized every means of working together including conference calls, FAX, e-mail, and document collaboration . . . we have truly tested the team approach and it works!

Leading the team from Irwin/McGraw-Hill are Kyle Lewis, Senior Sponsoring Editor, Trisha O'Shea, Sponsoring Editor, and Steve Fahringer, Developmental Editor. Their renewed commitment, direction, and support have infused the team with the excitement of a new project.

The production staff is headed by Beth Cigler, Senior Project Manager whose planning and attention to detail has made it possible for us to successfully meet a very challenging schedule. Members of the production team include: Gino Cieslik and Francis Owens, art and design, Pat Rogondino, layout, Susan Defosset and Joan Paterson, copy editing. While all have contributed immensely, I would particularly like to thank Pat and Susan . . . team members for many past editions whom I can always depend on to do a great job. My thanks also go to the project Marketing Manager, Jodi McPherson, for her enthusiastic promotion of this edition.

Finally, I am particularly grateful to a small but very dedicated group of people who helped me develop the manuscript. My deepest appreciation is to my co-author, consultant, and lifelong partner, Tim, for his help and support while I have been working on this edition. Colleen Hayes who has been assisting me from the beginning, continues to be my right arm, taking on more responsibility with each edition. Susan Demar and Carol Dean have also helped on the last several editions and continue to provide excellent developmental and technical support. New to the project this year are Bill Barth, Kathi Duggan, and Steve Willis, who have provided technical expertise and youthful perspective.

## Reviewers

We would also like to thank the reviewers for their insightful input and criticism. Their feedback has helped to make this edition even stronger.

Josephine A. Braneky, *New York City Technical College*
Robert Breshears, *Maryville University*

Gary Buterbaugh, *Indiana University of Pennsylvania*
Mitchell M. Charkiewicz, *Bay Path College*
Seth Hock, *Columbus State Community College*
Katherine S. Hoppe, *Wake Forest University*
Lisa Miller, *University of Central Oklahoma*
Anne Nelson, *High Point University*
Judy Tate, *Tarrant County Junior College*
Dottie Sunio, *Leeward Community College*
Charles Walker, *Harding University*
Mark E. Workman, *Blinn College*

Additionally, each semester I hear from students at Arizona State University who are enrolled in the Introduction to Computers course. They constantly provide great feedback from a student's perspective . . . I thank you all.

Finally, I would like to thank Keri Howard, Manager for the Coffee Plantation, for her evaluation and input into the Downtown Internet Café case study.

# Features of This Text

**Concept Boxes** identify the most important concepts in each Tutorial.

## Concept ⑤ Automatic Grammar Check

The automatic grammar-checking feature advises you of incorrect grammar as you create and edit a document, and proposes possible corrections. If Word detects grammatical errors in subject-verb agreements, verb forms, capitalization, or commonly confused words, to name a few, they are identified with a wavy green line. You can correct the grammatical error by editing it or you can display a suggested correction. Not all grammatical errors identified by Word are actual errors. Use discretion when correcting the errors. Grammar checking does not occur until after you enter punctuation or end a line.

**2** ▪ Right-click on Announcing four to display the Grammar shortcut menu.

Your screen should be similar to Figure 1–10.

suggested correction

related menu options

Grammar shortcut menu

**Tables** provide quick summaries of toolbar buttons, key terms, and procedures for specific tasks.

Yellow **Additional Information** boxes appear throughout each tutorial and explain additional uses of the application or of a specific topic.

**Figure 1–10**

A shortcut menu showing a suggested correction is displayed. The Grammar shortcut menu also includes several related menu options described below.

### Additional Information

A dimmed option means it is currently unavailable.

| Option | Effect |
|---|---|
| Ignore | Instructs Word to ignore the grammatical error in this sentence. |
| Grammar | Opens the Grammar Checker and displays an explanation of the error. |
| About this Sentence | If the Office Assistant feature is on, this option is available. It also provides a detailed explanation of the error. |

Because you cannot readily identify the reason for the error, you will open the Grammar Checker.

## Other Features

**Real World Case**—Each O'Leary Lab Manual provides students with a fictitious running case study. This case study provides students with the real-world capabilities for each software application. Each tutorial builds upon the gained knowledge of the previous tutorial with a single case study running throughout each Lab Manual.

**End-of-Chapter Material**—Each tutorial ends with a visual **Concept Summary**. This two-page spread presents a concept summary of the concepts presented in the tutorial and can be used as a study aid for

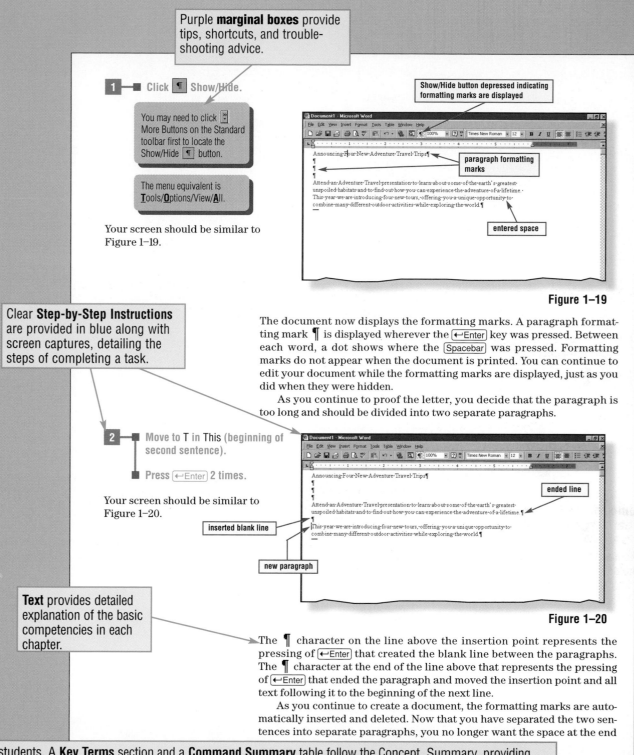

Purple **marginal boxes** provide tips, shortcuts, and trouble-shooting advice.

1 ■ Click ¶ Show/Hide.

You may need to click ⬝ More Buttons on the Standard toolbar first to locate the Show/Hide ¶ button.

The menu equivalent is **T**ools/**O**ptions/View/**A**ll.

Your screen should be similar to Figure 1–19.

Show/Hide button depressed indicating formatting marks are displayed

paragraph formatting marks

entered space

**Figure 1–19**

Clear **Step-by-Step Instructions** are provided in blue along with screen captures, detailing the steps of completing a task.

The document now displays the formatting marks. A paragraph formatting mark ¶ is displayed wherever the ⟨←Enter⟩ key was pressed. Between each word, a dot shows where the ⟨Spacebar⟩ was pressed. Formatting marks do not appear when the document is printed. You can continue to edit your document while the formatting marks are displayed, just as you did when they were hidden.

As you continue to proof the letter, you decide that the paragraph is too long and should be divided into two separate paragraphs.

2 ■ Move to T in This (beginning of second sentence).

■ Press ⟨←Enter⟩ 2 times.

Your screen should be similar to Figure 1–20.

ended line

inserted blank line

new paragraph

**Figure 1–20**

**Text** provides detailed explanation of the basic competencies in each chapter.

The ¶ character on the line above the insertion point represents the pressing of ⟨←Enter⟩ that created the blank line between the paragraphs. The ¶ character at the end of the line above that represents the pressing of ⟨←Enter⟩ that ended the paragraph and moved the insertion point and all text following it to the beginning of the next line.

As you continue to create a document, the formatting marks are automatically inserted and deleted. Now that you have separated the two sentences into separate paragraphs, you no longer want the space at the end

students. A **Key Terms** section and a **Command Summary** table follow the Concept Summary, providing a list of page-referenced terms and keyboard and toolbar shortcuts which can be a useful study aid for students. **Screen Identification, Matching, Multiple Choice**, and **True False Questions** provide additional reinforcement to the tutorial material. **Discussion Questions, Hands-on Practice Exercises**, and **On Your Own Exercises** develop critical thinking skills and offer step-by-step practice. These exercises have a rating system from Easy to Difficult and test the student's ability to apply the knowledge they have gained in each tutorial. Each O'Leary Lab Manual provides at least two **On the Web** exercises where students are asked to use the Web to solve a particular problem.

# Teaching Resources

The following is a list of supplemental material that can be used to help teach this course.

## Active Testing and Learning Assessment Software (ATLAS)

Available for The O'Leary Series is our cutting edge "Real Time Assessment" ATLAS software. ATLAS is web enabled and allows students to perform timed tasks while working live in an application. ATLAS will track how a specific task is completed and the time it takes to complete that task and so measures both proficiency and efficiency. ATLAS will provide full customization and authoring capabilities for professors and can include content from any of our application series.

## Instructor's Resource Kits

Instructor's Resource Kits provide professors with all of the ancillary material needed to teach a course. Irwin/McGraw-Hill is committed to providing instructors with the most effective instructional resources available. Many of these resources are available at our Information Technology Supersite, found at **www.mhhe.com**/**it**. Our Instructor's Resource Kits are available on CD-ROM and contain the following:

- **Diploma by Brownstone**—Diploma is the most flexible, powerful, and easy to use computerized testing system available in higher education. The Diploma system allows professors to create an exam as a printed version, as a LAN-based Online version, or as an Internet version. Diploma also includes grade book features, which automate the entire testing process.

- **Instructor's Manual**—The Instructor's Manual includes solutions to all lessons and end of the unit material, teaching tips and strategies, and additional exercises.

- **Student Data Files**—Students must have student data files in order to complete practice and test sessions. The instructor and students using this text in classes are granted the right to post student data files on any network or stand-alone computer, or to distribute the files on individual diskettes. The student data files may be downloaded from our IT Supersite at **www.mhhe.com**/**it**.

- **Series Web site**—Available at **www.mhhe.com**/**cit**/**oleary**.

## Digital Solutions

- **Pageout Lite**—This software is designed for you if you're just beginning to explore Web site options. Pageout Lite will help you to easily post your own material online. You may choose one of three templates, type in your material, and Pageout Lite will instantly convert it to HTML.

- **Pageout**—Pageout is our Course Web Site Development Center. Pageout offers a syllabus page, Web site address, Online Learning Center content, online exercises and quizzes, gradebook, discussion board, an area for students to build their own Web pages, plus all features of Pageout Lite. For more information please visit the Pageout Web site at **www.mhla.net/pageout**.

- **OLC/Series Web Sites**—Online Learning Centers (OLCs)/series sites are accessible through our Supersite at **www.mhhe.com/it**. Our Online Learning Centers/series sites provide pedagogical features and supplements for our titles online. Students can point and click their way to key terms, learning objectives, chapter overviews, PowerPoint slides, exercises, and Web links.

- **The McGraw-Hill Learning Architecture (MHLA)**—MHLA is a complete course delivery system. MHLA gives professors ownership in the way digital content is presented to the class through on-line quizzing, student collaboration, course administration, and content management. For a walk-through of MHLA, visit the MHLA Web site at **www.mhla.net**.

## Packaging Options

For more about our discount options, contact your local Irwin/McGraw-Hill sales representative at 1-800-338-3987 or visit our Web site at **www.mhhe.com/it**.

# Contents

# Introducing Common Office 2000 Features

This section will review several basic procedures and Windows features. In addition, you will learn about many of the features that are common to all Microsoft Office 2000 applications. Although Excel 2000 will be used to demonstrate how the features work, only common features will be addressed. The features that are specific to each application will be introduced individually in each tutorial.

## Turning on the Computer

If necessary, follow the procedure below to turn on your computer.

Do not have any disks in the drives when you start the computer.

**1** ■ **Turn on the power switch.** The power switch is commonly located on the back or right side of your computer. It may also be a button that you push on the front of your computer.

■ **If necessary, turn your monitor on and adjust the contrast and brightness.** Generally, the button to turn on the monitor is located on the front of the monitor. Use the dials (generally located in the panel on the front of the monitor) to adjust the monitor.

Press Tab to move to the next box.

■ **If you are on a network, you may be asked to enter your User Name and Password. Type the required information in the boxes. When you are done, press ←Enter.**

The Windows program is loaded into the main memory of your computer and the Windows desktop is displayed.

Your screen should be similar to Figure 1.

**Figure 1**

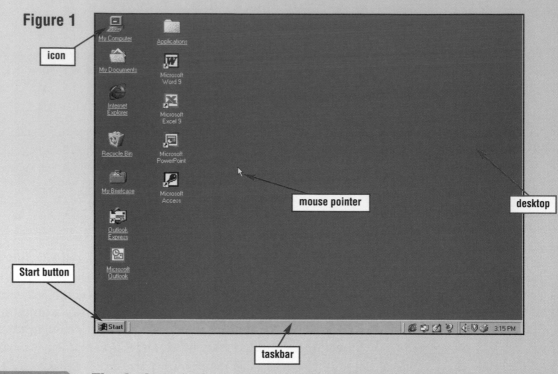

icon

mouse pointer

desktop

Start button

taskbar

If a Welcome box is displayed, click ☒ (in the upper right corner of the box) to close it.

The **desktop** is the opening screen for Windows and is the place where you begin your work using the computer. Figure 1 shows the Windows 98 desktop. If you are using Windows 95, your screen will look slightly different. Small pictures, called **icons**, represent the objects on the desktop. Your desktop will probably display many different icons than those shown here. At the bottom of the desktop screen is the **taskbar**. It contains buttons that are used to access programs and features. The **Start button** on the left end of the taskbar is used to start a program, open a document, get help, find information, and change system settings.

## Using a Mouse

If you are already familiar with using a mouse, skip to the section Loading an Office Application.

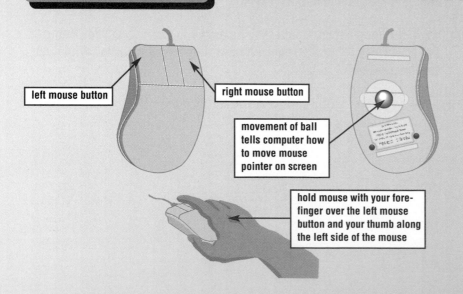

left mouse button

right mouse button

movement of ball tells computer how to move mouse pointer on screen

hold mouse with your forefinger over the left mouse button and your thumb along the left side of the mouse

The arrow-shaped symbol on your screen is the **mouse pointer**. It is used to interact with objects on the screen and is controlled by the hardware device called a **mouse** that is attached to your computer.

The mouse pointer changes shape on the screen depending on what it is pointing to. Some of the most common shapes are shown in the table below.

| Pointer Shape | Meaning |
| --- | --- |
| ⬐ | Normal select |
| 🖑 | Link select |
| ⧗ | Busy |
| ⊘ | Area is not available |

If your system has a stick, ball or touch pad, the buttons are located adjacent to the device.

On top of the mouse are two or three buttons that are used to choose items on the screen. The mouse actions and descriptions are shown in the table below.

| Action | Description |
| --- | --- |
| Point | Move the mouse so the mouse pointer is positioned on the item you want to use. |
| Click | Press and release a mouse button. The left mouse button is the primary button that is used for most tasks. |
| Double-click | Quickly press and release the left mouse button twice. |
| Drag | Move the mouse while holding down a mouse button. |

Throughout the labs, "click" means to use the left mouse button. If the right mouse button is to be used, the directions will tell you to right-click on the item.

**1** ▪ **Move the mouse in all directions (up, down, left, and right) and note the movement of the mouse pointer.**

▪ **Point to the** 🖥 **My Computer icon.**

Your screen should be similar to Figure 2.

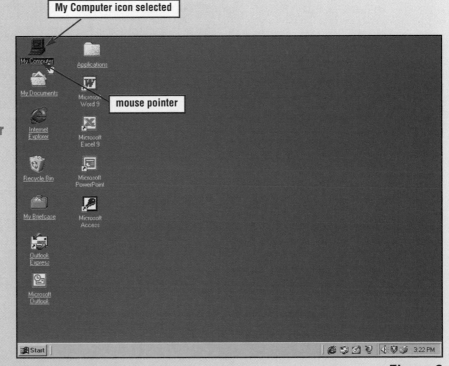

**Figure 2**

Depending on the version of Windows you are using and the setup, the mouse pointer may be ▷ and you will need to click on the icon to select it.

The pointer on the screen moved in the direction you moved the mouse and currently appears as a 🖑. The icon appears highlighted, indicating it is the selected item and ready to be used. A **ScreenTip** box containing a brief description of the item you are pointing to may be displayed.

## Loading an Office Application

There are several ways to start an Office application. One is to use the Start/New Office Document command and select the type of document you want to create. Another is to use Start/Documents and select the document name from the list of recently used documents. This starts the associated application and opens the selected document at the same time. The two most common ways to start an Office 2000 application are by choosing the application name from the Start menu or by clicking a desktop shortcut for the program if it is available.

Point to a Start menu option to select it; click it to choose it.

If you are using Windows 98, depending on your setup, you may only need to single-click the shortcut.

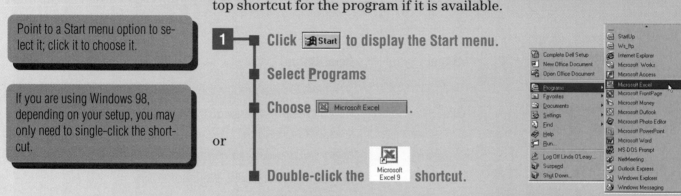

**1** ■ Click ⊞Start to display the Start menu.

■ Select **P**rograms

■ Choose [X] Microsoft Excel .

or

■ Double-click the [Microsoft Excel 9] shortcut.

After a few moments, the Excel application window is displayed, and your screen should be similar to Figure 3.

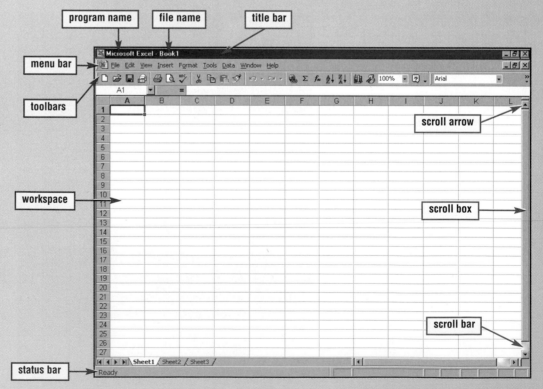

**Figure 3**

# Basic Windows Features

As you can see, many of the features in the Excel window are the same as in other Windows applications. Among those features is a title bar, a menu bar, toolbars, a document window, scroll bars, and mouse compatibility. You can move and size Office application windows, select commands, use Help, and switch between files and programs, just as you can in Windows. The common user interface makes learning and using new applications much easier.

## TITLE BAR

The Excel window title bar displays the program name, Microsoft Excel, followed by the file name Book1, the default name of the file displayed in the window. The left end of the title bar contains the Excel application window ⊠ Control-menu icon, and the right end displays the ▣ Minimize, ▣ Restore, and ⊠ Close buttons. They perform the same functions and operate in the same way as in Windows 95 and Windows 98.

**1** ■ If necessary, click ▢ in the title bar to maximize the application window.

## MENU BAR

The **menu bar** below the title bar displays the Excel program menu, which consists of nine menus. The right end displays the document window Minimize, Restore, and Close buttons. As you use the Office applications, you will see that the menu bar contains many of the same menus, such as File, Edit, and Help. You will also see several menus that are specific to each application. You will learn about using the menus in the next section.

## TOOLBARS

The **toolbar** located below the menu bar contains buttons that are mouse shortcuts for many of the menu items. Commonly, the Office applications will display two toolbars when the application is first opened: Standard and Formatting. They may appear together on one row, or on separate rows. You will learn about using the toolbars shortly.

## WORKSPACE

The **workspace** is the large center area of the Excel application window where documents are displayed in open windows. Currently, there is one open document window, which is maximized and occupies the entire area. Multiple documents can be open and displayed in the workspace at the same time.

## STATUS BAR

The **status bar** at the bottom of the window displays location information and the status of different settings as they are used. Different information is displayed in the status bar for different applications.

## SCROLL BARS

A **scroll bar** is used with a mouse to bring additional lines of information into view in a window. It consists of **scroll arrows** and a **scroll box**.

Clicking the scroll arrows moves the information in the direction of the arrows, allowing new information to be displayed in the workspace. You can also move to a general location within the area by dragging the scroll box up or down the scroll bar. The location of the scroll box on the scroll bar indicates your relative position within the area of available information. Scroll bars can run vertically along the right side or horizontally along the bottom of a window. The vertical scroll bar is used to move vertically, and the horizontal scroll bar moves horizontally in the space.

## Using Office 2000 Features

### MENUS

A **menu** is one of many methods you can use to tell a program what you want it to do. When opened, a menu displays a list of commands. Most menus appear in a menu bar. Other menus pop up when you right-click (click the right mouse button) on an item. This type of menu is called a **shortcut menu**.

**1** ■ **Click File to open the File menu.**

Your screen should be similar to Figure 4.

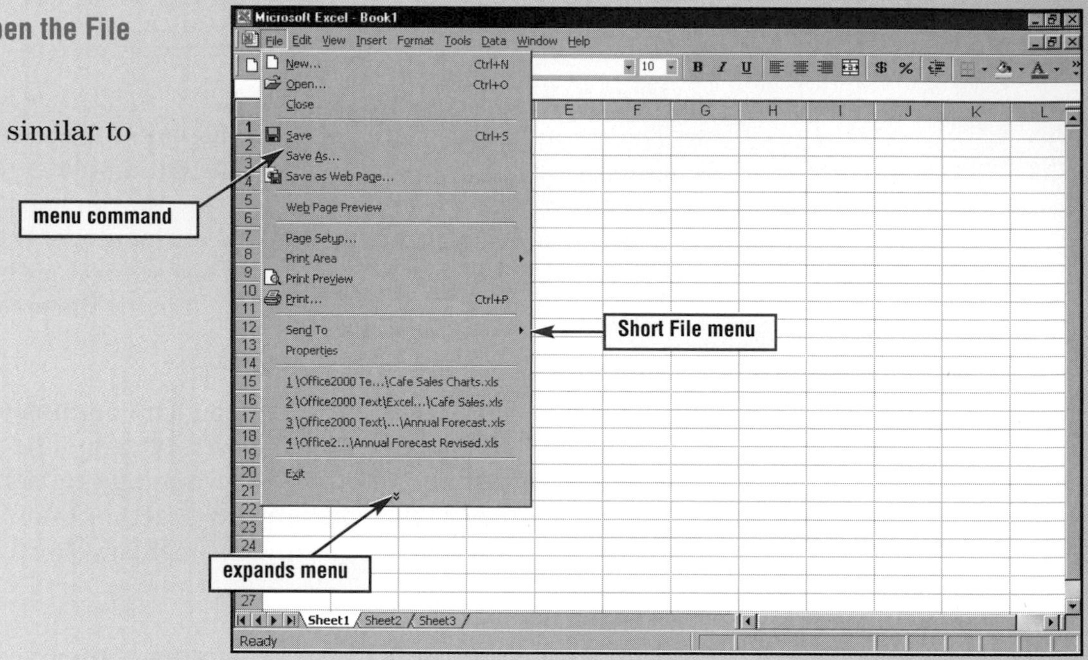

**Figure 4**

When a menu is first opened, it displays a short version of commands. The short menu displays basic commands when the application is first used. As you use the application, those commands you use frequently are listed on the short menu and others are hidden. Because the short menu is personalized automatically to the user's needs, different commands may be listed on your File menu than appear in Figure 4 above.

An expanded version will display automatically after the menu is open for a few seconds (see Figure 5). If you do not want to wait for the expanded version to appear, you can click ✴ at the bottom of the menu and the menu list will expand to display all commands.

You can double-click the menu name to show the expanded menu immediately.

Your screen should be similar to Figure 5.

**Figure 5**

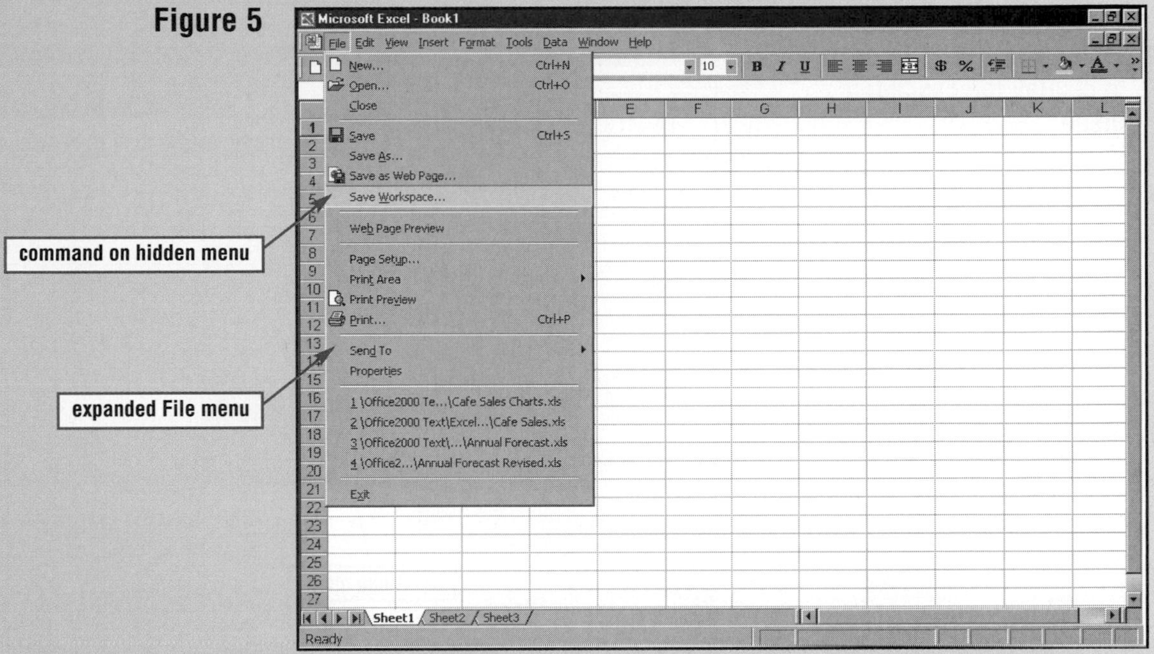

command on hidden menu

expanded File menu

The commands that are in the hidden menu appear on a light gray background. Once one menu is expanded, others are expanded automatically until you choose a command or perform another action.

**2** ■ Point to each menu in the menu bar to see the expanded menu for each.

■ Point to the File menu again.

Many commands have images next to them so you can quickly associate the command with the image. The same image appears on the toolbar button for that feature.

Menus may include the following features (not all menus include all features):

| Feature | Meaning |
| --- | --- |
| Ellipses (...) | Indicates a dialog box will be displayed |
| ▶ | Indicates a cascading menu will be displayed |
| Dimmed | Indicates the command is not available for selection until certain other conditions are met |
| Shortcut key | A key or key combination that can be used to execute a command without using the menu |
| Checkmark ✓ | Indicates a toggle type of command. Selecting it turns the feature on or off. A checkmark indicates the feature is on. |

Once a menu is open, you can *select* a command from the menu by pointing to it. A colored highlight bar, called the **selection cursor**, appears over the selected command. If the selected command line displays a right-facing arrow, a submenu of commands automatically appears when the command is selected. This is commonly called a **cascading menu**.

**3** ■ **Point to the Send To command to display the cascading menu.**

Your screen should be similar to Figure 6.

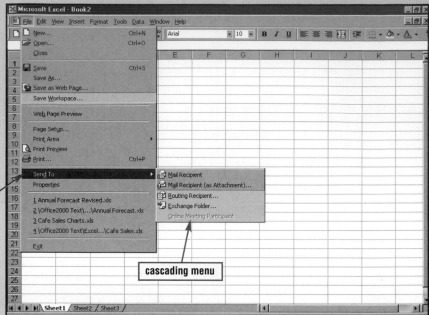

**selection cursor**

**cascading menu**

**Figure 6**

> You can also type the underlined command letter to choose a command. If the command is already selected, you can press ←Enter to choose it.

Then to *choose* a command, you click on it. When the command is chosen, the associated action is performed. You will use a command in the Help menu to access the Microsoft Office Assistant and Help feature.

*Note:* If your Office Assistant feature is already on, as shown in Figure 7, skip step 4.

**4** ■ **Point to Help.**

■ **Choose Show the Office Assistant.**

> If the Assistant does not appear, your school has disabled this feature. If this is the case, choose Help/Microsoft Excel Help and skip to the section Using Help.

Your screen should be similar to Figure 7.

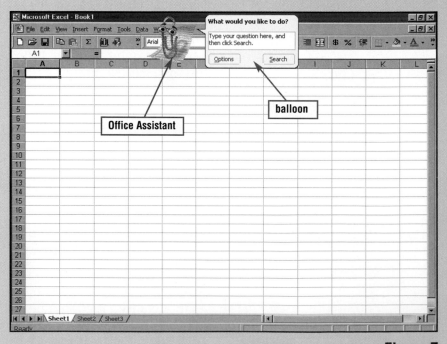

**Office Assistant**

**balloon**

**Figure 7**

The command to display the Assistant has been executed, and the Office Assistant character is displayed. Because there are a variety of Office Assistant characters, your screen may display a different character than shown here.

*Note:* If the Assistant does not appear, this feature has been disabled. If this is the case, Choose **H**elp/Microsoft Excel **H**elp or press [F1] and skip to the section Using Help.

## Using the Office Assistant

- - - - - - - - - - - - - - - - - - - - - - - - - - - - - - - - - - -

**Additional Information**

You can drag the Office Assistant to any location on the screen.

When the Office Assistant is on, it automatically suggests help topics as you work. It anticipates what you are going to do and then makes suggestions on how to perform the task. In addition, you can activate the Assistant at any time to get help on features in the Office application you are using. When active, the Office Assistant balloon appears and displays a prompt and a text box in which you can type the topic you want help on.

**1** ━■ **If the balloon is not displayed as in Figure 7 above, click the Office Assistant character to activate it.**

You will ask the Office Assistant to provide information on the different ways you can get help while using the program.

**2** ━ ■ Type **How do I get help?**

■ Click [ Search ] .

Your screen should be similar to Figure 8.

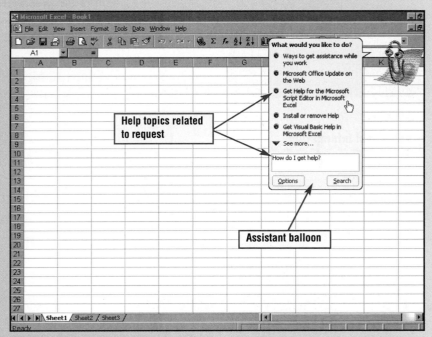

**Figure 8**

The balloon displays a list of related topics from which you can select.

**3** ■ **Choose** Ways to get assistance while you work.

Your screen should be similar to Figure 9.

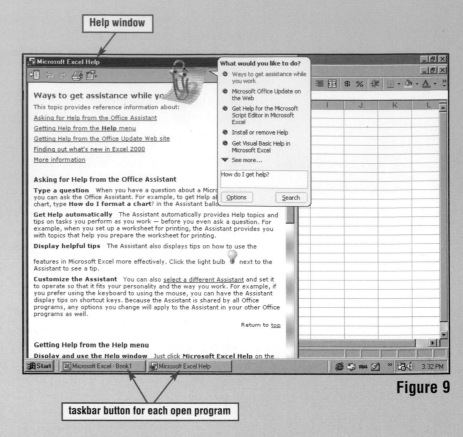

**Figure 9**

The Help program has been opened and displays the selected topic. Because Help is a separate program, it appears in its own window. The taskbar displays a button for both open windows. Now that Help is open, you no longer need to see the Assistant.

> You can also press [F1] to open Help if the Office Assistant is not on.

**4** ■ **Click** [Options] .

■ **Select U̲se the Office Assistant to clear the checkmarks.**

■ **Click** [ OK ] .

■ **Click** [Microsoft Excel Help] **in the taskbar to switch back to the Help window.**

> **Additional Information**
>
> The [Options] button is used to change the Office Assistant settings so it provides different levels of help, or to select a different Assistant character.

## Using Help

In the Help window, the toolbar buttons help you use different Help features and navigate within Help. The 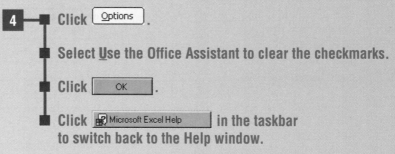 Show button displays the Help Tabs frame.

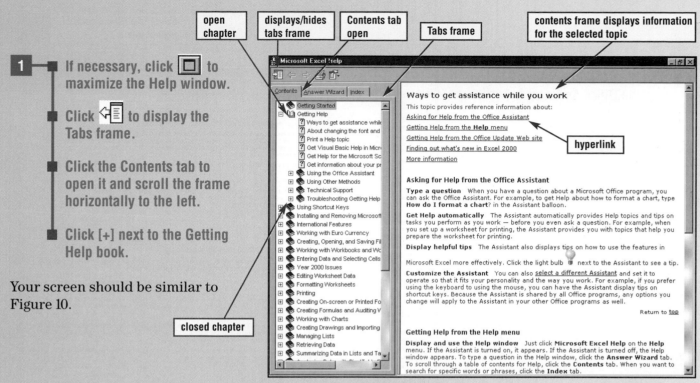

**Figure 10**

1. ■ If necessary, click □ to maximize the Help window.

   ■ Click ◀🗐 to display the Tabs frame.

   ■ Click the Contents tab to open it and scroll the frame horizontally to the left.

   ■ Click [+] next to the Getting Help book.

Your screen should be similar to Figure 10.

The Help window is divided into two vertical frames. **Frames** divide a window into separate, scrollable areas that can display different information. The left frame in the Help window is the Tabs frame. The three folder-like tabs—Contents, Index, and Search—are used to access the three different means of getting Help information. The open tab appears in front of the other tabs and displays the available options for the feature. The right frame is the content frame. It displays the content for the located information.

The Contents tab displays a table of contents listing of topics in Help. Clicking on an item preceded with a ❖ opens a "chapter," which expands to display additional chapters or specific Help topics. Chapters are preceded with a 📖 icon and topics with a ❓ icon.

The content frame displays the selected Help topic. It contains more information than can be displayed at one time.

2. ■ Using the scroll bar, scroll the right frame to the bottom of the Help topic.

   ■ Scroll back to the top of the Help topic.

### USING A HYPERLINK

Another way to move in Help is to click a hyperlink. A **hyperlink** is a connection to a location in the current document, another document, or the World Wide Web. It commonly appears as colored or underlined text. Clicking the hyperlink moves to the location associated with the hyperlink.

> The mouse pointer appears as 🖑 when pointing to a hyperlink.

**1** ▬ **Click the** Asking for Help from the Office Assistant **hyperlink.**

Your screen should be similar to Figure 11.

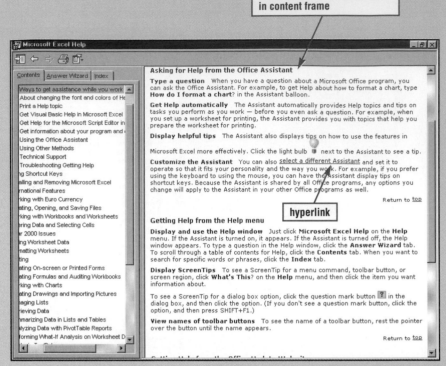

**Figure 11**

Help quickly jumps to the selected topic and displays the topic heading at the top of the frame.

**2** ▬ **Read the information displayed on this topic.**

▪ **Click the** select a different Assistant **hyperlink.**

Your screen should be similar to Figure 12.

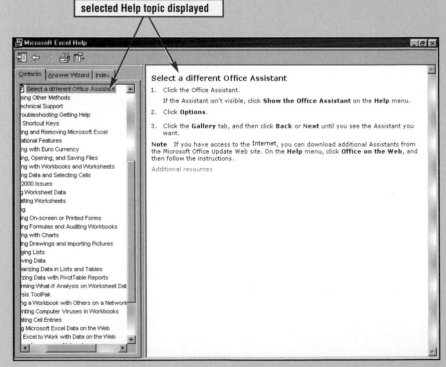

**Figure 12**

The Help topic about selecting a different Assistant is displayed. Notice the Contents list now highlights this topic, indicating it is the currently selected topic. Other hyperlinks may display a definition of a term.

**3** ■ Click the Internet hyperlink.

Your screen should be similar to Figure 13.

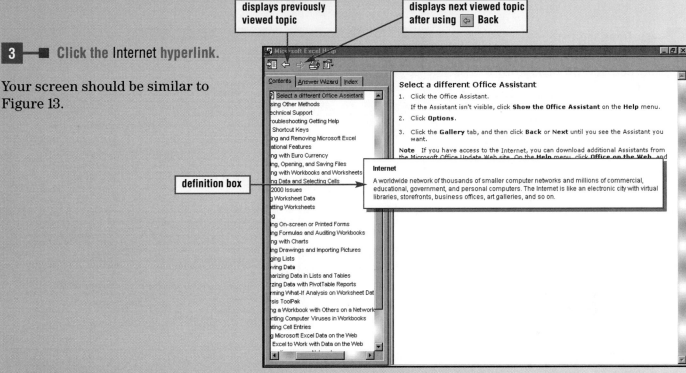

**Figure 13**

A box containing a definition of the Internet is displayed.

**4** ■ Click on the definition box to clear it.

To quickly return to the previous topic,

**5** ■ Click ⇦ Back.

The previous topic is displayed again.

The ⇨ Forward button is available after using ⇦ Back and can be used to move to the next viewed topic.

### USING THE INDEX TAB

To search for Help information by entering a word or phrase for a topic, you can use the Index tab.

**1** ■ Open the Index tab.

Your screen should be similar to Figure 14.

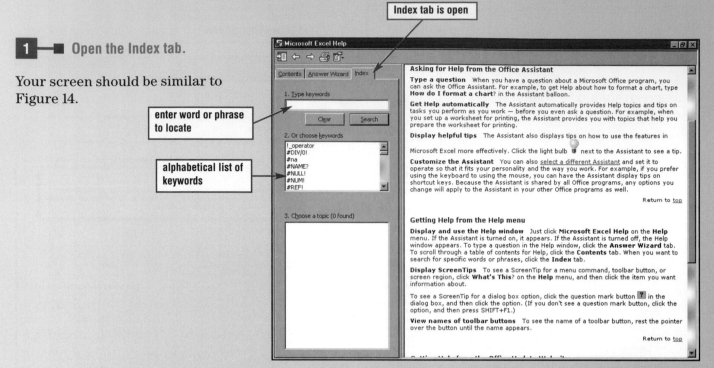

**Figure 14**

The Index tab consists of a text box where you can type a word or phrase that best describes the topic you want to locate. Below it is a list box displaying a complete list of Help keywords in alphabetical order. You want to find information about using the Index tab.

**2** ■ Type **index** in the text box.

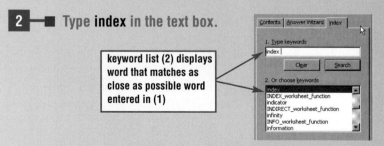

The keyword list jumps to the word "index." To locate all Help topics containing this word,

**3** ■ Click Search .

Your screen should be similar to Figure 15.

selected topic

located 11 topics containing keyword 'index'

selected topic displayed in Content frame

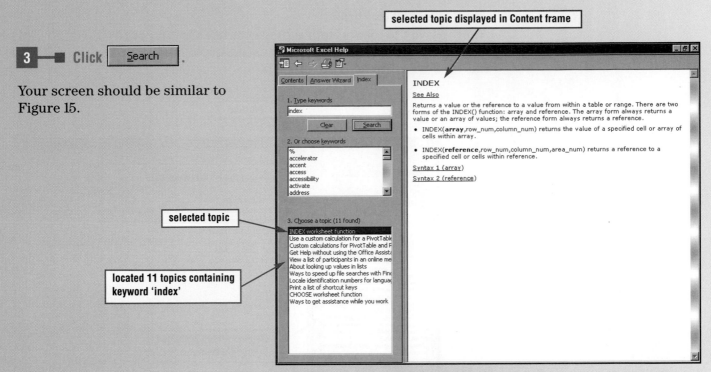

**Figure 15**

The topic list displayed the 11 located Help topics containing this word and displays the information on the first topic in the content frame. However, many of the located topics are not about the Help Index feature. To narrow the search more, you can add another word to the keyword text box.

**4** ■ Type **help** in the keyword text box following the word index.

■ Click Search .

Your screen should be similar to Figure 16.

three topics located that contain both words

selected topic

selected topic displayed

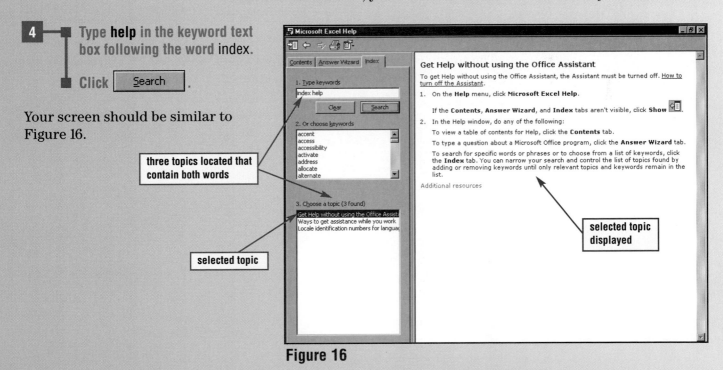

**Figure 16**

Now only three topics were located that contain both keywords. The first topic Get Help without using the Office Assistant is selected and displayed in the content frame.

### USING THE ANSWER WIZARD

Another way to locate Help topics is to use the Answer Wizard tab. This feature works just like the OfficeAssistant to locate topics. You will use this method to locate Help information on toolbars.

**1** ■ Open the <u>A</u>nswer Wizard tab.

■ Type **How do toolbars work?** in the text box.

■ Click [ <u>S</u>earch ] .

**Additional Information**
- - - - - - - - - - -
The search term does not need to be worded as a question. It can also be a word or phrase.

Your screen should be similar to Figure 17.

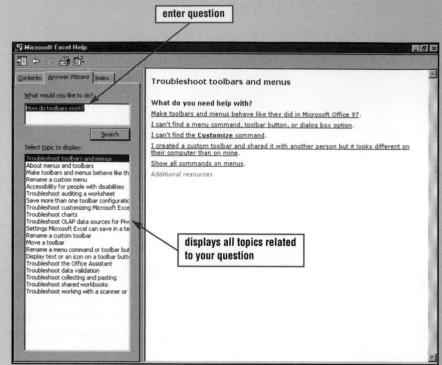

Figure 17

The topic list box displays all topics that the Answer Wizard considers may be related to the question you entered.

**2** ▪ Select About menus and toolbars
from the topic list.

Your screen should be similar to
Figure 18.

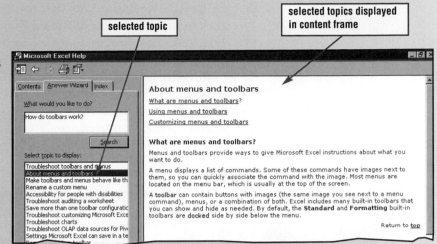

**Figure 18**

**3** ▪ Click 📑 to hide the Tabs frame
and, if necessary, maximize the
Help window again.

▪ Read the information about this
topic.

▪ Read the hyperlink topics "resize
a toolbar" and "show all buttons
on a toolbar."

▪ Click **X** to close Help.

Your screen should be similar to
Figure 19.

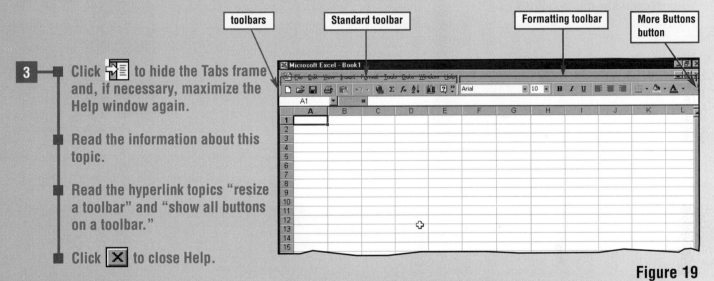

**Figure 19**

The Help window is closed, and the Excel window is displayed again.

## Using Toolbars

While using Office 2000, you will see that many toolbars open automatically as different tasks are performed. Toolbars initially display the basic buttons. Like menus they are personalized automatically, displaying those buttons you use frequently and hiding others. The More Buttons ⋙ button located at the end of a toolbar displays a drop-down button list of those buttons that are not displayed. When you use a button from this list, it then is moved to the toolbar, and a button that has not been used recently is moved to the More Buttons list.

Initially, Excel displays two toolbars, Standard and Formatting, on one row below the menu bar (See Figure 19). The Standard toolbar contains buttons that are used to complete the most frequently used menu commands. The Formatting toolbar contains buttons that are used to change the appearance or format of the document. However, your screen may display different toolbars in different locations. If you right-click on a toolbar, the toolbar shortcut menu is displayed. Using this menu, you can specify which toolbars are displayed. To see which toolbars are open,

**1**━■ **Right-click on any toolbar.**

> The menu equivalent is View/Toolbars.

Your screen should be similar to Figure 20.

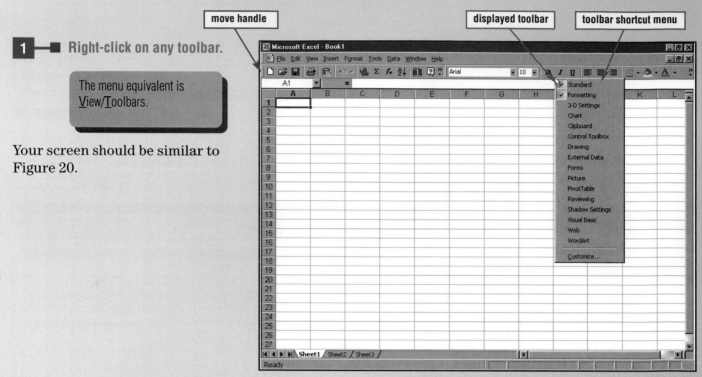

**Figure 20**

The toolbar shortcut menu displays a list of toolbar names. Those that are currently displayed are checked. Clicking on a toolbar from the list will display it onscreen. Clicking on a checked toolbar will hide the toolbar.

**2**━■ **If necessary, clear the checkmark from all toolbars other than the Standard and Formatting toolbars.**

There should now only be two open toolbars. When a toolbar is opened, it may appear docked or floating. A **docked** toolbar is fixed to an edge of the window and displays the move handle ▯. Dragging this bar up or down allows you to move the toolbar. If multiple toolbars share the same row, dragging the bar left or right adjusts the size of the toolbar. If docked, a toolbar can occupy a row by itself, or several can be on a row together. A **floating** toolbar appears in a separate window that can be moved by dragging the title bar.

**3** ■ Drag the move handle of the Standard toolbar into the workspace.

> The mouse pointer appears as ✥ when you point to the ▯ of any toolbar.

Your screen should be similar to Figure 21.

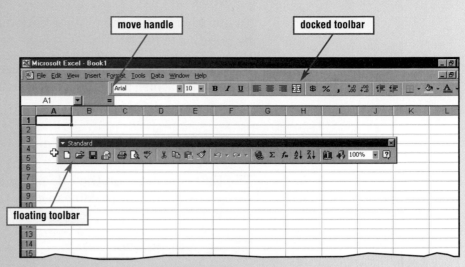

**Figure 21**

The Standard toolbar is now floating and can be moved to any location in the window by dragging the toolbar title bar. If you move it to the edge of the window, it will attach to that location and become a docked toolbar. A floating toolbar can also be sized by dragging the edge of the toolbar.

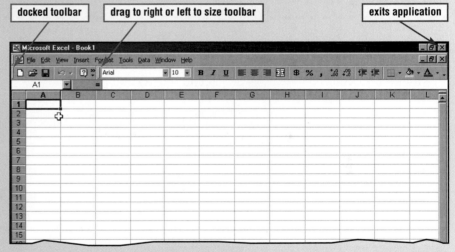

**Figure 22**

**4** ■ Move the floating toolbar to the left end of the row below the menu bar.

■ If necessary, move the Formatting toolbar to the right end of the same row as the Standard toolbar.

Your screen should be similar to Figure 22.

**Additional Information**

Double-clicking a toolbar when multiple toolbars share the same row minimizes or maximizes the toolbar size.

The two toolbars now occupy a single row. The size of each toolbar can be adjusted to show more or fewer buttons by dragging the move handle.

**5** ■ Drag the ▯ of the Formatting toolbar to the right or left as needed until each bar occupies approximately half the row space.

To quickly identify the toolbar buttons, you can display the button name by pointing to the button.

**6** ━■ Point to any button on the Standard toolbar to see the ScreenTip displaying the button name.

## Exiting an Office Application

The Exit command on the File menu can be used to quit most Windows programs. In addition, you can click the ☒ Close button in the application window title bar.

**1** ━■ Click ☒ Close.

The application window is closed, and the desktop is visible again.

# Key Terms

| | |
|---|---|
| cascading menu xxviii | ScreenTip xxiv |
| desktop xxii | scroll arrows xxv |
| docked xxxviii | scroll bar xxv |
| floating xxxviii | scroll box xxv |
| frame xxxi | selection cursor xxvii |
| hyperlink xxxi | shortcut menu xxvi |
| icon xxii | Start button xxii |
| menu xxvi | status bar xxv |
| menu bar xxv | taskbar xxii |
| mouse xxii | toolbar xxv |
| mouse pointer xxii | workspace xxv |

# Command Summary

| Command | Shortcut Keys | Button | Action |
|---|---|---|---|
| Start/Programs | | | Opens program menu |
| File/Exit | Alt + F4 | ☒ | Exits Excel program |
| View/Toolbars | | | Hides or displays toolbars |
| Help/Microsoft Excel Help | F1 | | Opens Help window |
| Help/Show the Office Assistant | | | Displays Help's Office Assistant |

# Overview

## What Is an Electronic Spreadsheet?

The electronic spreadsheet, or worksheet, is an automated version of the accountant's ledger. Like the accountant's ledger, it consists of rows and columns of numerical data. Unlike the accountant's ledger, which is created on paper using a pencil, an eraser, and a calculator, the electronic spreadsheet is created using a computer system and an electronic spreadsheet application software program.

In contrast to a word processor, which manipulates text, an electronic spreadsheet manipulates numerical data. The first electronic spreadsheet software program, VisiCalc, was offered on the market in 1979. Since then the electronic spreadsheet program has evolved into a powerful business tool that has revolutionized the business world.

The electronic spreadsheet eliminates the paper, pencil, and eraser. With a few keystrokes the user can quickly change, correct, and update the data. Even more impressive is the spreadsheet's ability to perform calculations from very simple sums to the most complex financial and mathematical formulas. The calculator is replaced by the electronic spreadsheet. Analysis of data in the spreadsheet has become a routine business procedure. Once requiring hours of labor and/or costly accountants' fees, data analysis is now available almost instantly using electronic spreadsheets.

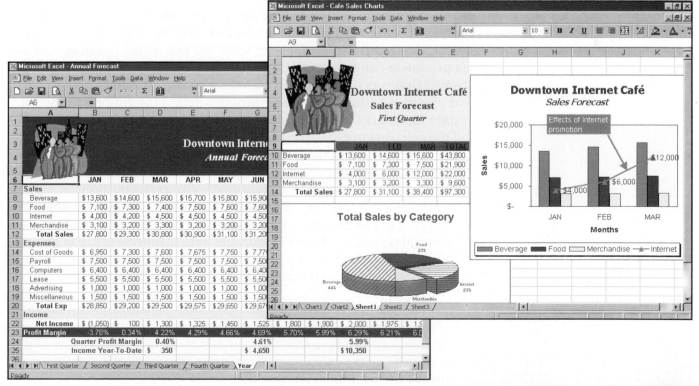

Nearly any job that uses rows and columns of numbers can be performed using an electronic spreadsheet. Typical uses of electronic spreadsheets are for budgets and financial planning in both business and personal situations.

## Excel 2000 Features

Excel 2000 helps you create well-designed spreadsheets that produce accurate results. The application not only makes it faster to create the spreadsheet, but produces a professional-appearing result. The advantages are in the ability of the spreadsheet program to quickly edit and format data, perform calculations, create charts, and print the spreadsheet.

The data entered in an electronic spreadsheet can be edited and revised using the program commands. Numeric or text data is entered into the worksheet in a location called a cell. These entries can then be erased, moved, copied, or edited. Formulas can be entered that perform calculations using data contained in specified cells. The results of the calculations are displayed in the cell containing the formula.

The design and appearance of the spreadsheet can be enhanced in many ways. There are several commands that control the format or display of a numeric entry in a cell. For instance, numeric entries can be displayed with dollar signs or with a set number of decimal places. Text or label entries in a cell can be displayed centered or left- or right-aligned to improve the spreadsheet's appearance. You can further enhance the appearance of the spreadsheet by changing the type style and size and by adding special effects such as bold, italic, borders, boxes, drop shadows, and shading around selected cells. Columns and rows can be inserted and deleted. The cell width can be changed to accommodate entries of varying lengths.

You can play with the values in the worksheet to see the effect of changing specific values on the worksheet. This is called what-if or sensitivity analysis. Questions that once were too expensive to ask or took too long to answer can now be answered almost instantly and with little cost. Planning that was once partially based on instinct has been replaced to a great extent with facts. However, any financial planning resulting from the data in a worksheet is only as accurate as that data and the logic behind the calculations.

Excel 2000 also has the ability to produce a visual display of the data in the form of graphs or charts. As the values in the worksheet change, a graph referencing those values automatically reflects the new values. These graphs are a tool for visualizing the effects of changing values in a worksheet. You can also include a graph with the spreadsheet data. This way you can display and print it with the data it represents. You can also enhance the appearance of a graph by using different type styles and sizes, adding three-dimensional effects, and including text and objects such as lines and arrows.

Another feature is the ability to open and use multiple spreadsheet files at the same time. Additionally, you can create multiple spreadsheets within a file, called 3-D spreadsheets. Even more important is the ability to link spreadsheets so that when data in one file changes, it automatically updates the linked data in another file.

## Case Study for Excel 2000 Tutorials

The Downtown Internet Café is a new concept in coffeehouses, combining the delicious aromas of a genuine coffeehouse with the fun of using the Internet. You are the new manager for the coffeehouse and are working with the owner, Evan, to develop a financial plan for the next year.

## Before You Begin

*To the Student*
The following assumptions have been made:

■ Microsoft Excel 2000 has been properly installed on your computer system.

■ The data disk contains the data files needed to complete the series of Excel 2000 tutorials and practice exercises. These files are supplied by your instructor.

■ You are already familiar with how to use Windows and a mouse.

*To the Instructor*
By default, Office 2000 installs the most commonly used components and leaves others, such as the Solver and Database Query, to be installed when first accessed. It is assumed that these additional features have been installed prior to students using the tutorials.

Please be aware that the following settings are assumed to be in effect for the Excel 2000 program. These assumptions are necessary so that the screens and directions in the manual are accurate.

■ The Standard and Formatting toolbars share one row. The ScreenTips feature is active. (Use Tools/Customize/Options.)

■ The Office Assistant feature is not on (Right click on the Assistant, Select **O**ptions and clear the Use the Office Assistant option.)

■ The Normal view is on. Zoom is 100 percent. (Use View/Normal; View/Zoom/100%.)

■ All default settings for a new workbook are in effect including a default font size of 10 pt.

In addition, all figures in the tutorials reflect the use of a standard VGA display monitor set at 800 by 600. If another monitor setting is used, there may be more or fewer rows and columns displayed in the window than in the figures. The 800 by 600 setting displays rows 1 through 27 and columns A through L. This setting can be changed using Windows setup.

## Microsoft Office Shortcut Bar

The Microsoft Office Shortcut Bar (shown below) may be displayed automatically on the Windows desktop. Commonly it appears in the right side of the desktop; however, it may appear in other locations, depending upon your setup. The Shortcut Bar on your screen may display different buttons. This is because the Shortcut Bar can be customized to display other toolbar buttons.

The Office Shortcut Bar makes it easy to open existing documents or to create new documents using one of the Microsoft Office applications. It can also be used to send e-mail, add a task to a to-do list, schedule appointments using Schedule[+], or add Contacts or Notes.

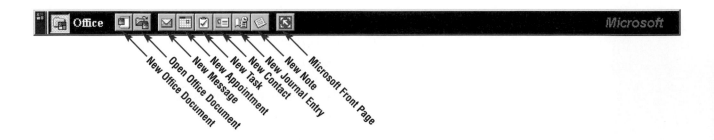

## Instructional Conventions

Hands-on instructions you are to perform appear as a sequence of numbered blue steps. Within each step, a series of pink bullets identifies the specific actions that must be performed. Step numbering begins over within each main topic heading throughout the tutorial.

Command sequences you are to issue appear following the word "Choose." Each menu command selection is separated by a /. If the menu command can be selected by typing a letter of the command, the letter will appear underlined and bold. Items that need to be highlighted will follow the word "Select." You can select items with the mouse or directional keys.

**EXAMPLE**

**1** ■ Choose **F**ile/**O**pen

■ **Select** Forecast.

Commands that can be initiated using a button and the mouse appear following the word "Click." The icon (and the icon name if the icon does not include text) is displayed following Click. The menu equivalent and keyboard shortcut appear in a margin note when the action is first introduced.

## EXAMPLE

The menu equivalent is **F**ile/**O**pen and the keyboard shortcut is Ctrl + O.

**1** ━━■ **Click**  **Open**

Black text identifies items you need to select or move to. Information you are asked to type appears in black and bold.

## EXAMPLE

**1** ━━■ **Move to** B3.

     ■ **Type Sales Forecast**.

# Creating and Editing a Worksheet

## Competencies

After completing this tutorial, you will know how to:

1. Enter, edit, and clear cell entries.
2. Save, close, and open workbooks.
3. Specify ranges.
4. Copy and move cell entries.
5. Enter formulas and functions.
6. Adjust column widths.
7. Change cell alignment.
8. Format cells.
9. Insert rows.
10. Insert and size a ClipArt graphic.
11. Enter and format a date.
12. Preview and print a worksheet.

**Case Study**  You are excited about your new position as manager and financial planner for a local coffeehouse. Evan, the owner, has hired you as part of a larger effort to increase business at the former Downtown Café. Evan began this effort by completely renovating his coffeehouse, installing Internet

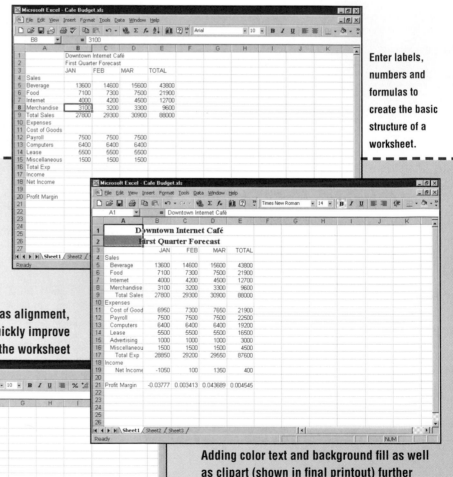

Enter labels, numbers and formulas to create the basic structure of a worksheet.

Basic formatting, such as alignment, indents, and numeric styles quickly improve the appearance of the worksheet

Adding color text and background fill as well as clipart (shown in final printout) further enhance the worksheet appearance.

hookups and outlets for laptops, and changing its name to the Downtown Internet Café. You and Evan expect to increase sales by attracting Internet-savvy café-goers, who, you hope, will use the Downtown Internet Café as a place to meet, study, or just relax.

Evan wants to create a forecast estimating sales and expenses for the first quarter. As part of a good business plan, you and Evan need a realistic set of financial estimates and goals.

In this tutorial, you will help with the first quarter forecast by using Microsoft Excel 2000, a spreadsheet application that can store, manipulate, and display numeric data. You will learn to enter numbers, perform calculations, copy data, label rows and columns as you create the basic structure of a worksheet for the Downtown Internet Café. You will then learn how to enhance the worksheet using formatting features and by inserting a ClipArt graphic as shown here.

### Downtown Internet Café
### First Quarter Forecast

| | JAN | FEB | MAR | TOTAL |
|---|---|---|---|---|
| **Sales** | | | | |
| Beverage | $13,600 | $14,600 | $15,600 | $43,800 |
| Food | $ 7,100 | $ 7,300 | $ 7,400 | $21,800 |
| Internet | $ 4,000 | $ 4,200 | $ 4,500 | $12,700 |
| Merchandise | $ 3,100 | $ 3,200 | $ 3,300 | $ 9,600 |
| **Total Sales** | $27,800 | $29,300 | $30,800 | $87,900 |
| | JAN | FEB | MAR | TOTAL |
| **Expenses** | | | | |
| Cost of Goods | $ 6,950 | $ 7,300 | $ 7,600 | $21,850 |
| Salary | $ 7,500 | $ 7,500 | $ 7,500 | $22,500 |
| Computers | $ 6,400 | $ 6,400 | $ 6,400 | $19,200 |
| Lease | $ 5,500 | $ 5,500 | $ 5,500 | $16,500 |
| Advertising | $ 1,000 | $ 1,000 | $ 1,000 | $ 3,000 |
| Miscellaneous | $ 1,500 | $ 1,500 | $ 1,500 | $ 4,500 |
| **Total Exp** | $28,850 | $29,200 | $29,500 | $87,550 |
| **Income** | | | | |
| **Net Income** | $ (1,050) | $ 100 | $ 1,300 | $ 350 |
| | | | | |
| **Profit Margin** | -3.78% | 0.34% | 4.22% | 0.40% |

S. Name
February 7, 2001

## Concept Overview

The following concepts will be introduced in this tutorial:

**1** **Worksheet Development** Worksheet development consists of four stages; planning, entering and editing, testing, and formatting.

**2** **Types of Entries** The information or data you enter in a cell can be text, numbers, or formulas.

**3** **Column Width** The size or width of a column controls how much information can be displayed in a cell.

**4** **Range** A selection consisting of two or more cells on a worksheet is a range.

**5** **Formulas** A formula is an entry that performs a calculation.

**6** **Relative Reference** A relative reference is a cell or range reference in a formula whose location is interpreted by Excel in relation to the position of the cell that contains the formula.

**7** **Functions** Functions are prewritten formulas that perform certain types of calculations automatically.

**8** **Automatic Recalculation** Excel automatically recalculates formulas whenever a change occurs in a referenced cell.

**9** **Alignment** Alignment settings allow you to change the horizontal and vertical placement and the orientation of an entry in a cell.

**10** **Fonts** Fonts consist of typefaces, point sizes, and styles that can be applied to characters to improve their appearance.

**11** **Character Effects** Different character effects can be applied to selections to add emphasis or interest to a document.

**12** **Number Formats** Number formats affect how numbers look onscreen and when printed.

**13** **Graphics** A graphic is a non-text element or object, such as a drawing or picture that can be added to a document.

## Exploring the Excel Window

### Additional Information

See Introducing Common Office 2000 Features for information on how to start the application and for a discussion of features common to all Office 2000 applications.

As part of the renovation of the Downtown Internet Café, new computers and the most current versions of software programs were installed, including the latest version of the Microsoft Office suite of applications, Office 2000. You will use the spreadsheet application Excel 2000 included in the Office suite to create the first quarter forecast for the Café.

**1** ■ Start Excel 2000.

■ If necessary, maximize the Excel application window.

After a few moments, the Excel application window is displayed. Your screen should be similar to Figure 1–1.

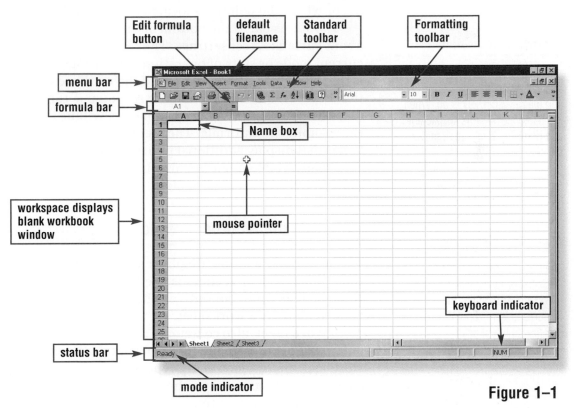

Edit formula button | default filename | Standard toolbar | Formatting toolbar

menu bar

formula bar

Name box

mouse pointer

workspace displays blank workbook window

keyboard indicator

status bar

mode indicator

Ready

**Figure 1–1**

The Excel window title bar displays the program name, Microsoft Excel, followed by the file name Book1, the default name of the file displayed in the workbook window. The menu bar below the title bar displays the Excel program menu. It consists of nine menus that provide access to the commands and features you will use to create and modify a worksheet.

The toolbars, normally located below the menu bar, contain buttons that are mouse shortcuts for many of the menu items. The **Standard toolbar** contains buttons that are used to complete the most frequently used menu commands. The **Formatting toolbar** contains buttons that are used to change the appearance or format of the document. Excel includes 23 different toolbars. Many of the toolbars appear automatically as you use different features. Your screen may display other toolbars if they were on when the program was last exited.

Because Excel remembers settings that were on when the program was last exited, your screen may look slightly different.

Below the toolbars is the **formula bar**. The formula bar displays entries as they are made and edited in the workbook window. The **Name Box**, located at the left end of the formula bar, provides information about the selected item. The Edit Formula button is used to create or edit a formula.

The **workspace** currently displays a blank workbook window, which is maximized and occupies the entire space. A **workbook** is an Excel file that stores the information you enter using the program. Excel calls a window that displays a workbook file a **workbook window**. You can have multiple workbook files open at once, each displayed in their own workbook window in the workspace. You will learn about the different parts of the workbook window shortly.

The mouse pointer probably appears as a ⬚ or ⬚ on your screen. The mouse pointer changes shape depending upon the task you are performing or where the pointer is located on the window.

The status bar at the bottom of the Excel window displays information about various Excel settings. The left side of the status bar displays the current mode or state of operation of the program (*M*) Ready. When Ready is displayed, you can move around the workbook, enter data, use the function keys, or choose a command. As you use the program, the status bar displays the current mode. The modes will be discussed as they appear throughout the tutorials. The right end of the status bar displays eight boxes that display additional information as features are used.

Finally, your screen may display the Office Assistant. This feature provides quick access to online Help.

## Exploring the Workbook Window

The workbook window displays a new blank workbook file containing three blank sheets. A sheet is used to display different types of information, such as financial data or charts. Whenever you open a new workbook, it displays a worksheet.

A **worksheet**, also commonly referred to as a **spreadsheet**, is a rectangular grid of **rows** and **columns** used to enter data. It is always part of a workbook and is the primary type of sheet you will use in Excel. The worksheet is much larger than the part you are viewing in the window. The worksheet actually extends 256 columns to the right and 65,536 rows down.

---

**Additional Information**

If your status bar displays NUM, this is a keyboard indicator that tells you the NumLock key is on. When on, using the numeric keypad enters numbers. When off, it moves the cell selector. Pressing Num Lock on your keyboard toggles between these settings.

---

**Additional Information**

The text assumes the Office Assistant is not activated. See Introducing Common Office 2000 Features to learn about this feature and how to turn it off.

---

The default workbook opens with three worksheets. The number of sheets in a workbook is limited only by the available memory on your computer.

**Workbook file**

column letters

cell selector
identifies active cell

column

row numbers

row

worksheet

cell

Sheet1 / Sheet2 / Sheet3

tab scroll buttons

sheet tabs

---

Do not be concerned if your workbook window displays more or less column letters and row numbers than shown here. This is a function of your computer monitor settings.

The **row numbers** along the left side and the **column letters** across the top of the workbook window identify each worksheet row and column. The intersection of a row and column creates a **cell**. Notice the heavy border, called the **cell selector**, surrounding the cell located at the intersection of column A and row 1. The cell selector identifies the **active cell**, which is the cell your next entry or procedure affects. Additionally, the Name box in the formula bar displays the **reference**, consisting of the column letter and row number of the active cell. The reference of the active cell is A1.

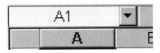

Each sheet in a workbook is named. The default names are Sheet1, Sheet2, and so on, displayed on **sheet tabs** at the bottom of the workbook window. The name of the **active sheet**, which is the sheet you can work in, appears bold. The currently displayed worksheet in the workspace, Sheet1, is the active sheet.

**1** ━━■ Click the Sheet 2 tab.

Your screen should be similar to Figure 1–2.

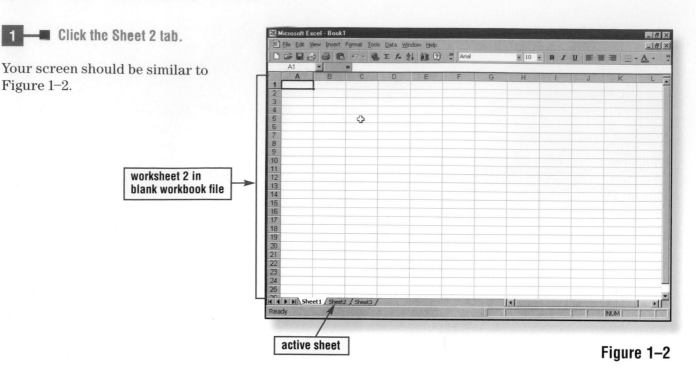

worksheet 2 in blank workbook file

active sheet

**Figure 1–2**

An identical blank worksheet is displayed in the window. The Sheet2 tab letters are bold, the background is highlighted, and it appears in front of the other sheet tabs to show it is the active sheet.

**2** ━━■ Click the Sheet 1 tab to make it the active sheet again.

The sheet tab area also contains **tab scroll buttons**, which are used to scroll tabs right or left when there are more worksheet tabs than there is available space. You will learn about these features throughout the tutorials.

## Moving Around the Worksheet

You can use the directional keys in the numeric keypad (with NumLock off) or, if you have an extended keyboard, you can use the separate directional keypad area.

Either the mouse or the keyboard can be used to move the cell selector from one cell to another in the worksheet. To move using a mouse, simply point to the cell you want to move to and click the mouse button. Depending upon what you are doing, using the mouse to move may not be as convenient as using the keyboard, in which case the directional keys can be used. To use the mouse, then the keyboard to move the cell selector,

**1** ■ Click cell B3.

■ Press →  (3 times).

■ Press ↓  (4 times).

Your screen should be similar to Figure 1–3.

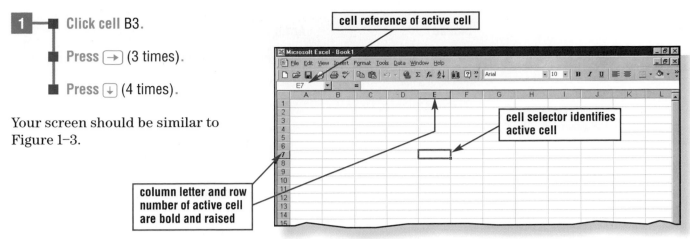

cell reference of active cell

cell selector identifies active cell

column letter and row number of active cell are bold and raised

**Figure 1–3**

The cell selector is now in cell E7, making this cell the active cell. The Name box displays the cell reference. In addition, the row number and column letter appear bold and raised to further identify the location of the active cell. To return quickly to the upper-left corner, cell A1, of the worksheet,

**2** ■ Press Ctrl + Home.

As you have learned, the worksheet is much larger than the part you are viewing in the window. To see an area of the worksheet that is not currently in view, you need to scroll the window. Either the keyboard or the mouse can be used to quickly scroll a worksheet Again, both methods are useful depending upon what you are doing. The key and mouse procedures shown in the table that follows can be used to move around the worksheet. In addition, if you hold down the arrow keys, the Alt + Page Up or Alt + Page Down keys, or the Page Up or Page Down keys, you can quickly scroll through the worksheet. As you scroll the worksheet using the keyboard, the cell selector moves to the new location. When you use the mouse and the scroll bar, however, the cell selector does not move until you click on a cell that is visible in the window.

| Keys | Action |
|---|---|
| Arrow keys ← ↑ → ↓ | Moves cell selector one cell in direction of arrow |
| Page Down | Moves cell selector down one full window |
| Page Up | Moves cell selector up one full window |
| Alt + Page Down | Moves cell selector right one full window |
| Alt + Page Up | Moves cell selector left one full window |
| Ctrl + Home | Moves cell selector to upper left corner cell of worksheet |
| Home | Moves cell selector to beginning of row |
| End → | Moves cell selector to last-used cell in row |
| End ↓ | Moves cell selector to last-used cell in column |

| Mouse | Action |
|---|---|
| Click cell | Moves cell selector to selected cell |
| Click scroll arrow | Scrolls worksheet one row/column in direction of arrow |
| Click above/below scroll box | Scrolls worksheet one full window up/down |
| Click right/left of scroll box | Scrolls worksheet one full window right/left |
| Drag scroll box | Scrolls worksheet multiple windows up/down or right/left |

**Additional Information**

The position of the scroll box indicates the relative location of the area you are viewing within the worksheet and the size indicates the proportional amount of the used area.

To see the rows immediately below row 27 and the columns to the right of column L,

**3** ■ Press Page Up.

■ Press Alt + Page Down.

Your screen should be similar to Figure 1–4.

Your screen may display more or fewer rows and columns depending on your screen and system settings.

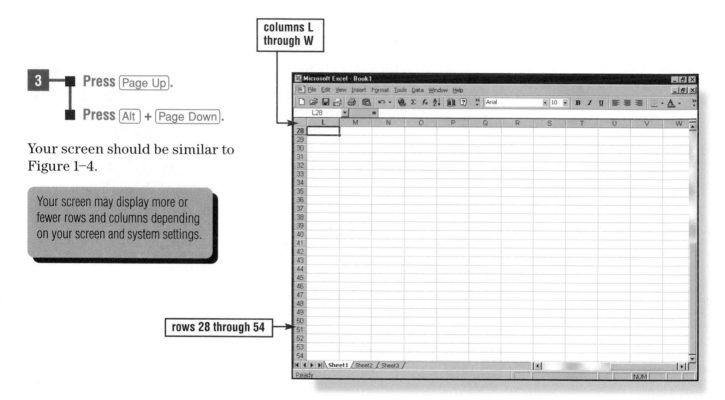

**columns L through W**

**rows 28 through 54**

**Figure 1–4**

The worksheet scrolled one full window upward and left and the window displays rows 28 through 54 and columns L through W of the worksheet.

**4** ■ Scroll the worksheet with the mouse using the scroll bar.

■ Practice moving the cell selector around the worksheet using each of the keys presented in the table above.

■ Move to A1.

**Additional Information**

When you use the scroll bar to scroll the worksheet, the cell selector does not move. When you drag the scroll box, a ScreenTip appears showing the column or row location that will appear when you stop scrolling.

Row: 1

You can use the mouse or the keyboard with most of the exercises in these tutorials. As you use both the mouse and the keyboard, you will find that it is more efficient to use one or the other in specific situations.

## Planning the Worksheet

Now that you are familiar with the parts of the worksheet, you are ready to create the worksheet showing the forecast for the first three months of operation for the Downtown Internet Café. As you create a worksheet, the development progresses through several stages.

### Concept  1 Worksheet Development

Worksheet development consists of four stages; planning, entering and editing, testing, and formatting. The objective is to create a well-designed worksheet that produces accurate results, and is clearly understood, adaptable, and efficient. You will find that you will generally follow these steps in order for your first draft of a worksheet. However, you will probably retrace steps such as editing and formatting as the worksheet develops.

**1. Plan**
Your first step is to specify the purpose of the worksheet and how it should be organized. This means clearly identifying the data that will be input, the calculations that are needed to achieve the results, and the output that is desired. As part of the planning step, it is helpful to sketch out a design of the worksheet to organize the worksheet's structure. The design should include the worksheet title and row and column headings that identify the input and output. Additionally, sample data can be used to help determine the formulas needed to produce the output.

**2. Enter and edit**
After planning the worksheet, your next step is to create the structure of the worksheet using Excel by entering the worksheet labels, data, and formulas. As you create the worksheet, you are bound to make errors that need to be corrected or edited or you will need to revise the content of what you have entered to make it clearer, or to add or delete information.

**3. Test**
Once your worksheet structure is complete, you are ready to test the worksheet for errors. Several sets of real or sample data are used as the input, and the resulting output is verified. The input data should include a full range of possible values for each data item to ensure the worksheet can function successfully under all possible conditions.

**4. Format**
Enhancing the appearance of the worksheet to make it more readable or attractive is called formatting. This step is usually performed when the worksheet is near completion. It includes many features such as boldfaced text, italics, and color.

As the complexity of the worksheet increases, the importance of following the design process increases. Even for simple worksheets like the one you will create in this tutorial, the design process is important.

During the planning phase, you have spoken with the café manager regarding the purpose of the worksheet and the content in general. The primary purpose is to develop a forecast for sales and expense for the next year. Evan first wants you to develop a worksheet for the first quarter forecast and to then extend it by quarters for the year. After reviewing past budgets and consulting with Evan, you have designed the basic layout for the first quarter forecast for the café as shown below.

Downtown Internet Café
First Quarter Forecast

Sales:

| Beverage | January | February | March | Total |
|---|---|---|---|---|
| | $13,600 | $14,600 | $15,600 | $43,800 (sum of beverage sales) |
| Food | XX,XXX | ___ | ___ | |
| Total Sales | $XX,XXX (sum of monthly sales) | $XX,XXX | $XX,XXX | $XXX,XXX (sum of total sales) |

Expenses:

Cost of Goods  $(.25 * beverage sales + 50 * food sales)  $(sum of cost of goods)
Salary  ___  ___  ___
___

Total Expenses  $XX,XXX  $XX,XXX  $XX,XXX  $XXX,XXX
(sum of monthly expenses)  (sum of total expenses)

Income
Net Income  $(Total Sales − Total Expenses) ___ ___
Profit Margin  $(Total Expenses ÷ Total Sales) ___ ___

## Entering Data

As you can see, the budget contains both descriptive text entries and numeric data. These are the two types of entries you can make in a worksheet.

## Concept **2** Types of Entries

The information or data you enter in a cell can be text, numbers, or formulas. **Text** entries can contain any combination of letters, numbers, spaces, and any other special characters. **Number** entries can include only the digits 0 to 9 and any of the special characters, + − ( ) , . / $ % E e. Number entries are used in calculations. An entry that begins with an equal sign (=) is a **formula**. Formula entries perform calculations using numbers or data contained in other cells. The resulting value is a **variable** value because it can change if the data it depends on changes. In contrast, a number entry is a **constant** value. It does not begin with an equal sign and does not change unless you change it directly by typing in another entry.

First you will enter the worksheet **headings**. Row and column headings are entries that are used to create the structure of the worksheet and describe other worksheet entries. Generally, headings are text entries. The column headings in this worksheet consist of the three months (January through March) and a total (sum of entries over three months) located in columns B through E. To enter data in a worksheet, you must first select the cell where you want the entry displayed. The column heading for January will be entered in cell B2.

**1** Move to B2.

Type **J**

Your screen should be similar to Figure 1–5.

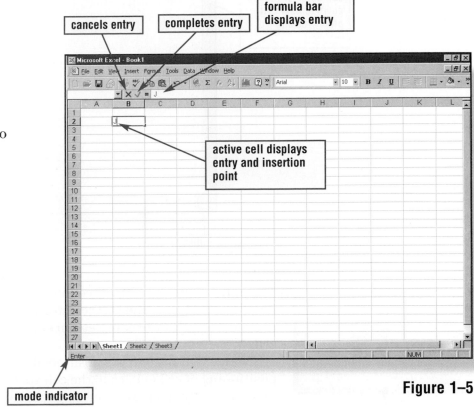

**Figure 1–5**

Several changes have occurred in the window. As you type, the entry is displayed both in the active cell and in the formula bar. An insertion point appears in the active cell and marks your location in the entry. Two new buttons, ☒ and ☑, appear in the formula bar. They can be used by the mouse to complete your entry or cancel it.

Notice also that the mode displayed in the status bar has changed from Ready to Enter. This notifies you that the current mode of operation in the worksheet is entering data. To continue entering the heading,

> If you made an error while typing the entry, use [Backspace] to erase the characters back to the error. Then retype the entry correctly.

**2** Type **anuary**

Although the entry is displayed in both the active cell and the formula bar, you need to press the [←Enter] key or click ☑ to complete your entry. If you press [Esc] or click ☒, the entry is cleared and nothing appears in the cell. Since your hands are already on the keyboard, it is quicker to press [←Enter] than it is to use the mouse to click ☑.

**3**━━■ Press ⌐←Enter⌐.

Your screen should be similar to Figure 1–6.

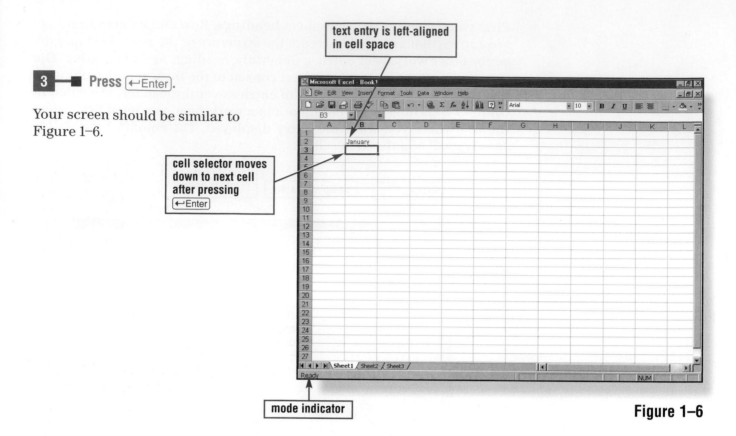

text entry is left-aligned in cell space

cell selector moves down to next cell after pressing ⌐←Enter⌐

mode indicator

**Figure 1–6**

Pressing ⌐⇧Shift⌐ + ⌐←Enter⌐ to complete an entry moves the cell selector up a cell, and ⌐Ctrl⌐ + ⌐←Enter⌐ completes the entry without moving the cell selector.

The entry January is displayed in cell B2, and the mode has returned to Ready. In addition, the cell selector has moved to cell B3. Whenever you use the ⌐←Enter⌐ key to complete an entry, the cell selector moves down one cell.

Notice that the entry is positioned to the left side of the cell space. The positioning of cell entries in the cell space is called alignment. By default, text entries are displayed left-aligned. You will learn more about this feature later in the tutorial.

## Clearing an Entry

- - - - - - - - - - - - - - - - - - - - - - - - - - - - - - - - - - - - -

After looking at the entry, you decide you want the column headings to be in row 3 rather than in row 2. This will leave more space above the column headings for a worksheet title.

The ⌐Delete⌐ key can be used to clear the contents from a cell. To remove the entry from cell B2 and enter it in cell B3,

The menu equivalent is **E**dit/Cle**a**r/**C**ontents. Clear Contents is also an option on the shortcut menu.

**1**━━■ Move to B2.

━■ Press ⌐Delete⌐.

━■ Move to B3.

━■ Type **January**

━■ Click  .

The cell selector remains in the active cell when you use ☑ to complete an entry. In Figure 1-7, because the cell selector is positioned on a cell containing an entry, the contents of the cell are displayed in the formula bar.

## Editing an Entry

You would like to change the heading from January to JAN. An entry in a cell can be entirely changed in the Ready mode or partially changed or edited in the Edit mode. To use the Ready mode, you move the cell selector to the cell you want to change and retype the entry the way you want it to appear. As soon as a new character is entered, the existing entry is cleared.

Generally, however, if you need to change only part of an entry, it is quicker to use the Edit mode. To change to Edit mode, double-click on the cell whose contents you want to edit.

**1** ■ Double-click B3.

> The mouse pointer must be ✛ when you double-click on the cell.

> Pressing the F2 key will also change to Edit mode.

Your screen should be similar to Figure 1-7.

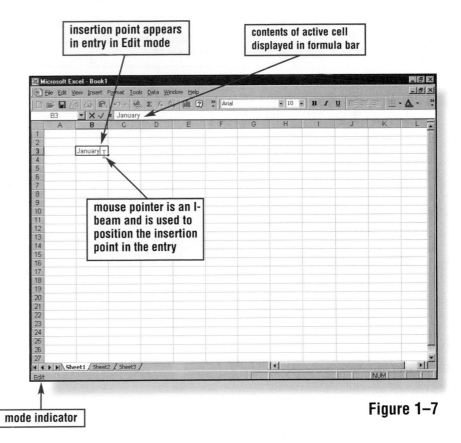

insertion point appears in entry in Edit mode

contents of active cell displayed in formula bar

mouse pointer is an I-beam and is used to position the insertion point in the entry

mode indicator

**Figure 1-7**

The status bar shows that the new mode of operation is Edit. The insertion point appears in the entry, and the mouse pointer changes to an I-beam when positioned on the cell. The mouse pointer can now be used to move the insertion point in the entry by positioning the I-beam and clicking.

In addition, in the Edit mode, the following keys can be used to move the insertion point:

| Key | Action |
|---|---|
| Home | Moves insertion point to beginning of entry |
| ←Enter | Moves insertion point to end of entry |
| → | Moves insertion point one character right |
| ← | Moves insertion point one character left |

**Additional Information**

You can also use Ctrl + Delete to delete everything to the right of the insertion point.

Once the insertion point is appropriately positioned, you can edit the entry by removing the incorrect characters and typing the correct characters. The Delete key erases characters at the insertion point, and the Backspace key erases characters to the left of the insertion point. To change this entry to JAN,

capital letters produced automatically when caps lock key is on

insertion point changes to a highlight when overwrite is on

**2** ▪ **If necessary, move** the insertion point to the end of the entry.

▪ **Press** Backspace **(4 times).**

▪ **Press** Home.

▪ **Press** Caps Lock.

▪ **Press** →.

▪ **Press** Insert.

▪ **Type A**

Your screen should be similar to Figure 1–8.

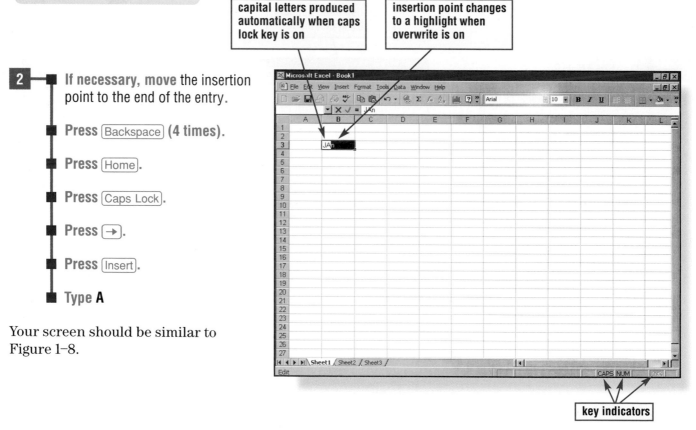

key indicators

**Figure 1–8**

The four characters at the end of the entry were deleted using Backspace. Turning on the Caps Lock feature produced an uppercase letter A without having to hold down ⇧Shift. Finally, by pressing Insert the program switched from inserting text to overwriting text as you typed. The insertion point changes to a highlight to show the character will be replaced. The status bar displays CAPS and OVR to let you know these features are on.

Overwrite is automatically turned off when you leave Edit mode or if you press [Insert] again.

**3** ■ Type **N**

■ Press (←Enter).

The new heading JAN is entered into cell B3, replacing January. As you can see, editing will be particularly useful with long or complicated entries.

Next you will enter the remaining three headings in row three. You can also complete an entry by moving to any other worksheet cell. To try this,

**4** ■ Move to C3.

■ Type **FEB**

■ Press (→) or click D3.

■ Complete the column headings by entering **MAR** in cell D3 and **TOTAL** in cell E3.

■ When you are done, turn off [Caps Lock].

Your screen should be similar to Figure 1–9.

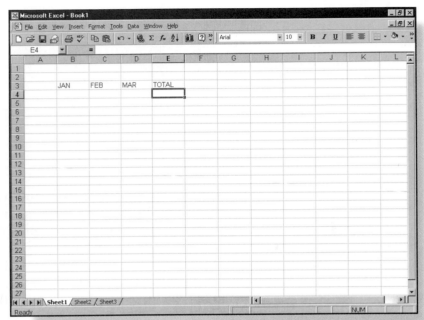

**Figure 1–9**

## Using AutoCorrect

Above the column headings, in rows 1 and 2, you want to enter a title for the worksheet. While entering the title, you will intentionally misspell the words First and Quarter to demonstrate how the AutoCorrect feature of Office works. The **AutoCorrect** feature automatically corrects common typing errors as they are made. Office 2000 contains a list of words that are commonly spelled incorrectly or typed incorrectly. When you misspell one of the words in the list, Excel will automatically correct the spelling for you. For example, it will automatically capitalize the days of the week. If you commonly spell a word wrong that is not in the AutoCorrect list, you can manually add it to the list. This word is added to the list on the computer you are using and will be available to anyone who uses the machine after you.

1 ▬▬ ■ Move to B1.

■ Type **Downtown Internet Cafe**

■ Press ⏎Enter.

■ Type **Firts Quater Forecast**

■ Press ⏎Enter.

Your screen should be similar to Figure 1–10.

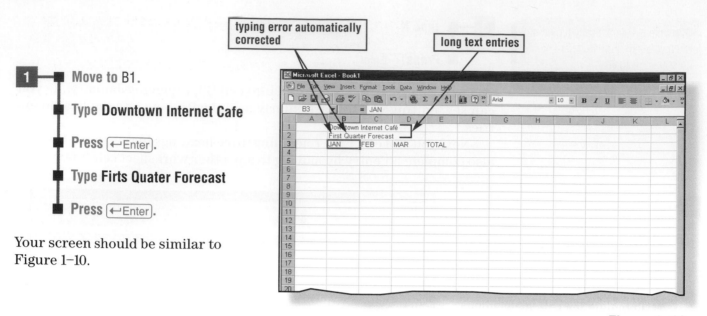

**Figure 1–10**

The two typing errors were automatically corrected when you completed the entry. When a text entry is longer than the cell's column width, Excel will display as much of the entry as it can. If the cell to the right is empty, the whole entry will be displayed. If the cell to the right contains an entry, the overlapping part of the entry is not displayed.

Next the row headings need to be entered into column A of the worksheet. The row headings and what they represent are shown below:

| Heading | Represents |
| --- | --- |
| **Sales** | |
| Beverage | Income from sale of drinks (espresso, gourmet coffee, cold drinks) |
| Food | Income from sales of sandwiches and salads |
| Internet | Income from Internet connection time charges |
| Merchandise | Income from sale of Café tee-shirts, mugs, and so forth |
| Total Sales | Sum of all sales |
| **Expenses** | |
| Cost of Goods | Cost of beverage and food items sold |
| Salary | Personnel expenses |
| Computers | Monthly payment for computer hardware |
| Lease | Monthly lease expense |
| Miscellaneous | Monthly expenses for T1 line, phone, electricity, water, trash removal, etc. |
| **Income** | |
| Net Income | Total sales minus total expenses |
| Profit Margin | Net income divided by total sales. |

**2** Complete the row headings for the Sales portion of the worksheet by entering the following headings in the indicated cells:

| Cell | Heading |
|------|---------|
| A4 | **Sales** |
| A5 | **Beverage** |
| A6 | **Food** |
| A7 | **Internet** |
| A8 | **Merchandise** |
| A9 | **Total Sales** |

Remember to press ⏎Enter or an arrow key to complete the last entry.

Your screen should be similar to Figure 1–11.

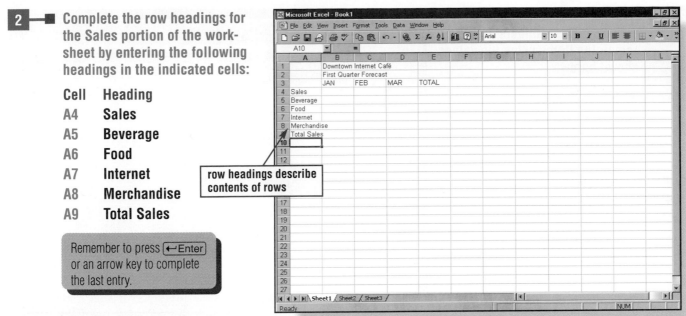

**Figure 1–11**

## Entering Numbers

Next you will enter the expected beverage sales numbers for January through March into cells B5 through D5. As you learned earlier, number entries can include the digits 0 to 9 and any of these special characters: + − ( ), . / $ % E e. When entering numbers, it is not necessary to type the comma to separate thousands or the currency ($) symbol. You will learn about adding these symbols later.

To enter the expected beverage sales for January,

**1** Move to B5.

■ Type **13600**

■ Press ⏎Enter.

You can use the number keys above the alphabetic keys or the numeric keypad area to enter numbers. If you use the numeric keypad, the Num Lock key must be on.

Your screen should be similar to Figure 1–12.

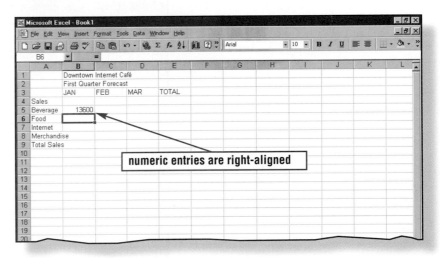

**Figure 1–12**

Unlike text entries, Excel displays number entries right-aligned in the cell space by default.

**2** ■ In the same manner, enter the January sales numbers for the remaining items using the values shown below.

| Cell | Number |
|------|--------|
| B6 | 7100 |
| B7 | 3600 |
| B8 | 3100 |

Your screen should be similar to Figure 1–13.

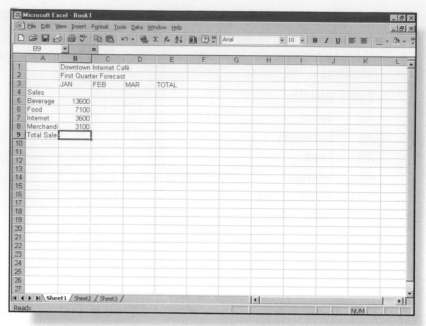

**Figure 1–13**

## Adjusting Column Widths

After entering the numbers for January in column B, any long headings in column A were cut off or interrupted. Notice that the entry in cell A8 is no longer completely displayed. It is a long text entry and because the cell to the right (B8) now contains an entry, the overlapping part of the entry is shortened.

**1** ■ Move to A8.

Your screen should be similar to Figure 1–14.

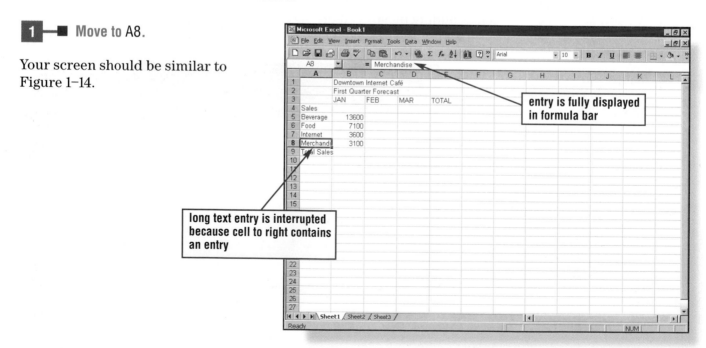

entry is fully displayed in formula bar

long text entry is interrupted because cell to right contains an entry

**Figure 1–14**

You can now see the entire entry is fully visible in the formula bar and that only the display of the entry in the cell has been shortened. To allow the long text entries in column A to be fully displayed, you can increase the column's width.

## Concept ③ Column Width

The size or width of a column controls how much information can be displayed in a cell. A text entry that is larger than the column width will be fully displayed only if the cells to the right are blank. If the cells to the right contain data, the text is interrupted. On the other hand, when numbers are entered in a cell, the column width is automatically increased to fully display the entry.

The default column width setting in Excel is 8.43. The number represents the average number of digits that can be displayed in a cell using the standard font. The column width can be any number from 1 to 255.

When the worksheet is printed, it appears as it does currently on the screen. Therefore, you want to increase the column width to display the largest entry. Likewise, you can decrease the column width when the entries in a column are short.

### Additional Information

You can also adjust the size of any row by dragging the row divider line or by using F**o**rmat/**R**ow/H**e**ight.

The menu equivalent is F**o**rmat/**C**olumn/**W**idth.

The column width can be quickly adjusted by dragging the boundary line located to the right of the column letter. Dragging it to the left decreases the column width, while dragging it to the right increases the width. As you drag, a temporary column reference line shows where the new column will appear and a ScreenTip displays the width of the column.

**2** ■ Point to the boundary line to the right of the column letter A and drag the mouse pointer to the right.

> The mouse pointer changes to ↔ when you can size a column.

■ When the ScreenTip displays 15.00, release the mouse button.

Your screen should be similar to Figure 1–15.

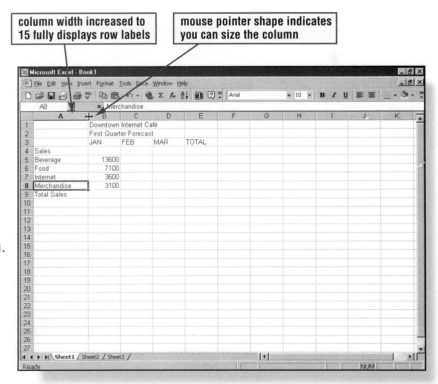

column width increased to 15 fully displays row labels

mouse pointer shape indicates you can size the column

**Figure 1–15**

Now, however, the column width is wider than you need. Another way to change the column width is to automatically adjust the width to fit the column contents.

**3** ■ **Double-click the A column boundary line.**

> The menu equivalent is **F**ormat/**C**olumn/**A**utoFit Selection.

Your screen should be similar to Figure 1–16.

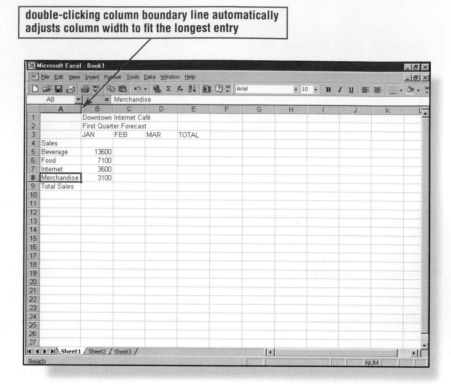

**Figure 1–16**

The column width is sized to just slightly larger than the longest cell contents.

## Saving and Closing a Workbook

The rest of the row headings, sales values, and several of the expense numbers for the month of January have already been entered and saved on your data disk in a file called Café Forecast. Before opening this workbook file, you will save and close the current workbook.

**Additional Information**

As a backup against the accidental loss of work due to power failure or other mishap, you may want to install the AutoSave add-in feature. This feature automatically saves your work at the set time intervals you specify.

While working on a document, your changes are stored in memory. Not until you save the document as a file on a disk are you safe from losing your work due to a power failure or other mishap. When you save a file, you need to specify the location where you want the file stored and a file name. The Save and Save As commands on the File menu can be used to save a file. The Save command saves a document using the same path and file name by replacing the contents of the existing disk file with the changes you have made. The Save As command allows you to select the path and provide a different file name. This command lets you save both an original version of a document and a revised document as two separate files. When a workbook is saved for the first time, either command can be used.

**1** ■ Place your data disk in drive A (or the appropriate drive for your system).

■ Click 🖫 Save

> The menu equivalent is **F**ile/**S**ave and the keyboard shortcut is Ctrl + S.

Your screen should be similar to Figure 1–17.

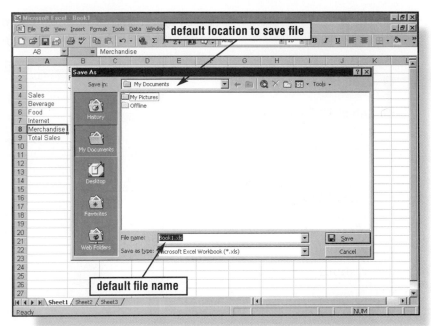

**Figure 1–17**

### Additional Information

Windows documents can have up to 256 characters in the file name. Names can contain letters or numbers. Special symbols cannot be used with the exception of the underscore.

The Save As dialog box is displayed in which you specify the location to save the file and the file name. The Save In list box displays the default location where files are stored. The list box displays the names of any Excel files stored in that location. The File Name list box displays the default workbook file name, Book1. Notice the default name is highlighted, indicating it is selected and will be replaced as you type the new name. First you will change the file name to Forecast.

**2** ■ Type **Forecast**

Your screen should be similar to Figure 1–18.

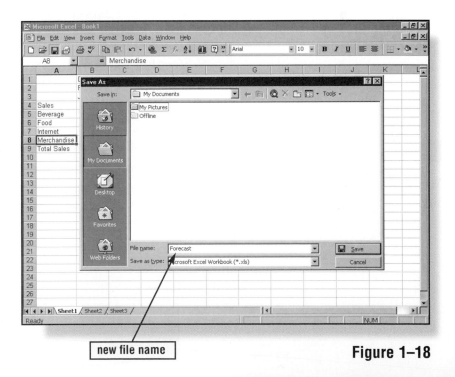

**Figure 1–18**

The default file name is replaced with new file name. Next you need to change the location to the drive containing your data disk.

**3** ■ Open the Save In list box.

■ Select 3½ Floppy (A:) (or the appropriate drive for your system) from the Save In drop-down list.

If an error message is displayed, check that your disk is properly inserted in the drive and click [ Retry ].

Your screen should be similar to Figure 1–19.

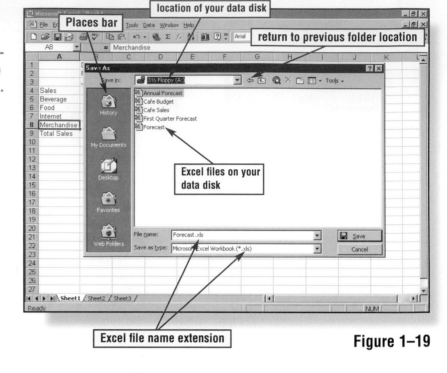

**Figure 1–19**

Your file list may display more file names than shown here.

Now the name list box displays the names of all Excel files on your data disk. You can also select the location to save from the Places bar along the left side of the dialog box. The icons bring up a list of recently accessed files and folders, the contents of the My Documents and Favorites folder, the Windows desktop, and the remote WebFolders list. Selecting a folder from one of these lists changes to that location. You can also click the [⇦] button in the toolbar to return to folders that were previously opened during the current session.

Notice that Excel added the xls file extension to the file name. This is the default extension for Excel workbook documents.

**4** ■ Click [🖫 Save].

Your screen should be similar to Figure 1–20.

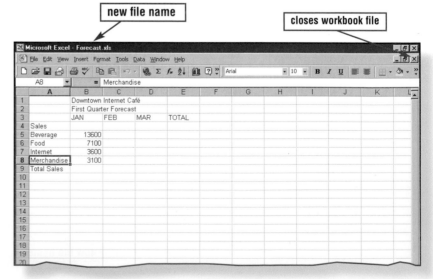

**Figure 1–20**

The new file name is displayed in the worksheet window title bar. The worksheet data that was on your screen and in the computer's memory is now saved on your data disk in a new file called Forecast. You are now ready to close the workbook file.

The menu equivalent is **F**ile/**C**lose.

**5** ■ **Click ☒ Close Window (in the menu bar).**

Because you did not make any changes to the document since saving it, the document window is closed immediately and the Excel window displays an empty workspace. If you had made additional changes, Excel would ask if you wanted to save the file before closing it. This prevents the accidental closing of a file that has not been saved first.

*Note:* If you are running short on lab time, this is an appropriate place to end your session.

## Opening a Workbook File

You are now ready to open the workbook file named Café Budget.

**1** ■ **Click ☞ Open.**

The menu equivalent is **F**ile/**O**pen and the keyboard shortcut is Ctrl + O.

■ **If necessary, select the drive containing your data disk from the Look In drop-down list.**

Your screen should be similar to Figure 1–21.

location to find file

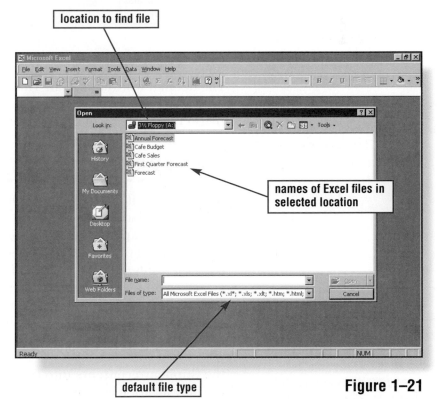

names of Excel files in selected location

default file type

**Figure 1–21**

If your screen does not display file extensions, your Windows program has this option deactivated.

From the Open dialog box, you specify the name and location of the file to open. The file list area displays the names of all Microsoft Excel files on your data disk. Only Excel files are displayed; this is the default setting in the Files of Type text box. The file you want to open is Café Budget.

**2** ■ Select Café Budget.

> You can double-click on the file name to both select it and choose ☞ Open ▾ .

■ Click ☞ Open ▾ .

Your screen should be similar to Figure 1–22.

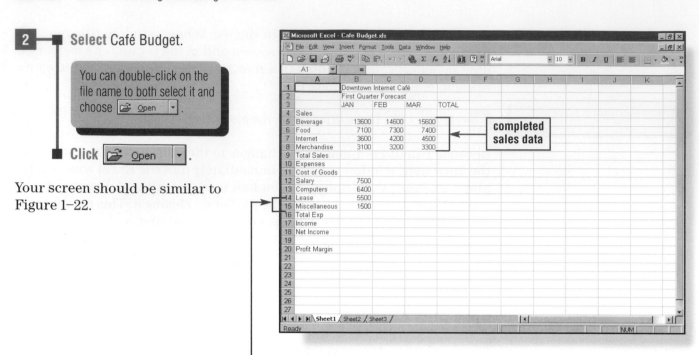

completed sales data

new row labels and expense values

**Figure 1–22**

The new workbook file is loaded and displayed in the workbook window. The opened workbook, Café Budget, contains the additional sales values for February and March, the expense row headings, and several of the expense values for the month of January.

## Copying Data

Next you want to enter the estimated expenses for salary, computers, lease, and miscellaneous for February and March. They are the same as the January expense numbers. Because these values are the same, instead of entering the same number repeatedly into each cell you can quickly copy the contents of one cell to another.

The contents of worksheet cells can be duplicated (copied) to other locations in the worksheet using the Copy and Paste commands on the Edit menu or their toolbar shortcuts. First you use the Copy command to copy the cell contents to the Clipboard. Then you move to the new location where you want the contents copied and use the Paste command to insert the Clipboard contents into the selected cells. Be careful when pasting to the new location because any existing entries are replaced.

To use the Copy command, you first must select the cell or cells containing the data to be copied. This is called the **copy area** or **source**.

First you will copy the value in cell B12 into cells C12 and D12.

### Additional Information

Office 2000 contains an Office clipboard in addition to the Windows clipboard. Only one item can be stored in the Windows clipboard while up to 12 items can be stored in the Office 2000 clipboard. The Office 2000 clipboard allows you to copy multiple items from various Office documents and paste all or part of the collection of copied items into another Office document.

**1** ■ Move to B12.

■ Click 📋 Copy.

> The menu equivalent is **E**dit/**C**opy and the shortcut key is Ctrl + C. Copy is also available on the shortcut menu.

Your screen should be similar to Figure 1–23.

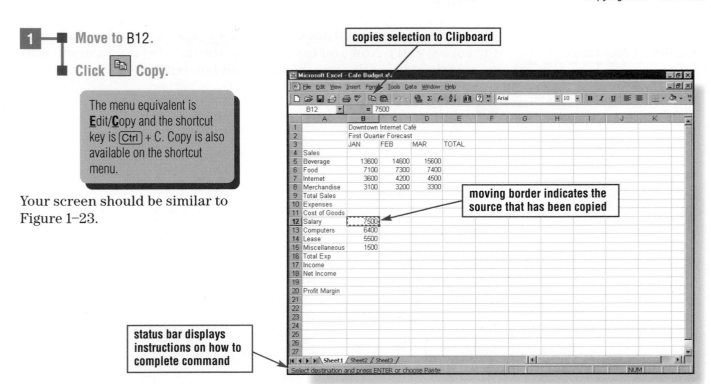

*copies selection to Clipboard*

*moving border indicates the source that has been copied*

*status bar displays instructions on how to complete command*

**Figure 1–23**

**Additional Information**

While the moving border is still displayed, you can also simply press ←Enter to paste. However, using this method clears the contents of the Clipboard immediately so it can only be used once.

A moving border identifies the source and indicates that the contents have been copied to the Clipboard. The instructions displayed in the status bar tell you to select a **destination**, also called the **paste area**, where you want the contents copied. To specify cell C12 as the destination,

**2** ■ Move to C12.

■ Click 📋 Paste.

> The menu equivalent is **E**dit/**P**aste and the shortcut key is Ctrl + V. Paste is also available on the shortcut menu.

Your screen should be similar to Figure 1–24.

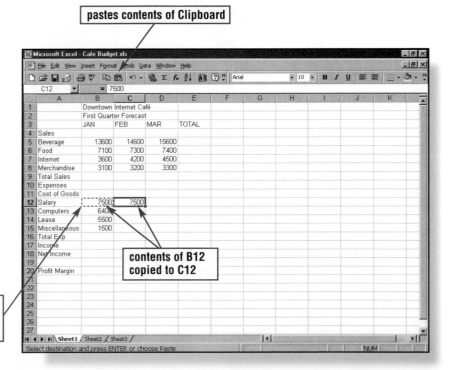

*pastes contents of Clipboard*

*contents of B12 copied to C12*

*moving border indicates source can be pasted again*

**Figure 1–24**

The moving border is still displayed indicating the Clipboard still contains the copied entry. Now you can complete the data for the Salary row by pasting the value again from the Clipboard into cell D12.

**3** — ■ Move to D12.

    ■ Click  Paste.

## Selecting a Range

Now you need to copy the Computers value in cell B13 to February and March. You could copy and paste the contents individually into each cell. It is much faster, however, to select a paste area that consists of multiple cells, called a range, and paste the contents to all cells in the selection at once.

**Concept 4 Range**

A selection consisting of two or more cells is a **range.** The cells in a range can be adjacent or nonadjacent. An **adjacent range** is a rectangular block of adjoining cells. In the example shown below, the shaded areas show valid and invalid adjacent ranges. A **nonadjacent range** is two or more selected cells or ranges that are not adjoining.

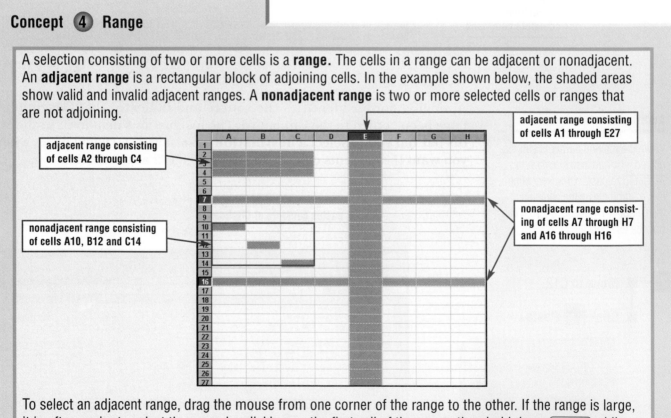

adjacent range consisting of cells A2 through C4

adjacent range consisting of cells A1 through E27

nonadjacent range consisting of cells A10, B12 and C14

nonadjacent range consisting of cells A7 through H7 and A16 through H16

To select an adjacent range, drag the mouse from one corner of the range to the other. If the range is large, it is often easier to select the range by clicking on the first cell of the range, then hold down [⇧ Shift] while clicking on the last cell of the range. You can quickly select an entire column or row by clicking the column or row letter or number. Dragging across the row or column heading selects adjacent rows and columns.

To select nonadjacent cells or cell ranges, after selecting the first cell or range hold down [Ctrl] while selecting each additional range. To select nonadjacent rows or columns, hold down [Ctrl] while selecting the rows or columns.

To complete the data for the Computer row, you want to copy the value in cell B13 to the Clipboard and then copy the Clipboard contents to the range of cells C13 through D13.

**1** ■ Move to B13

■ Click 📋 Copy

■ Drag to select cells C13 to D13.

> You can also hold down ⇧ Shift and use the directional keys to select a range.

■ Click 📋 Paste.

> The paste area does not have to be adjacent to the copy area.

Your screen should be similar to Figure 1–25.

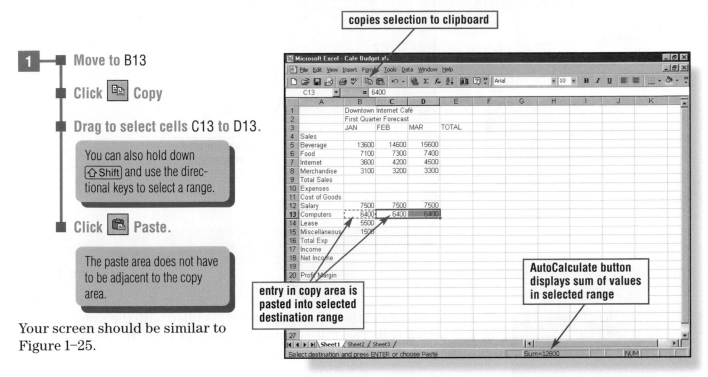

**Figure 1–25**

The destination range is highlighted and identified by a dark border surrounding the selected cells. The entry copied from cell B13 was pasted into the selected destination range. Also notice the AutoCalculate button in the status bar is now active. This button displays the sum of values in a selected range of cells. It can also display the average, count, minimum, or maximum values in a range by selecting the appropriate option from the button's shortcut menu.

## Copying Using the Fill Handle

Next you will copy the January Lease expenses to cells C14 through D14 and Miscellaneous expenses to cells C15 through D15. You can copy both values at the same time across the row by first specifying a range as the source area.

**1** ■ Drag to select cells B14 through B15.

Another way to copy is to drag the **fill handle,** the black box in the lower-right corner of the selection.

**2** ■ **Point to the fill handle and when the mouse pointer is a ✛, drag the mouse to extend the selection to cells C14 through D15.**

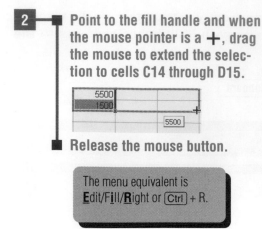

■ **Release the mouse button.**

The menu equivalent is **E**dit/Fi**ll**/**R**ight or Ctrl + R.

Your screen should be similar to Figure 1–26.

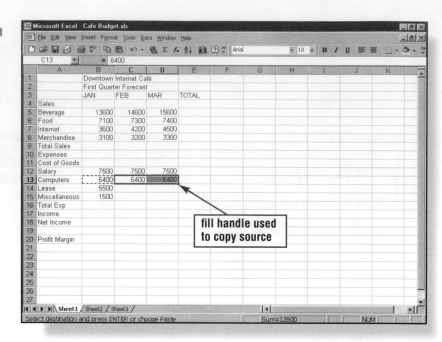

fill handle used to copy source

**Figure 1–26**

If a range is not selected, the contents of the cell to the left or above are copied into the active cell.

The range of cells to the right of the source is filled with the same value as in the active cell. The Fill command does not copy the source to the Clipboard; therefore, you cannot paste the source multiple times.

### Review of Copying Methods

To review, you have learned two methods to copy an entry:

1.   Use the Copy and Paste commands: **E**dit/**C**opy (Ctrl +C) or 📋 and **E**dit/**P**aste (Ctrl + V) or 📋.

2.   Use the **E**dit/Fi**ll** command: **R**ight, **L**eft, **U**p, or **D**own or drag the fill handle.

When you use the Copy command, the contents are copied to the Clipboard and can be copied to any location in the worksheet, another workbook, or another application. When you use **E**dit/Fi**ll** or drag the fill handle, the destination must be in the same row or column as the source, and the source is not copied to the Clipboard.

## Entering Formulas

The remaining entries that need to be made in the worksheet are formula entries.

---

### Concept ⑤ Formulas

A **formula** is an entry that performs a calculation. The result of the calculation is displayed in the cell containing the formula. A formula always begins with an equal sign (=), which defines it as a numeric entry. Formulas use the following arithmetic operators to specify the type of numeric operation to perform:

| Symbol | Operation |
|--------|-----------|
| + | addition |
| – | subtraction |
| / | division |
| * | multiplication |
| ^ | exponentiation |

In a formula that contains more than one operator, Excel performs the calculation in the following **order of precedence:**

Exponentiation

Multiplication and division

Addition and subtraction.

This order can be overridden by enclosing the operation you want performed first in parentheses. Excel evaluates operations in parentheses working from the innermost set of parentheses out. For example, in the formula =5*4–3, Excel first multiplies 5 times 4 to get 20, and then subtracts 3 for a total of 17. If you enter the formula as =5*(4–3), Excel first subtracts 3 from 4 because the operation is enclosed in parentheses. Then Excel multiplies the result, 1, by 5, for a final result of 5. If two or more operators have the same order of precedence, calculations are performed in order from left to right.

The values on which a numeric formula performs a calculation are called **operands**. Numbers or cell references can be operands in a formula. Usually cell references are used, and when the numeric entries in the referenced cell(s) change, the result of the formula is automatically recalculated. You can also use single-word row and column headings in place of cell references and formulas.

The first formula you will enter will calculate the total Beverage sales for January through March by summing the numbers in cells B5 through D5. You will use cell references in the formula as the operands and the + arithmetic operator to specify addition. A formula is entered in the cell where you want the calculated value to be displayed.

**1** ■ Move to E5.

■ Type =

■ Type b5+c5+d5

> Cell references can by typed in either uppercase or lower-case letters. Spaces between parts of the formulas are optional.

■ Press ←Enter.

> If you enter a formula incor-rectly, Excel displays an error in the cell or message box proposing a correction.

■ Move to E5.

Your screen should be similar to Figure 1-27.

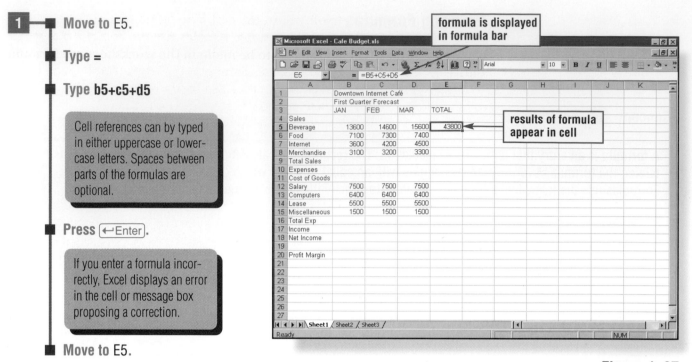

**Figure 1-27**

The number 43800 is displayed in cell E5 and the formula that calculates this value is displayed in the formula bar.

## Copying Formulas

The formulas to calculate the total sales for rows 5 through 8 can be entered next. Just like text and numeric entries, you can copy formulas from one cell to another.

**1** ■ Copy the formula in cell E5 to cells E6 through E8 using any of the copying methods.

■ Move to E6.

Your screen should be similar to Figure 1-28.

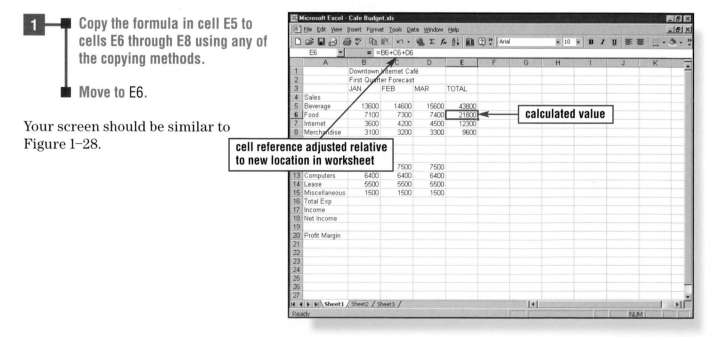

**Figure 1-28**

The number 21800 is displayed in the cell. The formula displayed in the formula bar is =B6+C6+D6. The formula to calculate the Food total sales is not an exact duplicate of the formula used to calculate the Beverage total sales (=B5+C5+D5). Instead the cells referenced in the formula have been changed to reflect the new location of the formula in row 6. This is because the references in the formula are relative references.

## Concept ⑥ Relative Reference

A **relative reference** is a cell or range reference in a formula whose location is interpreted by Excel in relation to the position of the cell that contains the formula. For example, in the formula to calculate total beverage sales in cell E5, the cell reference to B5 tells Excel to use the contents of the cell three cells to the left of the cell containing the formula. When a formula is copied, the referenced cells in the formula automatically adjust to reflect the new worksheet location. The relative relationship between the referenced cell and the new location is maintained. Because relative references automatically adjust for the new location, the relative references in a copied formula refer to different cells than the references in the original formula. The relationship between cells in both the copied and pasted formula is the same although the cell references are different.

|   | B | C | D | |
|---|---|---|---|---|
| 6 | 13600 | 14600 | 15600 | =B6+C6+D6 |
| 7 | 7100 | 7300 | 7500 | =B7+C7+D7 |
| 8 | 4000 | 4200 | 4500 | =B8+C8+D8 |
| 9 | 3100 | 3200 | 3300 | =B9+C9+D9 |
|   |   |   |   |   |
|   |   |   |   |   |

**2** — ■ Move to E7 and E8.

The formulas in these cells have also changed to reflect the new row location and to appropriately calculate the total based on the sales.

## Entering Functions

Next you will calculate the monthly total sales. The formula to calculate the total sales for January needs to be entered in cell B9 and copied across the row. You could use a formula similar to the formula used to calculate the category sales in column E. The formula would be =B5+B6+B7+B8. However, it is faster and more accurate to use a function.

## Concept ⑦ Functions

**Functions** are prewritten formulas that perform certain types of calculations automatically. The **syntax** or rules of structure for entering all functions is:

Function name (argument1, argument2,...)

The function name identifies the type of calculation to be performed. Most functions require that you enter one or more arguments following the function name. An **argument** is the data the function uses to perform the calculation. The type of data the function requires depends upon the type of calculation being performed. Most commonly, the argument consists of numbers or references to cells that contain numbers. The argument is enclosed in parentheses, and multiple arguments are separated by commas. If a function starts the formula, enter an equal sign before the function name (=SUM(D5:F5)/25).

Excel includes several hundred functions* divided into 9 categories. Some common functions and the results they calculate are shown below.

| Category | Function | Calculates |
|---|---|---|
| Financial | PMT | Calculates the payment for a loan based on constant payments and a constant interest rate |
| | PV | Returns the present value of an investment; the total amount that a series of future payments is worth now |
| Time & Date | TODAY | Returns the serial number that represents today's date |
| | DATE | Returns the serial number of a particular date |
| | NOW | Returns the serial number of the current date and time |
| Math & Trig | SUM | Adds all the numbers in a range of cells |
| | ABS | Returns the absolute value of a number, a number without its sign |
| Statistical | AVERAGE | Returns the average (arithmetic mean) of its arguments |
| | MAX | Returns the largest value in a set of values; ignores logical values and text |
| Lookup & Reference | COLUMNS | Returns the number of columns in an array or reference |
| | CHOOSE | Chooses a value or action to perform from a list of values, based on an index number |
| Database | DSUM | Adds the numbers in the field (column) or records in the database that match the conditions you specify |
| | DAVERAGE | Averages the values in a column in a list or database that match conditions you specify |
| Text | DOLLAR | Converts a number to text, using currency format |
| | UPPER | Converts text to uppercase |
| Logical | IF | Returns one value if a condition you specify evaluates to True and another value if it evaluates to False |
| | AND | Returns True if all its arguments are True; returns False if any arguments are False |
| Information | ISLOGICAL | Returns True if value is a logical value, either True or False. |
| | ISREF | Returns True if value is a reference |

*Use Help for detailed explanations of every function.

You will use the SUM function to calculate the total sales for January. Because the SUM function is the most commonly used function, it has its own toolbar button.

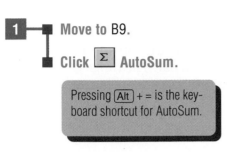

**1** ■ Move to B9.

■ Click Σ AutoSum.

> Pressing [Alt] + = is the keyboard shortcut for AutoSum.

Your screen should be similar to Figure 1–29.

**Figure 1–29**

### Additional Information

The AutoSum button can also calculate a grand total if your worksheet contains subtotals. Select a cell below or to the right of a cell that contains a subtotal and then click [Σ] AutoSum.

Excel automatically proposes a range based upon the data above or to the left of the active cell. The name of the function followed by the range argument enclosed in parentheses is displayed in the formula bar. Excel displays a range reference as the topmost cell and bottommost cell in the range separated by a colon (B5:B8). To accept the proposed range and enter the function,

**2** ■ Click ✓ Enter.

> If you used the [←Enter] key, move to B9.

Your screen should be similar to Figure 1–30.

**Figure 1–30**

The result, 27400, calculated by the SUM function is displayed in cell B9.

Next you need to calculate the total sales for February and March and the Total column.

**3**— ■ **Copy the function from cell B9 to cells C9 through E9.**

■ **Move to C9.**

The result calculated by the function, 29300, is displayed in cell C9 and the copied function is displayed in the formula bar. The range reference in the function adjusted relative to its new cell location because it is a relative reference.

## Testing the Worksheet

Now that you have created the worksheet structure and entered some sample data for the forecasted sales for the first quarter, you want to test the formulas to verify they are operating correctly. A simple way to do this is to use a calculator to verify that the correct result is displayed. You can then further test the worksheet by changing values and verifying that all cells containing formulas that reference the value are appropriately recalculated.

After considering the sales estimates for the three months, you decide that the estimated Internet sales for January are too low and you want to increase this number from 3600 to 4000.

**1**— ■ **Change the entry in cell B7 to 4000.**

Your screen should be similar to Figure 1–31.

increasing sales value by 400 increases total sales in B9, E7 and E9 by 400

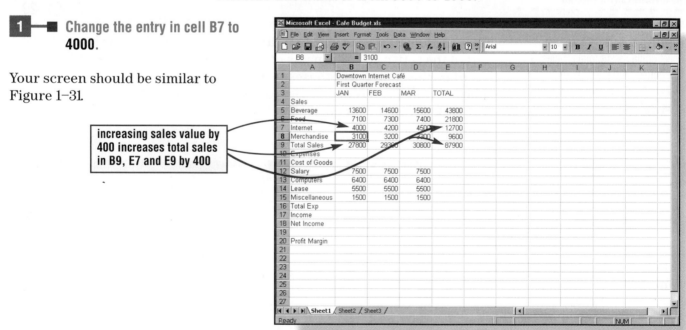

**Figure 1–31**

The Internet total in cell E7 has been automatically recalculated. The number displayed is now 12700. Likewise, the January total in cell B9 and the grand total in cell E9 have increased by 400 to reflect the change in cell B7.

### Concept 8 Automatic Recalculation

The **automatic recalculation** of a formula whenever a number in a referenced cell in the formula changes is one of the most powerful features of electronic worksheets. Only those formulas directly affected by a change in the data are recalculated. This is called **minimal recalculation**. Without this feature, in large worksheets it could take several minutes to recalculate all formulas each time a number is changed in the worksheet. The minimal recalculation feature decreases the recalculation time by only recalculating dependent formulas.

The formulas in the worksheet are correctly calculating the desired result. The Sales portion of the worksheet is now complete.

## Using Pointing to Enter a Formula

Next you will enter the formula to calculate the cost of goods sold expenses. These numbers are estimated by using a formula to calculate the number as a percent of sales. As a general rule, the Café calculates Beverage expenses at 25 percent of beverage sales and food expenses at 50 percent of food sales.

**Additional Information**

The cells can be adjacent or non-adjacent.

Rather than typing in the cell references for the formula, you will enter them by selecting the worksheet cells. In addition, to make the process of entering and copying entries even easier, you can enter data into the first cell of a range and have it copied to all other cells in the range at the same time by using Ctrl + ←Enter to complete the entry. You will use this feature to enter the formulas to calculate the beverage expenses for January through March. This formula needs to first calculate the beverage cost of goods at 25 percent and add it to the food cost of goods calculated at 50 percent.

**1** ■ Select B11 through D11.

■ Type =

■ Click cell B5.

Even when a range is selected, you can still point to specify cells in the formula. You can also use the direction keys to move to the cell.

Your screen should be similar to Figure 1–32.

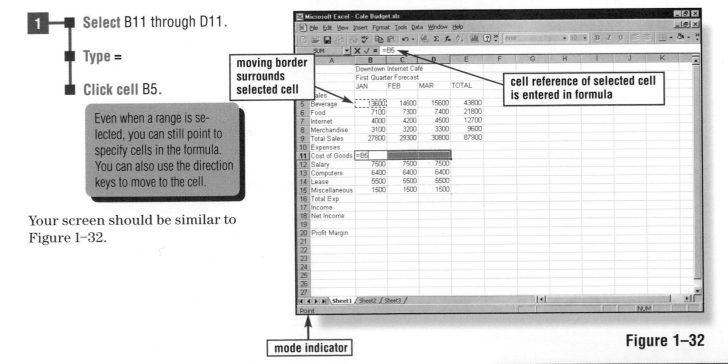

**Figure 1–32**

Notice that the status bar displays the current mode as Point. This tells you the program is allowing you to select cells by highlighting them. The cell reference, B5, is entered following the = sign. To continue the formula and enter the percentage value to multiply by,

**2** ■ Type **\*25%**

Next you need to add the Food percentage to the formula,

**3** ■ Type **+**

■ Click on B6.

■ Type **\*50%**

■ Press Ctrl + ←Enter.

Your screen should be similar to Figure 1–33.

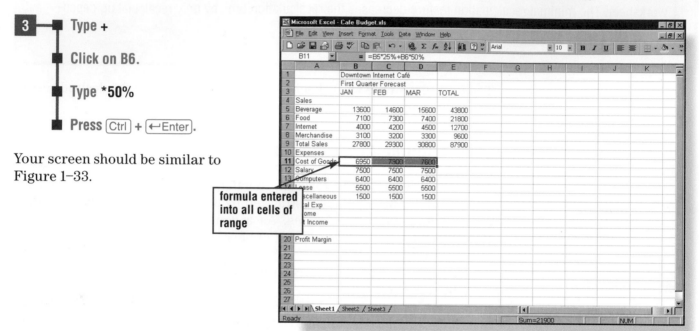

formula entered into all cells of range

**Figure 1–33**

The formula to calculate the January cost of goods expense was entered in cell B11 and copied to all cells of the selected range. You can now calculate the total expenses in row 11 and column E. To do this quickly, you will pre-select the range and use the AutoCalculate button.

**4** ■ Select B16 through D16.

■ Click Σ.

■ In a similar manner, enter sum functions to calculate the expenses in column E.

The next formula to be entered will calculate the net income. Net income is calculated by subtracting total expenses from total sales.

**Select** B18 through E18.

**Enter the formula =B9-B16**

**Press** Ctrl + ←Enter.

Your screen should be similar to Figure 1–34.

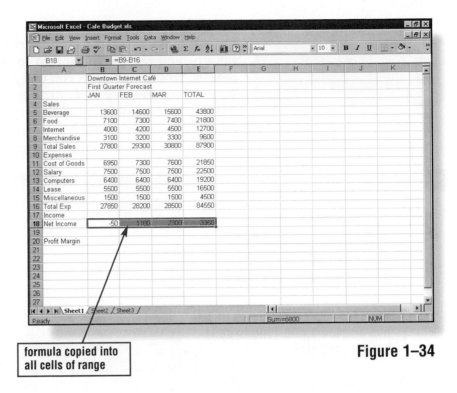

**formula copied into all cells of range**

**Figure 1–34**

The formula is quickly entered into all cells of the range. The final formula you need enter is to calculate the profit margin.

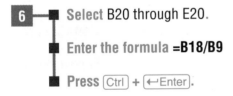

**Select** B20 through E20.

**Enter the formula =B18/B9**

**Press** Ctrl + ←Enter.

Your screen should be similar to Figure 1–35.

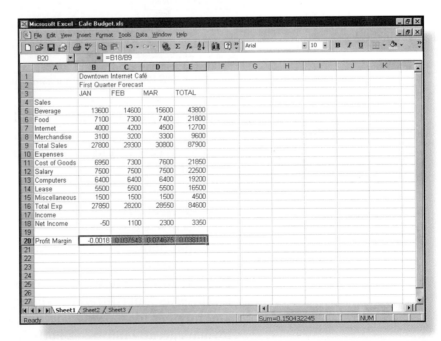

**Figure 1–35**

The profit margins are calculated and displayed in cells B20 through E20.

## Inserting Rows

To delete a cell, row or column, select it and choose **E**dit/**D**elete/Entire
**R**ow or Entire **C**olumn.

Finally, you realize you forgot to include a row for the Advertising expenses. To add this data, you will insert a blank row below the Lease row.
To indicate where you want to insert a single blank row, move the cell
pointer to the row immediately below the row where you want the new
row inserted. If you want to insert multiple rows, select a range of rows
and Excel inserts the same number of rows you selected in the range.

**1** ■ Move to A15.

■ Choose **I**nsert/**R**ows.

The Insert and Delete commands are also available on
the shortcut menu.

■ Enter the label **Advertising** in cell
A15 and the value **1000** in cells
B15 through D15.

■ Copy the function from cell E14
to E15 to calculate the Total
Advertising expense.

Your screen should be similar to
Figure 1–36.

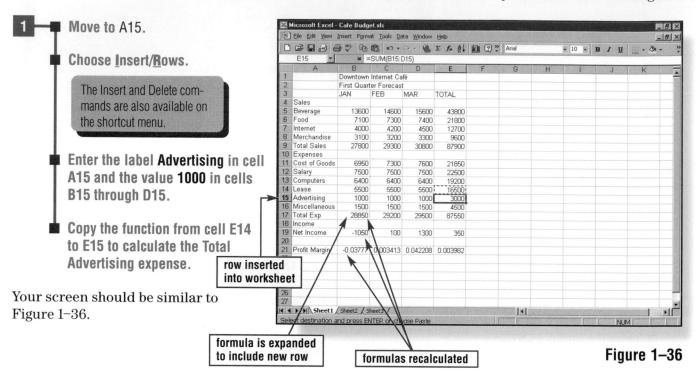

**row inserted
into worksheet**

**formula is expanded
to include new row**

**formulas recalculated**

**Figure 1–36**

### Additional Information

In a similar manner, you can insert
blank columns by moving the cell
pointer to the right of the column
where you want to insert the new
column and use **I**nsert/**C**olumn.

The range in the formula to calculate monthly total expenses in row 17 has
been revised to include the data in the inserted row. Additionally the net
income in row 19 and profit margin in row 21 have been recalculated to reflect the change in data.

## Formatting the Worksheet

Now that many of the worksheet values are entered, you want to improve
the appearance of the worksheet by changing the format of the headings.
**Format** controls how information is displayed in a cell and includes such
features as font (different type styles and sizes), color, patterns, borders,
and number formats such as commas and dollar signs. Applying different
formats greatly improves both the appearance and readability of the data
in a worksheet.

## Changing Cell Alignment

You decide the column headings would look better if they were right-aligned in their cell spaces. Then they would appear over the numbers in the column. Alignment is a basic format setting that is used in most worksheets.

**Concept ⑨ Alignment**

**Alignment** settings allow you to change the horizontal and vertical placement and the orientation of an entry in a cell. Horizontal placement allows you to left-, center-, or right-align text and number entries in the cell space. Entries can also be indented within the cell space, centered across a selection, or justified. You can also fill a cell horizontally with a repeated entry. Vertical placement allows you to specify whether the cell contents are displayed at the top, centered, or at the bottom of the vertical cell space or justified vertically. Orientation changes the angle of text in a cell by varying the degrees of rotation. Examples of the basic alignment settings are shown below.

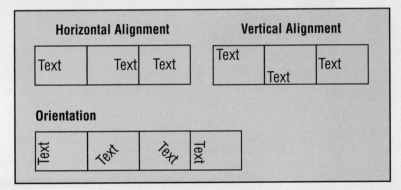

The default horizontal alignment is left for a text entry and right for a number entry. Vertical alignment is bottom for both types of entries.

First you will change the column heading in cell B3 to right-aligned using the Format menu.

**1** ■ **Move to B3.**

■ **Choose F̲ormat/Ce̲lls.**

> The shortcut key is Ctrl + 1. Format Cells is also an option on the shortcut menu.

■ **Open the Alignment tab.**

Your screen should be similar to Figure 1–37.

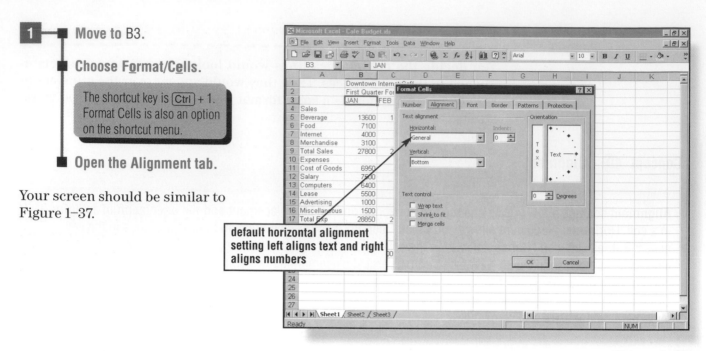

**Figure 1–37**

The Alignment tab shows the default horizontal alignment setting is General. This setting left-aligns text entries and right-aligns number entries. You want to change the horizontal alignment of the entry to right-aligned.

**2** ■ **Open the Horizontal drop-down list box.**

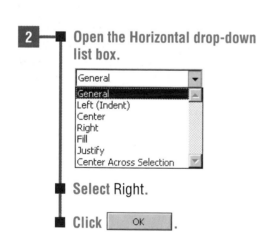

■ **Select Right.**

■ **Click** OK **.**

Your screen should be similar to Figure 1–38.

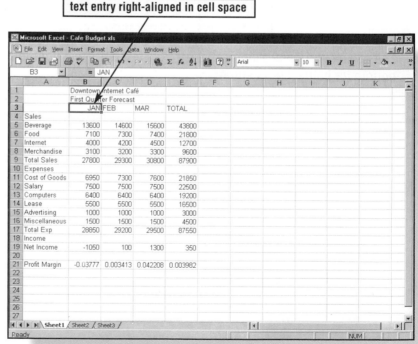

**Figure 1–38**

A quicker way to change the alignment is to use the Formatting toolbar shortcuts shown below:

| Shortcut | Action |
|----------|--------|
| | Align Left |
| | Center |
| | Align Right |

> If you do not hold down ⬆Shift while double-clicking on a border, the cell selector moves to the last-used cell in the direction indicated.

You can quickly align a range of cells by selecting the range and then using the command or button. A quick way to select a range of filled cells is to hold down ⬆Shift and double-click on the edge of the active cell in the direction in which you want the range expanded. For example, to select the range to the right of the active cell, you would double-click the right border. To right-align the remaining column entries,

**3** ■ Move to cell C3.

■ Hold down ⬆Shift and double-click the right cell border of cell C3.

■ Click ▤ Align Right.

> The menu equivalent is F**o**rmat/C**e**lls/Alignment/**H**orizontal/Right.

The entries in the selected range are right-aligned in their cell spaces.

## Indenting Entries

Next you would like to indent the row headings in cells A5 through A9 and A11 through A16 from the left edge of the cell. You want to indent the headings in both ranges at the same time. To select a nonadjacent range, you select the first cell or range of cells and then hold down Ctrl and select the other cells. To select the cells and indent them,

**1** — Select A5 through A8.

■ Hold down Ctrl.

■ Select A11 through A16.

■ Click 🔲 Increase Indent.

> The menu equivalent is Format/Cells/Alignment/ Horizontal/Left(Indent)/1.

Your screen should be similar to Figure 1–39.

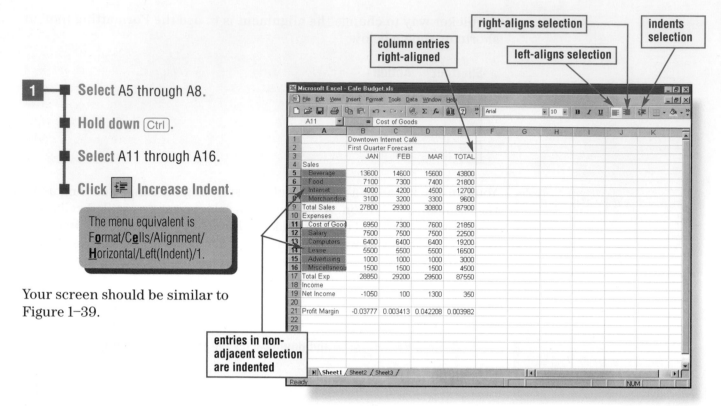

Figure 1–39

Each entry in the selected range is indented two spaces from the left edge of the cell. You would also like to indent the Total Sales, Total Exp, and Net Income headings four spaces.

**2** — Select A9, A17 and A19.

■ Click 🔲 Increase Indent (2 times).

Your screen should be similar to Figure 1–40.

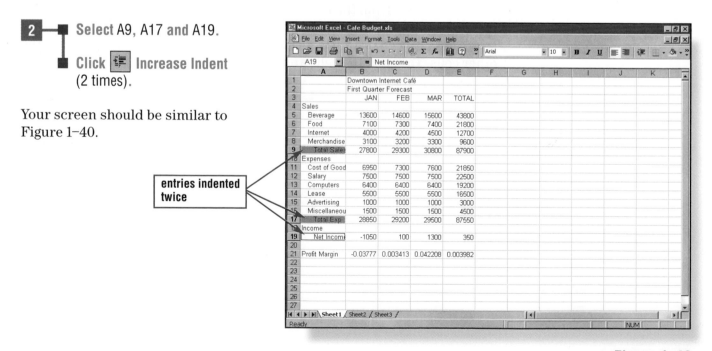

Figure 1–40

## Moving Cell Contents

**Additional Information**

If you move cells containing formulas, the formulas are not adjusted relative to their new worksheet location.

As you drag, an outline of the cell appears and the mouse pointer displays the cell reference to show its new location in the worksheet.

Next you want to center the worksheet titles across columns A through E so they are centered over the worksheet data. Before you can do this however, you need to first move the two titles into the leftmost cell of the range. You could cut and paste the contents, or you can drag the cell border to move the cell contents. This is similar to copying by dragging. Dragging is quickest and most useful when the distance between cells is short and they are visible within the window, whereas Cut and Paste is best for long-distance moves.

**1** ▪ Select cells B1 and B2.

▪ Point to the border of the range selection and when the mouse pointer shape is ↖ , drag the mouse pointer to cell A1:A2 and release the mouse button.

Your screen should be similar to Figure 1-41.

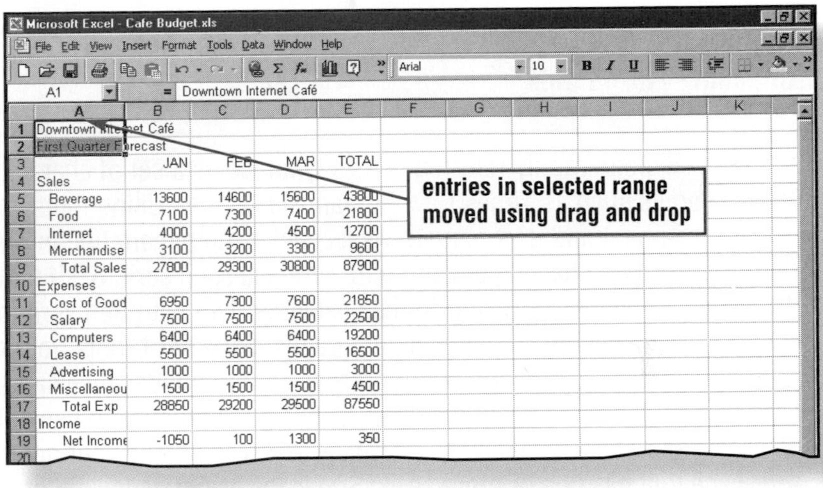

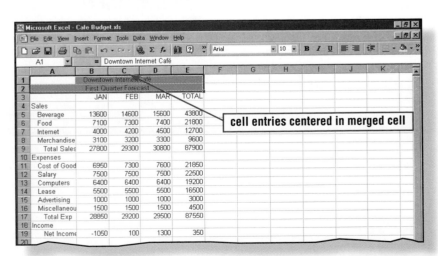

**Figure 1-41**

The cell contents are copied into cells A1 and A2 and cleared from the original cells.

## Centering Across a Selection

Now you are ready to center the worksheet title across cells A1 through E2.

**1** ▪ Select A1 through E2.

▪ Choose Format/Cells

▪ From the Horizontal drop-down list, select Center Across Selection.

▪ Click  OK  .

Your screen should be similar to Figure 1-42.

**Figure 1-42**

Excel has created a **merged cell** by combining all cells in the selected range into one and the contents of the leftmost cell of the range are centered within the merged cell space. The cell reference for the merged cell is the upper-left cell in the range. If you are centering a single row, you can use the toolbar shortcut ▦ for this feature.

## Changing Fonts and Font Styles

**Additional Information**

The Font settings are common to all Office 2000 programs.

Finally, you want to improve the worksheet appearance by enhancing the appearance of the title. One way to do this is to change the font and font size used in the title.

### Concept 10 Fonts

A **font**, also commonly referred to as a **typeface**, is a set of characters with a specific design. The designs have names such as Times New Roman and Courier. Using fonts as a design element can add interest to your document and give readers visual cues to help them find information quickly.

There are two basic types of fonts, serif and sans serif. **Serif** fonts have a flair at the base of each letter that visually leads the reader to the next letter. Two common serif fonts are Roman and Times New Roman. Serif fonts generally are used in paragraphs. **Sans serif** fonts do not have a flair at the base of each letter. Arial and Helvetica are two common sans serif fonts. Because sans serif fonts have a clean look, they are often used for headings in documents. It is good practice to use only two types of fonts in a document, one for text and one for headings. Too many styles can make your document look cluttered and unprofessional.

Each font has one or more sizes. Size is the height and width of the character and is commonly measured in points, abbreviated pt. One point equals about 1/72 inch, and text in most documents is 10 pt or 12 pt.

Here are several examples of the same text in various fonts and sizes.

| Typeface | Font Size (12 pt/18 pt) |
|---|---|
| Arial | This is 12 pt. This is 18 pt. |
| Courier New | This is 12 pt. This is 18 pt. |
| Times New Roman | This is 12 pt. This is 18 pt. |

The fonts on your computer system will be either printer or TrueType fonts. TrueType fonts appear onscreen as they will appear when printed. They are installed when Windows is installed. Printer fonts are supported by your printer and are displayed as close as possible to how they will appear onscreen, but may not match exactly when printed.

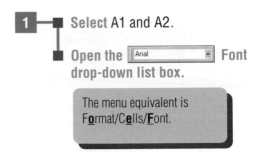

**1** ■ Select A1 and A2.

■ Open the [Arial ▼] Font drop-down list box.

The menu equivalent is F**o**rmat/C**e**lls/**F**ont.

Your screen should be similar to Figure 1–43.

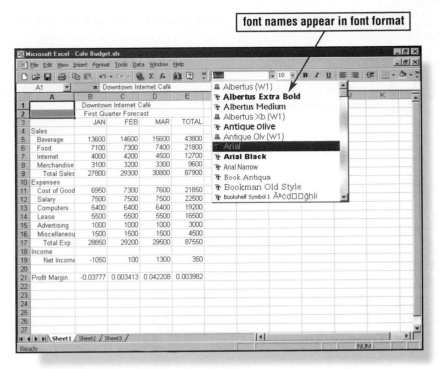

**Figure 1–43**

The Font drop-down menu displays examples of the available fonts in alphabetical order. The default worksheet font, Arial, is highlighted.

**2** ■ Select Times New Roman.

Your screen should be similar to Figure 1–44.

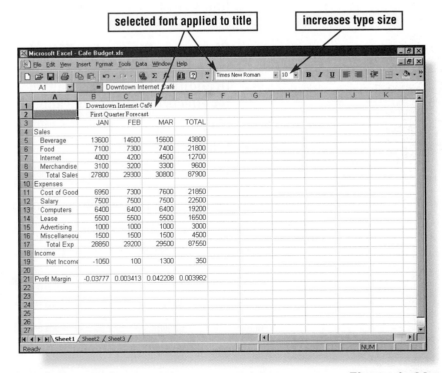

**Figure 1–44**

The title appears in the selected typeface and the Font button displays the name of the font in the active cell.

Next you will increase the font size to 14.

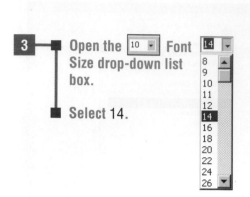

3   ■ Open the 10 ▾ Font
       Size drop-down list
       box.

    ■ Select 14.

Your screen should be similar to
Figure 1–45.

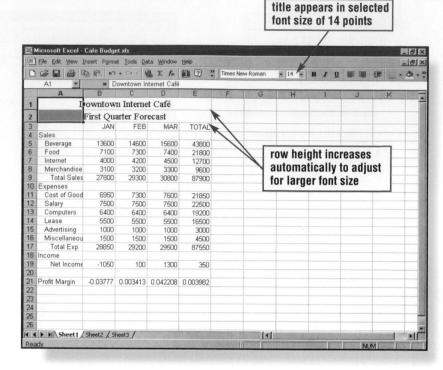

**Figure 1–45**

Notice that the height of the row has increased to accommodate the larger
font size of the heading.

## Changing Character Effects

In addition to changing font and font size, you can apply different character effects to enhance the appearance of text.

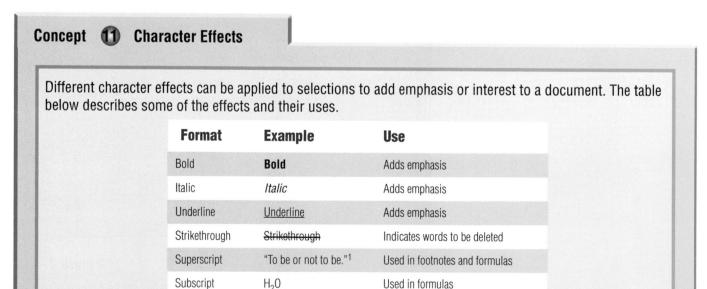

**Concept  11  Character Effects**

Different character effects can be applied to selections to add emphasis or interest to a document. The table
below describes some of the effects and their uses.

| Format | Example | Use |
| --- | --- | --- |
| Bold | **Bold** | Adds emphasis |
| Italic | *Italic* | Adds emphasis |
| Underline | Underline | Adds emphasis |
| Strikethrough | ~~Strikethrough~~ | Indicates words to be deleted |
| Superscript | "To be or not to be."[1] | Used in footnotes and formulas |
| Subscript | $H_2O$ | Used in formulas |
| Color | Color Color Color | Adds interest |

You want to add bold, italic, and underlines to several worksheet entries. First you will bold the two title lines.

**1** ■ Click **B** Bold.

Your screen should be similar to Figure 1–46.

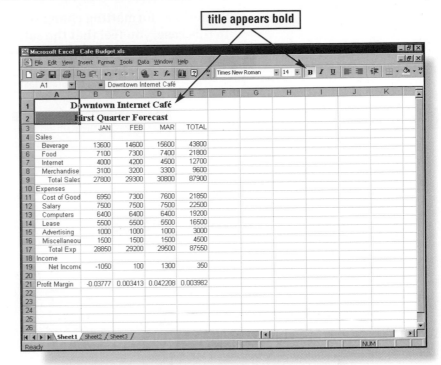

**Figure 1–46**

Next you would like to bold, underline, and italicize some of the other entries in the worksheet.

**2** ■ Select B3 through E3.

■ Click **B** Bold

■ Click **U** Underline

■ Bold and italicize the entries in cells A5 through A8.

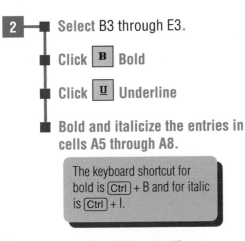

The keyboard shortcut for bold is Ctrl + B and for italic is Ctrl + I.

Your screen should be similar to Figure 1–47.

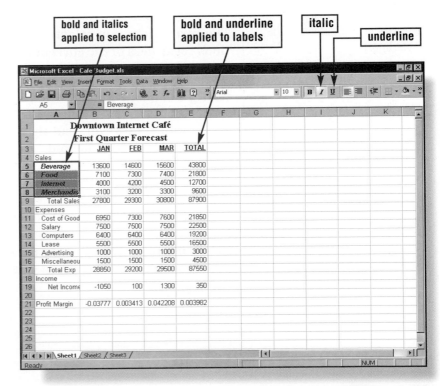

**Figure 1–47**

## Using Undo

Sometimes formatting changes you make do not have the expected result. In this case, you feel that the sales category names would look better without the formatting. To quickly undo the last two actions you performed,

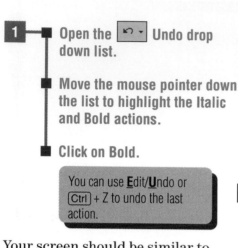

**1** ─■ Open the 🔄▾ Undo drop down list.

■ Move the mouse pointer down the list to highlight the Italic and Bold actions.

■ Click on Bold.

> You can use **E**dit/**U**ndo or Ctrl + Z to undo the last action.

Your screen should be similar to Figure 1–48.

### Additional Information

If you change your mind, use Edit/Redo ( 🔄▾ or Ctrl + y). Repeatedly using the Undo or Redo buttons performs the actions in the list one by one.

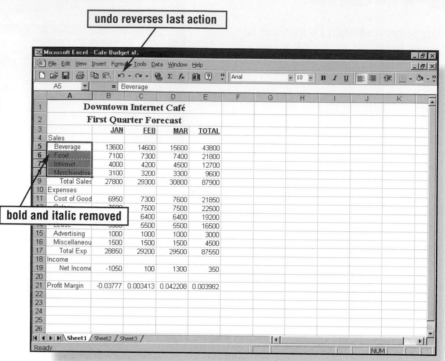

**undo reverses last action**

**bold and italic removed**

**Figure 1–48**

The two actions you selected are undone. Undo reverses the selected actions regardless of the current cell pointer location.

## Using Format Painter

You do think, however, that the Total Sales, Total Exp, and Net Income labels would look good in bold.

**1** ─■ Apply bold to cell A9.

You could repeat the same sequence for cell A16, but a quicker method is to copy the format from one cell to another using 🖌 Format Painter on the Standard toolbar. To copy the format of the active cell to the other cells and turn off the feature when you are done,

**2** ■ Double-click 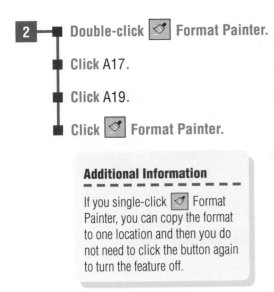 Format Painter.

■ Click A17.

■ Click A19.

■ Click ✎ Format Painter.

**Additional Information**

If you single-click ✎ Format Painter, you can copy the format to one location and then you do not need to click the button again to turn the feature off.

Your screen should be similar to Figure 1–49.

**Figure 1–49**

The formatting was quickly added to each cell as it was selected and the feature is off.

## Formatting Numbers

You also want to improve the appearance of the numbers in the worksheet by changing their format.

**Concept 12    Number Formats**

**Number formats** affect how numbers look onscreen and when printed. They do not affect the way Excel stores or uses the values in calculations. The default number format setting in a worksheet is General. In most cases when you enter numbers, the numbers appear just as you enter them, unformatted. Unformatted numbers are displayed without a thousands separator such as a comma, with negative values preceded by a – (minus sign), and with as many decimal place settings as cell space allows.

In some cases, formats are applied to number entries depending on the symbols you used when entering the data. The table below shows samples of how Excel automatically formats a number based on how it appears when you enter it.

| Entry | Format |
|---|---|
| 10,000 | Comma |
| $102.20 | Currency with two decimal places |
| 90% | Percent with zero decimal places |
| 10/30/98 | Date |
| 9:10 | Time |

First you will change the number format of cells B5 through E8 to display dollar signs, commas, and decimal places.

**1**   ■ Select cells B5 through E9.

   ■ Choose F**ormat/C**ells.

   ■ If necessary, open the Number tab.

   ■ From the Category list box, select Currency.

Your screen should be similar to Figure 1–50.

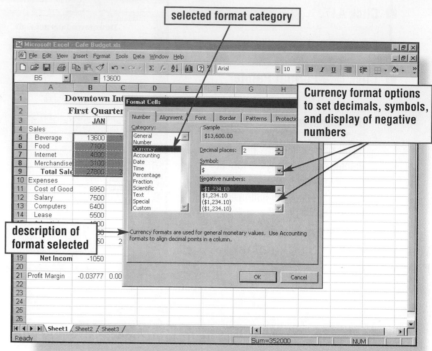

Figure 1–50

The Currency category includes options that allow you to specify the number of decimal places, how negative numbers will appear, and whether a currency symbol such as a dollar sign will be displayed.

**2**   ■ Click 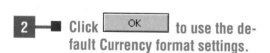 to use the default Currency format settings.

Your screen should be similar to Figure 1–51.

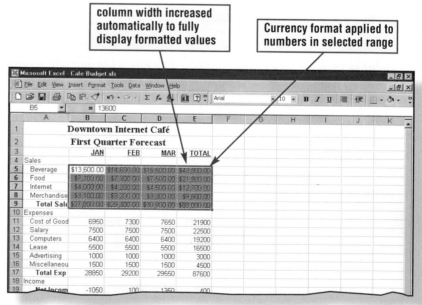

Figure 1–51

The number entries in the selected range appear with a currency symbol, comma, and two decimal places. The column widths increased automatically to fully display the formatted values.

A second format category that displays numbers as currency is Accounting. To see how this format looks,

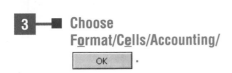

**3** ─■ Choose
F**o**rmat/C**e**lls/Accounting/
OK .

Your screen should be similar to Figure 1–52.

Accounting format
applied to range

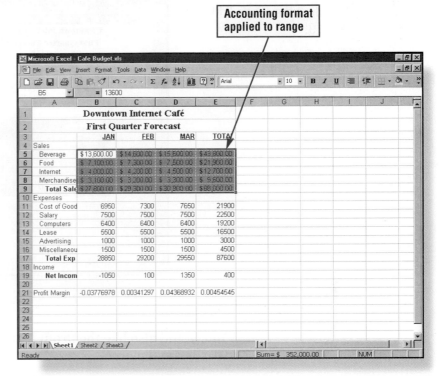

**Figure 1–52**

The numbers now appear in Accounting format. The primary difference between the Accounting and the Currency formats is that the Accounting format aligns numbers at the decimal place and places the dollar sign in a column at the left edge of the cell space. In addition, it does not allow you to select different ways of displaying negative numbers but displays them in black in parentheses. You decide the Accounting format will make it easier to read the numbers in a column.

As you look at the numbers, you decide it is not necessary to display the decimal places since most of the values are whole numbers. To do this,

> The button increases the number of decimal places.

**4** ─■ Click Decrease decimal (2 times).

You want to quickly apply the same formats to the expense range of cells.

**5** Click 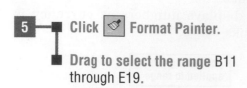 Format Painter.

Drag to select the range B11 through E19.

Your screen should be similar to Figure 1–53.

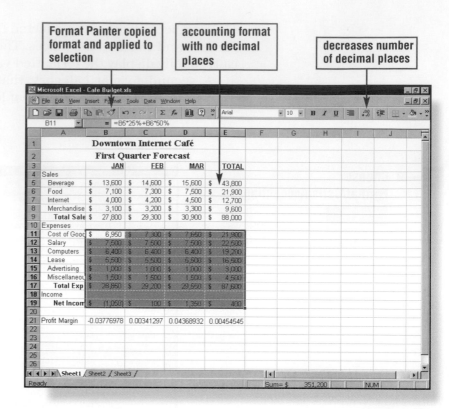

Figure 1–53

You would also like the Profit Margin to be displayed as a percentage with two decimal places.

**6** Select B21 through E21.

Choose Format/Cells Percentage/ OK .

Your screen should be similar to Figure 1–54.

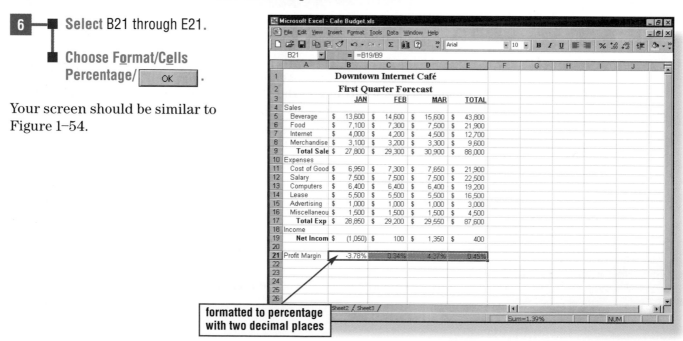

Figure 1–54

Now that the numbers are displayed as a percentage and the number of decimal places has been decreased, the column widths are larger than they need to be. Because Excel does not automatically reduce column widths, you need to make this change yourself. You will use the AutoFit feature to adjust the column widths for all cells in columns A through E.

**7** Click the A column letter and drag to the right to expand the selection to include column E.

Double-click any column border line in the selection to AutoFit the selection.

**Additional Information**

You could also press Ctrl + A or click the button at the intersection of the row numbers and column letters to select the entire worksheet and then double-click on any border line to adjust the column widths of all columns containing entries.

Your screen should be similar to Figure 1-55.

column A increased to display longest entry

column B to E decreased to the minimum column width needed to display entries

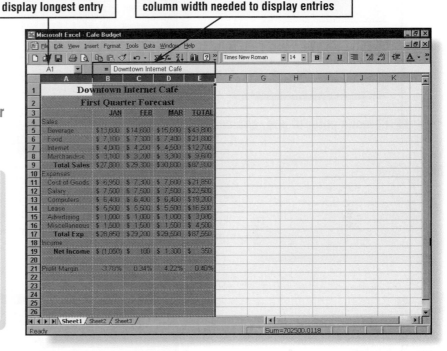

**Figure 1-55**

The width of columns B through E automatically decreased to the minimum column width needed to fully display the entries. The width of column A increased to accommodate the longest entry.

## Adding Color

The last formatting change you would like to make to the worksheet is to add color to the text and to the background of selected cells. First you will change the color of the text.

**1** Select A1 through A2.

Open the ◤ ▾ Font Color palette.

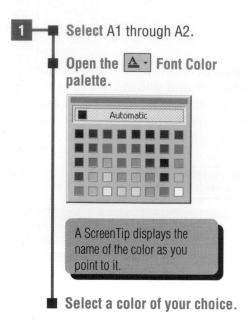

A ScreenTip displays the name of the color as you point to it.

Select a color of your choice.

Your screen should be similar to Figure 1–56.

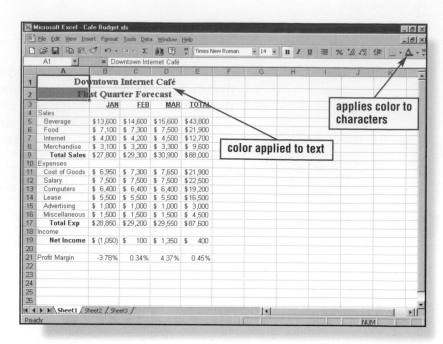

**Figure 1–56**

This text will use the cell fill color of yellow and the title text of blue.

The selected color appears in the button and can be applied again simply by clicking the button. Next you will change the cell background color, also called the fill color.

**2** Select A1 through E2.

Open the ✎ ▾ Fill Color palette.

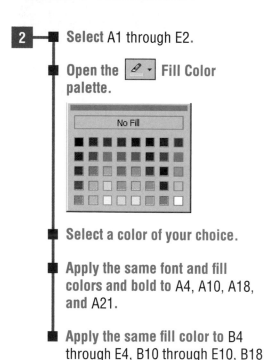

Select a color of your choice.

Apply the same font and fill colors and bold to A4, A10, A18, and A21.

Apply the same fill color to B4 through E4, B10 through E10, B18 through E18, and B21 through E21.

Your screen should be similar to Figure 1–57.

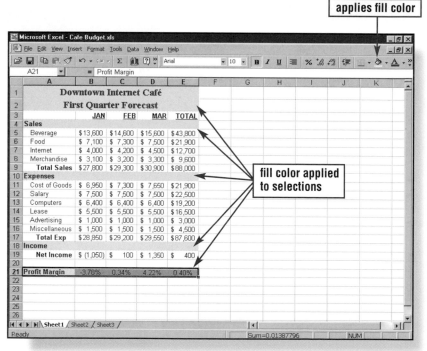

**Figure 1–57**

## Inserting Copied Cells

Although the formatting you added to the titles makes the worksheet easier to read, you decide you need to display month headings above the expense columns. To do this quickly, you can insert copied data between existing data. To indicate where to place the copied text, you move the cell pointer to the upper-left cell of the area where you want the selection inserted and specify the direction you want to shift the surrounding cells.

**1** ■ Copy the contents of cells A3 through E3.

■ Move to A10.

■ Choose Insert/Copied Cells.

■ If necessary, select Shift cells down from the Insert Paste dialog box.

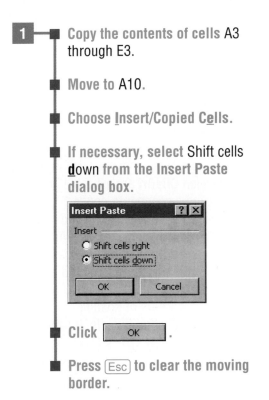

■ Click OK.

■ Press Esc to clear the moving border.

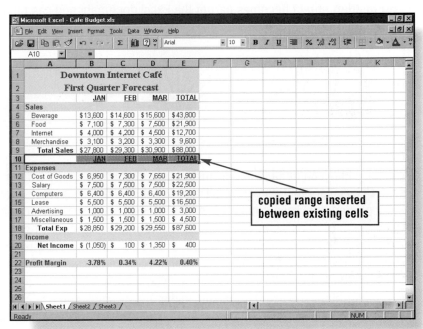

**Figure 1–58**

Your screen should be similar to Figure 1–58.

### Additional Information

You can also insert moved text between existing cells by cutting the selection and choosing Cut Cells from the Insert menu.

The copied data is inserted into the existing row (10) and all entries below are moved down one row. The formats applied to the selection you copied are also copied.

## Inserting and Sizing Graphics

Finally you want to add a graphic to add interest. A ClipArt image is one of several different graphic objects that can be added to an Excel document.

## Concept  Graphics

A **graphic** is a non-text element or object, such as a drawing or picture, that can be added to a document. An **object** is an item that can be sized, moved, and manipulated. A graphic can be a simple drawing object consisting of shapes such as lines and boxes that can be created using features on the Drawing toolbar. A **drawing object** is part of your Excel document. A **picture** is an illustration such as a scanned photograph. They are graphics that were created from another program. Pictures are inserted as embedded objects. An **embedded object** becomes part of the Excel document and can be opened and edited using the source program, the program in which it was created.

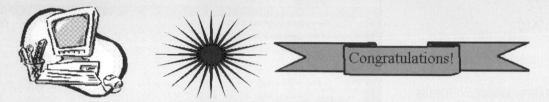

Picture files can be obtained from a variety of sources. Many simple drawings called **ClipArt** are available in the Clip Gallery that comes with Office 2000. You can also create graphic files using a scanner to convert any printed document, including photographs, to an electronic format. Most images that are scanned and inserted into documents are stored as Windows bitmap files (.bmp). All types of graphics, including ClipArt, photographs, and other types of images can be found on the Internet. These files are commonly stored as .jpg or .pcx files. Keep in mind that any images you locate on the Internet may be copyrighted and should only be used with permission. You can also purchase CDs containing graphics for your use.

A graphic object can be manipulated in many ways. You can change its size, add borders or shading, or move it to another location on the page, including in the margins or on top of or below other objects. It cannot, however, be placed behind the worksheet data.

You want to insert a ClipArt graphic to the right of the data in the worksheet.

**1** Move to F4.

Choose **I**nsert/**P**icture/**C**lipArt

Your screen should be similar to
Figure 1–59.

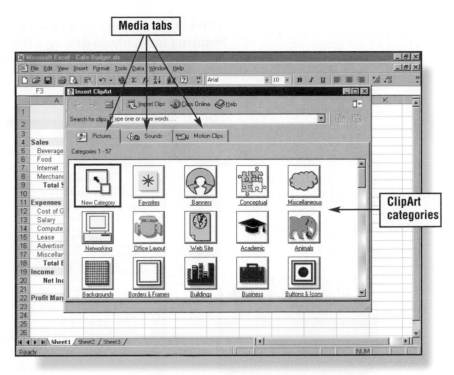

Figure 1–59

Your ClipArt categories may be different than shown in Figure 1–59.

The Insert ClipArt dialog box Media tabs organize the different media by
type. The Pictures tab contains clip art, photographs, scanned images,
drawings, and other graphics. Sound effects and music files are in the
Sounds tab and videos and animation files are in the Motion Clips tab. The
clip art you want is in the People category in the Pictures tab.

**2** If necessary, open the
Pictures tab.

Click ▦.

This picture can also be
found in the People at Work
category.

Your screen should be similar to
Figure 1–60.

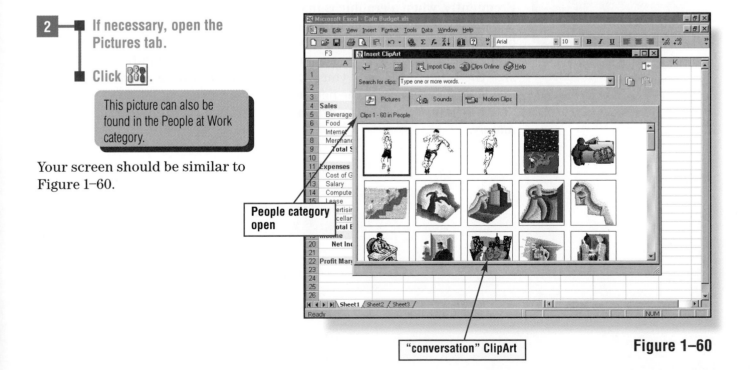

Figure 1–60

Icons of the ClipArt images available in the People category are displayed. Pointing to an image displays the image name in a ScreenTip. You want to insert the ClipArt named "conversation."

**3** ■ Click 📇 conversation.

■ From the Common Task pop-up menu click 📇 Insert Clip.

■ Click ☒ to close the dialog box.

> If this graphic is not available in the Clip Gallery, choose **I**nsert/**P**icture and select Conversation.wmf from your data disk.

Your screen should be similar to Figure 1–61.

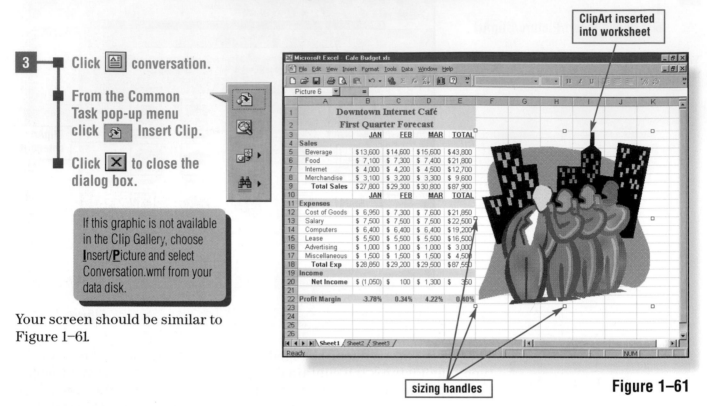

**ClipArt inserted into worksheet**

**sizing handles**

**Figure 1–61**

> The Picture toolbar may automatically display when a graphic object is selected.

The ClipArt image is inserted in the document at the current cell. Frequently, when a graphic is inserted, its size will need to be adjusted. In this case you want to reduce its size. The picture is surrounded by eight boxes, called **sizing handles**, indicating it is a selected object and can now be sized and moved anywhere in the document. The handles are used to size the object, much as you would size a window. A graphic object is moved by dragging it to the new location.

You want to reduce the graphic size to cells F4 through J22, approximately.

**4** ■ **Point to the lower-right corner handle.**

> The mouse pointer changes to ↖, just as it does when resizing a window.

■ **Drag the mouse to reduce the size of the graphic to cover cells F4 through J20.**

> Dragging a corner handle maintains the original proportions of the picture.

■ **Move to A1.**

Your screen should be similar to Figure 1–62.

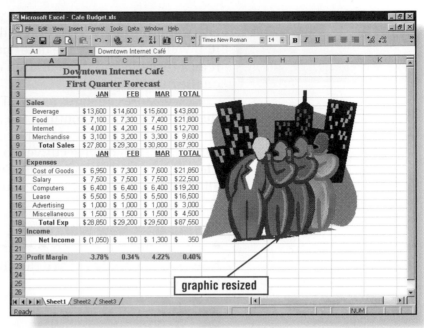

**Figure 1–62**

The three-month forecast is now complete.

## Entering a Date

Now that the worksheet is complete, you want to include your name and the date in the worksheet as documentation.

**1** ■ **Enter your first initial and last name in cell A24.**

■ **Enter the current date in cell A25 in the format mm/dd/yyyy (for example, 10/10/2001).**

■ **Move to A25.**

Your screen should be similar to Figure 1–63.

> Your date may be formatted differently, depending on the last-used date format on your system.

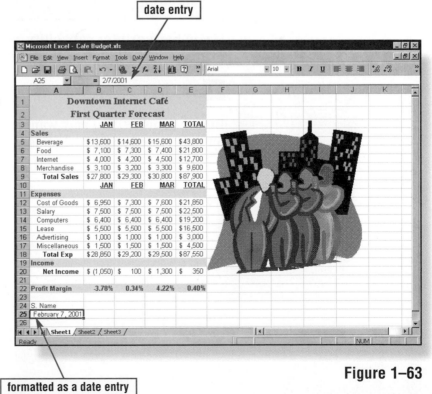

**Figure 1–63**

> Use Format/Cells/Number/Date to change the date format.

Excel automatically recognized your entry as a date and formatted the entry appropriately. The entry is displayed in the formula bar as you enter it. If you had preceded the date entry with =, Excel would have interpreted it as a formula and a calculation of division would have been performed on the numbers.

Excel stores all dates as serial numbers with each day numbered from the beginning of the century; the date serial number 1 corresponds to the date January 1, 1900, and the integer 65380 is December 31, 2078. The integers are assigned consecutively beginning with 1 and ending with 65,380. They are called **date numbers**. Conversion of the date to a serial number allows dates to be used in calculations.

## Saving as a New Workbook

Now you are ready to save the changes you have made to the workbook file to your data disk.

1 ■ Choose File/Save As

■ Edit the file name to **Café Forecast**.

■ If the Save In location is not correct, select the appropriate location from the drop-down list.

■ Click 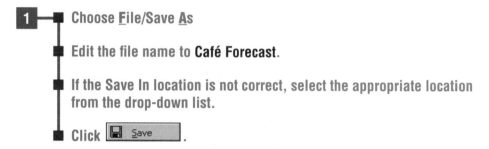 .

## Previewing and Printing a Workbook

If you have printer capability, you can print a paper copy, also called a printout or hard copy, of the worksheet.

1 ■ If necessary, turn the printer on and check to see that it is on-line.

Before printing, you may want to preview how the worksheet will appear on the printed page. To do this,

**2** ■ Click  Print Preview.

The menu equivalent is **F**ile/Print Pre**v**iew.

Your screen should be similar to Figure 1–64.

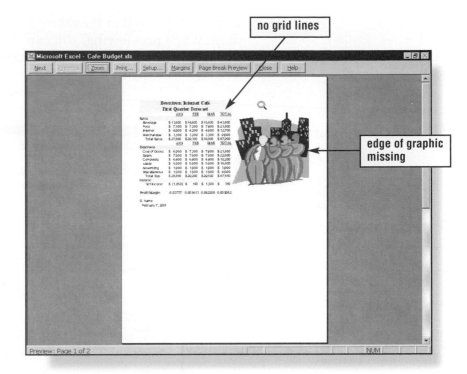

**Figure 1–64**

The Print Preview window displays the worksheet as it will appear on the printed page. Notice that the row and column lines are not displayed and will not print. Also notice that the right edge of the graphic is cut off because it is too large to fit on the page. You need to make the graphic smaller so that it will all print on one page.

**3** ■ Click  .

Your screen should be similar to Figure 1–65.

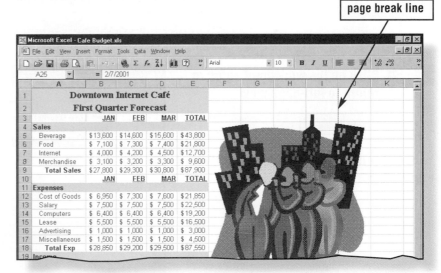

**Figure 1–65**

Notice the dotted line between columns I and J. This line indicates the location of the page break.

Click on the graphic to select it.

**4** ■ Select the graphic and reduce it in size to just fit within the page break.

■ Preview the worksheet again.

You can now see that the entire graphic is displayed and will print on the page. While previewing, you can change from full-page view to a magnified view by clicking on the preview page when the mouse pointer appears as a 🔍.

**magnified view**

**5** ■ **Click the worksheet title.**

The area you click on is the area that will display in the Preview window.

Your screen should be similar to Figure 1–66.

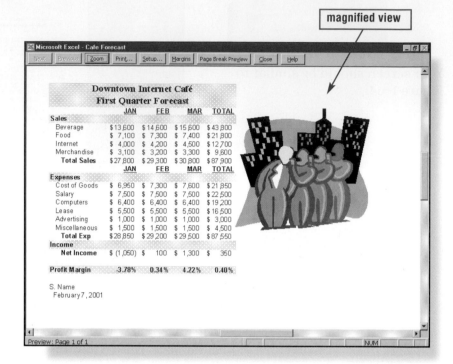

**Figure 1–66**

The worksheet is displayed in the actual size it will appear when printed.

**selected printer**

**6** ■ **Click on the worksheet again to return to full-page view.**

■ Click Print... .

Your screen should be similar to Figure 1–67.

**prints entire worksheet**

**prints active sheet**

**prints one copy**

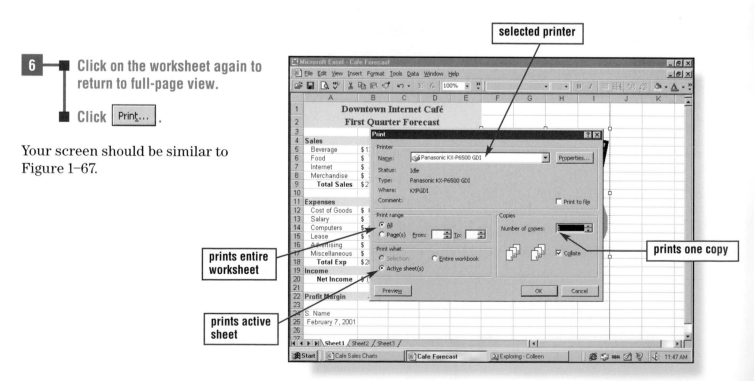

**Figure 1–67**

From the Print dialog box, you need to specify the printer you will use and the document settings. The printer that is currently selected is displayed in the Name drop-down list box in the Printer section of the dialog box.

**7** ■ If you need to change the selected printer to another printer, open the Na**m**e drop-down list box and select the appropriate printer (your instructor will tell you which printer to select).

The Print Range area of the Print dialog box lets you specify how much of the document you want printed. The All setting prints the entire document and Pages prints only the pages you specify. The Print what options are used to restrict the printing to a selection, the active sheet, or the entire workbook. The default settings of All and Active sheet are correct. In the Copies section, the default setting of one copy of the document is acceptable. To begin printing using the settings in the Print dialog box,

> The menu equivalent is **F**ile/**P**rint and the keyboard shortcut is Ctrl + P. You can also click 🖨 to print using the default print settings.

**8** ■ Click  .

Your printer should be printing out the worksheet. Your printed output should look like the figure shown in the Case Study at the beginning of the tutorial. If you do not have a color printer, the colors appear as shades of gray.

## Exiting Excel

If you want to quit or exit the Excel program at this time,

**1** ■ Move to A1.

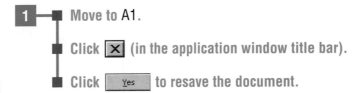

> The menu equivalent is **F**ile/E**x**it.

### Additional Information

Excel saves the file with the cell selector positioned in the same cell it was in when saved.

# Concept Summary

## Tutorial 1: Creating and Editing a Worksheet

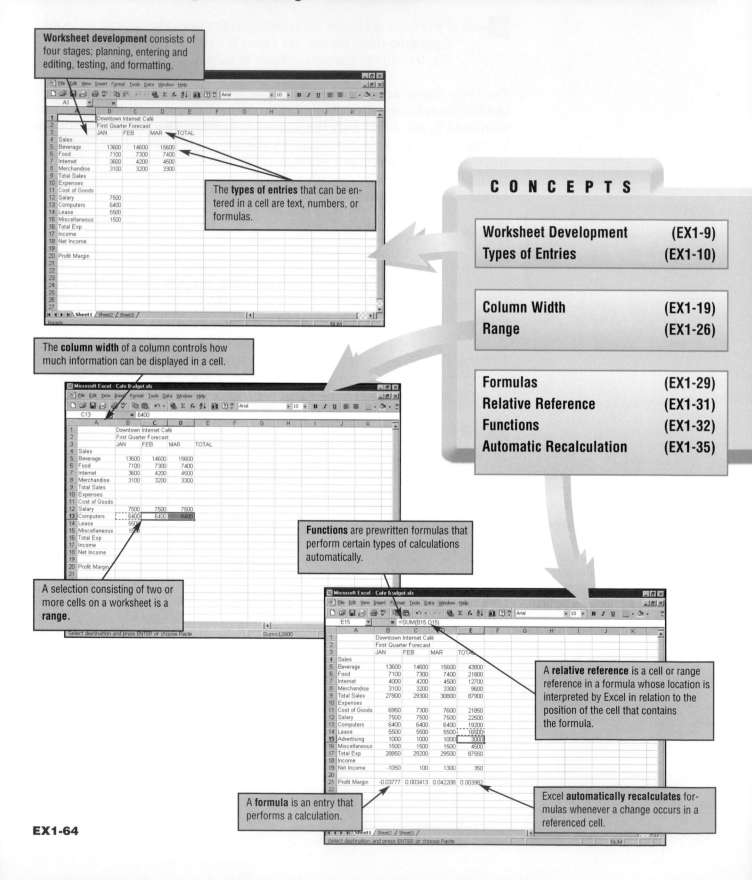

**Worksheet development** consists of four stages; planning, entering and editing, testing, and formatting.

The **types of entries** that can be entered in a cell are text, numbers, or formulas.

## CONCEPTS

| | |
|---|---|
| **Worksheet Development** | (EX1-9) |
| **Types of Entries** | (EX1-10) |
| | |
| **Column Width** | (EX1-19) |
| **Range** | (EX1-26) |
| | |
| **Formulas** | (EX1-29) |
| **Relative Reference** | (EX1-31) |
| **Functions** | (EX1-32) |
| **Automatic Recalculation** | (EX1-35) |

The **column width** of a column controls how much information can be displayed in a cell.

**Functions** are prewritten formulas that perform certain types of calculations automatically.

A selection consisting of two or more cells on a worksheet is a **range.**

A **relative reference** is a cell or range reference in a formula whose location is interpreted by Excel in relation to the position of the cell that contains the formula.

A **formula** is an entry that performs a calculation.

Excel **automatically recalculates** formulas whenever a change occurs in a referenced cell.

**Fonts** consist of typefaces, point sizes, and styles that can be applied to characters to improve their appearance.

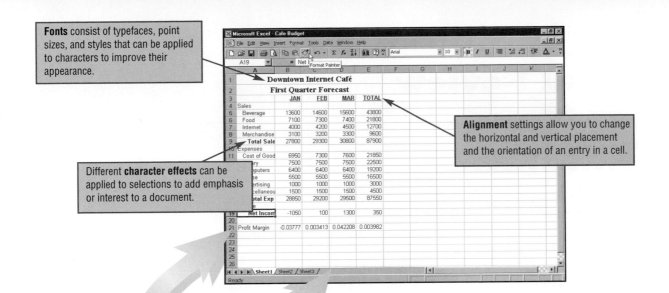

**Alignment** settings allow you to change the horizontal and vertical placement and the orientation of an entry in a cell.

Different **character effects** can be applied to selections to add emphasis or interest to a document.

| Alignment | (EX1-39) |
| Fonts | (EX1-44) |
| Character Effects | (EX1-46) |
| Number Formats | (EX1-49) |
| Graphics | (EX1-56) |

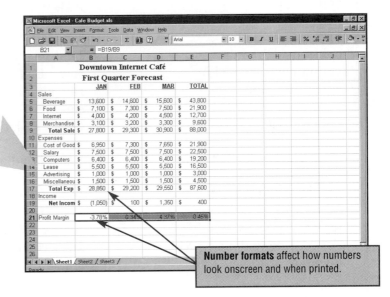

**Number formats** affect how numbers look onscreen and when printed.

A **graphic** is a non-text element or object, such as a drawing or picture that can be added to a document.

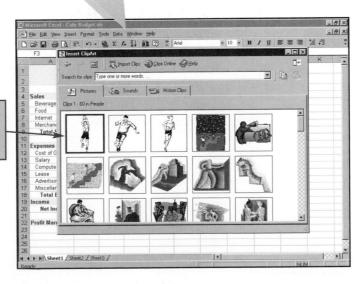

# Tutorial Review

## Key Terms

# Command Summary

| Command | Shortcut Keys | Button | Action |
|---|---|---|---|
| **F**ile/**O**pen <file name> | Ctrl + O | | Opens an existing workbook file |
| **F**ile/**C**lose | | | Closes open workbook file |
| **F**ile/**S**ave <file name> | Ctrl + S | | Saves current file on disk using same file name |
| **F**ile/**S**ave As <file name> | | | Saves current file on disk using a new file name |
| **F**ile/Print Pre**v**iew | | | Displays worksheet as it will appear when printed |
| **F**ile/**P**rint | Ctrl + P | | Prints a worksheet |
| **F**ile/E**x**it | | | Exits Excel |
| **E**dit/**U**ndo | Ctrl + Z | | Undoes last editing or formatting change |
| **E**dit/**R**edo | Ctrl + Y | | Restores changes after using Undo |
| **E**dit/**C**opy | Ctrl + C | | Copies selected data to Clipboard |
| **E**dit/**P**aste | Ctrl + V | | Pastes selections stored in Clipboard |
| **E**dit/Fi**l**l | | | Fills selected cells with contents of source cell |
| **E**dit/Cle**a**r/**C**ontents | Delete | | Clears cell contents |
| **E**dit/**D**elete/Entire **R**ow | | | Deletes selected rows |
| **E**dit/**D**elete/Entire **C**olumn | | | Deletes selected columns |
| **V**iew/**T**oolbars | | | Displays or hides selected toolbar |
| **I**nsert/Copied C**e**lls | | | Inserts row and copies text from Clipboard |
| **I**nsert/**R**ows | | | Inserts a blank row |
| **I**nsert/**C**olumns | | | Inserts a blank column |
| **I**nsert/**P**icture/**F**rom File | | | Inserts picture at insertion point from disk |
| F**o**rmat/C**e**lls/Number/Currency | | | Applies Currency format to selection |
| F**o**rmat/C**e**lls/Number/Accounting | | | Applies Accounting format to selection |
| F**o**rmat/C**e**lls/Number/Date | | | Applies Date format to selection |
| F**o**rmat/C**e**lls/Number/Percent | | | Applies Percent format to selection |
| F**o**rmat/C**e**lls/Number/Decimal places | | | Increases or decreases the number of decimal places associated with a number value |
| F**o**rmat/C**e**lls/Alignment/**H**orizontal/ Left (Indent) | | | Left-aligns entry in cell space |

| Command | Shortcut Keys | Button | Action |
|---|---|---|---|
| F**o**rmat/C**e**lls/Alignment/**H**orizontal/Center | | ≣ | Center-aligns entry in cell space |
| F**o**rmat/C**e**lls/Alignment/**H**orizontal/Right | | ≣ | Right-aligns entry in cell space |
| F**o**rmat/C**e**lls/Alignment/**H**orizontal/Left (Indent)/1 | | ≣ | Left-aligns and indents cell entry one space |
| F**o**rmat/C**e**lls/Alignment/Horizontal/Center Across Selection | | 🔳 | Centers cell contents across selected cells |
| F**o**rmat/C**e**lls/**F**ont | | | Changes font and attributes of cell contents |
| F**o**rmat/C**e**lls/Font/**F**ont Style/Bold | Ctrl + B | **B** | Bolds selected text |
| F**o**rmat/C**e**lls/Font/**F**ont Style/Italic | Ctrl + I | *I* | Italicizes selected text |
| F**o**rmat/C**e**lls/Font/**U**nderline/Single | Ctrl + U | U | Underlines selected text |
| F**o**rmat/C**e**lls/Font/**C**olor | | A ▾ | Adds color to text |
| F**o**rmat/C**e**lls/Patterns/**C**olor | | ✎ ▾ | Adds color to cell background |
| F**o**rmat/**R**ow/H**ei**ght | | | Changes height of selected rows |
| F**o**rmat/**C**olumn/**W**idth | | | Changes width of columns |
| F**o**rmat/**C**olumn/**A**utofit Selection | | | Changes column width to match widest cell entry |

# Screen Identification

In the following worksheet, several items are identified by letters. Enter the correct term for each item in the space provided.

a. _____

b. _____

c. _____

d. _____

e. _____

f. _____

g. _____

h. _____

i. _____

j. _____

k. _____

l. _____

m. _____

n. _____

o. _____

p. _____

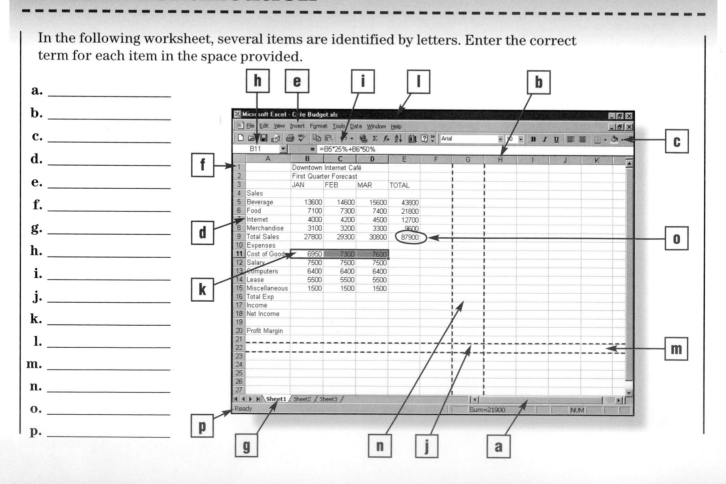

# Matching

Match the lettered item on the right with the numbered item on the left.

1. source _____
2. * _____
3. ▤ _____
4. Ctrl + Home _____
5. .xls _____
6. ▦ _____
7. =C19+A21 _____
8. range _____
9. D11 _____
10. formula bar _____

a. right-aligns cell entry

b. moves cell selector to upper-left corner of worksheet

c. the cell you copy from

d. two or more worksheet cells

e. a cell reference

f. displays current cell entry

g. an arithmetic operator

h. centers text across a selection

i. a formula summing two cells

j. Excel workbook file name extension

# Fill-In

Complete the following statements by filling in the blanks with the correct terms.

1. The _____ occupies the center of the Excel window and can display multiple windows.

2. The worksheet displays a rectangular grid of _____ and _____.

3. A(n) _____ consists of two or more worksheet cells.

4. The intersection of a row and column creates a(n)_____.

5. _____ are text entries that are used to create the structure of the worksheet.

6. By default, text entries are _____ -aligned and number entries are _____ - aligned.

7. A(n) _____ consists of the column letter and row number used to identify a cell.

8. A(n) _____ is an entry that performs a calculation.

9. Without _____ recalculation, large worksheets would take several minutes to recalculate all formulas each time a number was changed.

10. _____ control how information is displayed in a cell.

# Multiple Choice

Circle the correct response to the questions below.

1. The four steps in the document design planning process are:
   a. specify purpose, design and build, test, document
   b. outline, design, enter data, save
   c. specify purpose, enter data, build, document
   d. outline, enter data, design and build, document

2. _____entries can contain any combination of letters, numbers, spaces, and any other special characters.
   a. Number
   b. Variable
   c. Constant
   d. Text

3. The _____ of a column controls how much information can be displayed in a cell.
   a. size
   b. shape
   c. width
   d. alignment

4. A(n) _____ range is a rectangular block of adjoining cells.
   a. selected
   b. adjacent
   c. nonadjacent
   d. block

5. The values on which a numeric formula performs a calculation are called:
   a. operators
   b. operands
   c. accounts
   d. data

6. Whenever a formula containing _____ references is copied, the referenced cells are automatically adjusted.
   a. relative
   b. automatic
   c. fixed
   d. variable

7. A_____ is a set of characters with a specific design.
   a. font
   b. formula
   c. text entry
   d. function

8. _____can be applied to selections to add emphasis or interest to a document.

    **a.** Alignments

    **b.** Pictures

    **c.** Character effects

    **d.** Text formats

9. The currency number format can display:

    **a.** dollar signs

    **b.** commas

    **c.** decimal places

    **d.** all the above

10. A non-text element or object, such as a drawing or picture that can be added to a document, is called a(n):

    **a.** picture

    **b.** drawing

    **c.** graphic

    **d.** image

# True/False

Circle the correct answer to the following questions.

| | | |
|---|---|---|
| **1.** Formulas are used to create, edit, and position graphics. | True | False |
| **2.** The default column width setting in Excel is 15.0. | True | False |
| **3.** A nonadjacent range is two or more selected cells or ranges that are adjoining. | True | False |
| **4.** A formula is an entry that performs a calculation. | True | False |
| **5.** Because relative references automatically adjust for the new location, the relative references in a copied formula refer to different cells than the references in the original formula. | True | False |
| **6.** Formulas are prewritten statements that perform certain types of calculations automatically. | True | False |
| **7.** The automatic recalculation is one of the most powerful features of electronic worksheets. | True | False |
| **8.** Font settings allow you to change the horizontal and vertical placement and the orientation of an entry in a cell. | True | False |
| **9.** Number formats affect how numbers look onscreen and when printed. | True | False |
| **10.** An embedded object becomes part of the Excel document and can be opened and edited using the source program. | True | False |

# Discussion Questions

1. Discuss why it is important to design a worksheet before you begin entering actual data into it.

2. What types of entries are used in worksheets? Discuss the uses of each type of entry.

3. Discuss how formulas are created. Why are they the power behind worksheets?

4. Discuss the formatting features presented in the lab. Why are they important to the look of the worksheet?

# Hands-On Practice Exercises

**Step by Step**

| Rating System | |
|---|---|
| ☆ | Easy |
| ☆ ☆ | Moderate |
| ☆ ☆ ☆ | Difficult |

**1.** Lisa Sutton is an employment analyst working for the state of New Jersey. One of her responsibilities is to collect and analyze data on future job opportunities in the state. Lisa has compiled a list of the jobs that are expected to offer the most new positions. Follow the directions below to complete the worksheet shown here.

a. Open the workbook file New Positions.

b. Begin with the title of the worksheet: Modify the label in cell B2 so that the first letter of each word is capitalized; move the label in cell B2 to A2; move the label in cell B3 to A3; center the titles in cells A2 and A3 across the columns A through D; and finally, increase the font size to 14 point.

| | A | B | C | D |
|---|---|---|---|---|
| 1 | | | | |
| 2 | | **Jobs With Most New Positions** | | |
| 3 | | **1994-2005** | | |
| 4 | | | | |
| 5 | | N.J. Projected | Avg Pay | Percent Above |
| 6 | | New Positions | Per Hour | National Average |
| 7 | | | | |
| 8 | Systems Analysts/Programmers | 27,000 | $26.59 | 14.4% |
| 9 | Nursing Aides and Orderlies | 15,400 | $9.17 | 18.3% |
| 10 | Waiters and Waitresses | 13,600 | $6.09 | 8.4% |
| 11 | Home Health Aides | 13,400 | $7.97 | 1.8% |
| 12 | Marketing and Sales Supv. | 12,900 | $19.81 | 25.9% |
| 13 | Janitors and Cleaners | 12,500 | $8.79 | 11.3% |
| 14 | Salespersons, retail | 11,300 | $8.66 | 4.8% |
| 15 | Cashiers | 11,300 | $7.44 | 13.1% |
| 16 | Guards and watch guards | 10,200 | $8.21 | 2.8% |
| 17 | Nurse: Registered, Practitioner etc. | 9,100 | $22.46 | 15.9% |

c. Adjust the column widths so that all the data is fully displayed.

d. Format the numbers in column B as number with a comma to separate thousands and 0 decimal places. Format the numbers in column C as currency with dollar signs and two decimal places. Format the numbers in column D as percent with one decimal place.

e. Insert a new row below row 3 and a new row below row 6.

f. Bold the titles in rows 5 and 6. Underline the titles in row 6.

g. Center the values in columns B, C and D.

**h.** Add font and fill colors to the worksheet as you like.

**i.** Insert a ClipArt graphic of your choice from the Clip Gallery. Size and position it appropriately to fit the page.

**j.** Enter your name and the current date on separate rows just below the worksheet.

**k.** Move to cell A1. Save the workbook file as Jobs. Preview and print the worksheet.

**2.** Lisa Sutton, employment analyst for New Jersey, has collected data on the highest paying jobs in New Jersey and the country. Follow the directions below to complete the worksheet shown here.

**a.** Open the workbook file Highest Paying Jobs. Increase the column widths to fully display the data.

**b.** Center the titles in cells A1 and A2 over the worksheet data. Change the font of the main title line to New Times Roman 16 points. Change the font of the subtitle line to Times New Roman 14 points.

**c.** Insert a new row below row 2.

**d.** Calculate the percentage differential for Physicians and Surgeons in New Jersey to the U.S. average in cell D5. Copy the formula down the column. *Hint:* Subtract the U.S. value from the N.J. value and divide by the U.S. value.

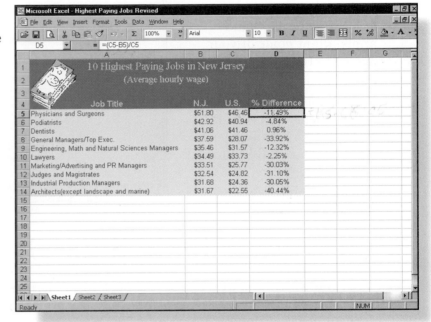

**e.** Format the data in columns B and C as currency with two decimal places. Format the data in column D as a percent with two decimal places.

**f.** Add a column heading, Job Title, in A4. Center and bold all column headings.

**g.** Add formatting, such as color fill and font color of your choice, to the worksheet.

**h.** Insert the ClipArt image of currency (located in the Business category of the Clip Gallery or on your data disk). Move and size it to fit to the left of the title.

**i.** Enter your name and the current date on separate rows just below the worksheet.

**j.** Move to cell A1. Save the workbook file as Highest Paying Jobs Revised. Preview and print the worksheet.

**3.** Mark Ernster works for a national real estate company. To compare housing prices in different areas of the country, he has collected data on the average prices of existing homes in four national regional areas. Follow the directions below to complete the worksheet shown here.

**a.** Open the workbook file Real Estate Prices.

**b.** Edit the title in cell B3 so that the first letter of each word is uppercase. Center the title across columns A through G. Increase the font size to 14 and bold and apply a font color of your choice to the title.

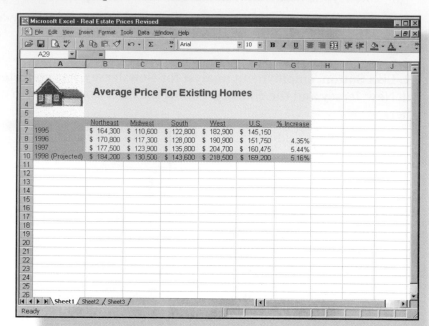

**c.** Center-align and underline the column headings in row 5. Right-align cells B7 through E10. Left-align cells A7 through A10. Best-fit column A.

**d.** Calculate the U.S. average for 1995 in cell F7 by summing the four regional averages in the row and dividing by 4. Be careful not to include the year row headings in your calculation. Copy the formula to the other two years in cells F8 and F9.

**e.** Next, you would like to calculate the percent of increase from 1995 to 1996 and from 1996 to 1997. Enter the formula **=(F8−F7)/F8** in cell G8. Format the formula as a percentage with two decimal places. Copy the formula to G9.

**f.** To calculate the 1998 projected average price, enter **=B9+B9*((B9−B8)/B9)** in cell B10. Copy the formula to cells C10 through F10. Copy the formula in G9 to G10.

**g.** Format all the prices as Accounting with zero decimal places. Increase the width of columns B through F to 10. Best-fit column G.

**h.** Delete row 6 and insert another blank row below the title.

**i.** Add fill colors to the worksheet as you like.

**j.** Insert the picture House.bmp from your data disk. Size and position it to fit on the left side of the title.

**k.** Enter your name and the current date on separate rows just below the worksheet.

**l.** Move to cell A1. Save and replace the workbook file Real Estate Prices. Preview and adjust the size of the picture. Print the worksheet.

**4.** Will Bloomquist is a writer for his college newspaper. He has been researching an article on student athletes and has found some interesting data on student athletic participation in high school and college by men and women. Follow the directions below to complete the worksheet shown here.

a. Open the workbook Athlete Data on your data disk.

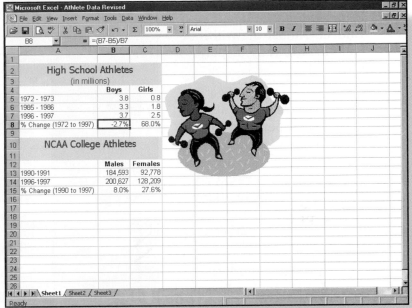

b. Center the titles in rows 2 and 3 over the worksheet data. Format the title in row 2 to Tahoma 14 points. Apply a font color and fill color of your choice to row 2. Format the subtitle in row 3 to 12 points and apply the same font and fill color as the main title.

c. Make the same changes you made to rows 2 and 3 to rows 9 and 10.

d. Bold and center the column labels in rows 4 and 11.

e. Adjust the width of column A to fully display the labels.

f. Format the data in B12 through C13 as Numbers with a thousands separator and no decimal places.

g. Calculate the % change for each column of data. Format the data as a percentage with one decimal place. (*Hint:* subtract the oldest year's data from the most recent year's and divide the result by the most recent year value.)

h. Insert a blank row above row 9.

i. Insert the Weightlifting ClipArt graphic (located in the Sports and Leisure category of the Clip Gallery or on your data disk) to the right of the worksheet. Adjust the size and location of the picture as necessary.

j. Enter your name and the current date on separate rows below the worksheet.

k. Move to cell A1. Save and replace the workbook file as Athlete Data. Preview and print the worksheet.

☆☆☆

**5.** Kent Allen works for The Mountain Lakes Homeowners Association. Using last year's final budget numbers, he is to create a projected budget for 2002. Follow the directions below to complete the worksheet shown here.

**a.** Open the workbook file Homeowners Association Budget. Adjust the width of column A to fully display the labels.

**b.** In column C calculate a 5 percent increase for all the income numbers for the year 2002. Calculate a 10 percent increase in administrative expenditures, a 20 percent decrease in Maintenance, and a 15 percent increase in Miscellaneous expenditures.

**c.** Format the data with the Accounting number format.

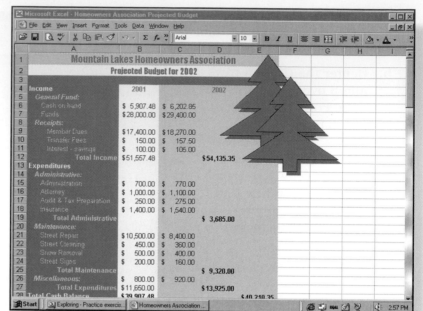

**d.** In column D calculate the totals for Total Income, Total Administrative, Total Maintenance and Total Expenditures for 2002. In column E, calculate the Total Cash Balance by subtracting the total income from the total expenditures for 2002.

**e.** Indent the row label subheads and further indent the items under each subhead. Right-align the total labels.

**f.** Delete rows 13 and 14.

**g.** Change the font type, size, and color of the title lines to a format of your choice.

**h.** Apply character effects and color of your choice to the worksheet.

**i.** Insert a ClipArt image of your choice from the Clip Gallery. Position and size it to fit the page.

**j.** Enter your name and the current date on separate rows just below the worksheet.

**k.** Move to cell A1. Save and replace the workbook file as Homeowners Association Projected Budget. Preview and print the worksheet.

**6.** Ian Pario is a financial assistant for Clark Office Supply. He is preparing a budgeted income statement for the first quarter (January through March). Follow the directions below to complete the worksheet shown here.

**a.** Open the workbook file Clark Office Supply. Expand column A to fully display the labels.

**b.** Enter **80000** for January sales, **85000** for February sales, and **80000** for March sales.

**c.** Enter **1500** for each month's fixed cost.

**d.** Using the following information, enter formulas to calculate the other items in the budgeted income statement:

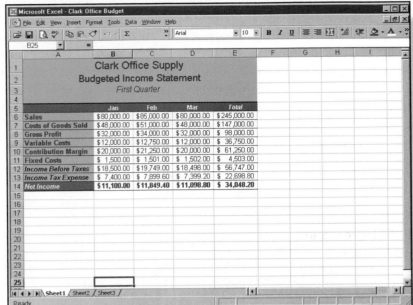

Cost of Goods Sold = 60% of Sales
Gross Profit = Sales – Cost of Goods Sold
Variable Costs = 15% of Sales
Contribution Margin = Gross Profit – Variable Costs
Income Before Taxes = Contribution Margin – Fixed Costs
Income Tax Expense = 40% of Income Before Taxes
Net Income = Income Before Taxes – Income Tax Expense

**e.** Calculate the first quarter totals.

**f.** Use the formatting features you learned in the tutorial to enhance the worksheet.

**g.** Enter your name and the current date on separate rows just below the worksheet.

**h.** Move to cell A1. Save the workbook file as Clark Income Statement. Preview and print the worksheet.

### On Your Own

**7.** Hank's girlfriend noticed that he gained a few extra pounds over Christmas and tactfully has suggested that he cut down on his snack foods. Hank has decided to eliminate all snacks that contain 30 percent of their calories from fat. To help him, you are to create a worksheet that lists his favorite foods, their calories per serving, and their fat grams per serving. The worksheet will use this data to calculate the percent of calories from fat for each snack.

The table below shows Hank's favorite foods and their calorie and fat content per serving. Each gram of fat contains nine calories. To calculate the percent of fat for each food, multiply the fat grams by nine and divide by the number of calories. Use the formatting features you learned in the tutorial to enhance the worksheet and to identify the snack items that have less than 30 percent calories from fat. Enter your name and the current date on separate rows just below the worksheet. Preview, save, and print the worksheet.

| Food | Fat grams per serving | Calories per serving |
| --- | --- | --- |
| Bagel | 1 | 240 |
| Cream Cheese | 9 | 110 |
| Hotdog | 13 | 140 |
| Muffin | 6 | 200 |
| Cookies | 4.5 | 130 |
| Pretzels | 1 | 110 |
| Chips | 9 | 140 |

**8.** Create a personal six-month budget using a worksheet. Enter an appropriate title and use descriptive labels for your monthly expenses (food, rent, car payments, insurance, credit card payments, etc.). Enter your monthly expenses (or, if you prefer, any reasonable sample data). Use formulas to calculate total expenses for each month and to calculate the average monthly expenditures for each expense item. Enhance the worksheet using features you learned in this tutorial. Enter your name and the current date on separate rows just below the worksheet. Preview, save, and print the worksheet.

**9.** Lee DeLuca is the new owner and manager of a candy store called Confectionery Delights. She has four salespeople (Ann, John, Robert, and Sally) and is planning a month-long sales promotion for August. Using the four steps in the planning process, you are to plan and create a worksheet for Lee that can be used to record and analyze sales for that month.

Weekly sales data for each employee will be entered into the worksheet. Using that data, the worksheet will calculate the average and total monthly sales for each person. Additionally, it will calculate the average and total weekly sales for the store. Write a short paragraph describing how you used each of the four planning steps. With sample data in the worksheet, enter your name and the current date on separate rows just below the worksheet. Preview, save, and print the worksheet.

☆ ☆ ☆

**10.** Use the library and/or the Web to locate information on employment opportunities and salary trends related to your area of study. Create a worksheet to display information relating to job titles, years of experience, and starting and top salaries for positions in your field. Calculate the median salary (the average of the starting and the top salary). Enhance the worksheet using features you learned in this tutorial. Enter your name and the current date on separate rows just below the worksheet. Preview, save, and print the worksheet.

# Charting Worksheet Data

## Competencies

After completing this tutorial, you will know how to:

1. Select a chart data range.
2. Change the type of chart.
3. Move the chart location.
4. Format chart elements.
5. Add chart titles and move the legend.
6. Create a combination chart.
7. Change worksheet data.
8. Add data labels, text boxes, and arrows.
9. Create, explode, and rotate a pie chart.
10. Apply patterns and color.
11. Size and align a sheet on a page.
12. Add predefined headers and footers.
13. Document, preview and print a workbook.

**Many different types of charts can be created and modified to visually represent worksheet data.**

## Case Study

After creating the first quarter forecast for the Downtown Internet Café, you contacted several other Internet cafes to inquire about their startup experiences. You heard many exciting success stories! Internet connections attract more customers and the typical customer stays longer at an Internet café than at a regular café. As a result, they end up spending more money.

**The Chart Wizard makes it easy to create a chart from data in a worksheet.**

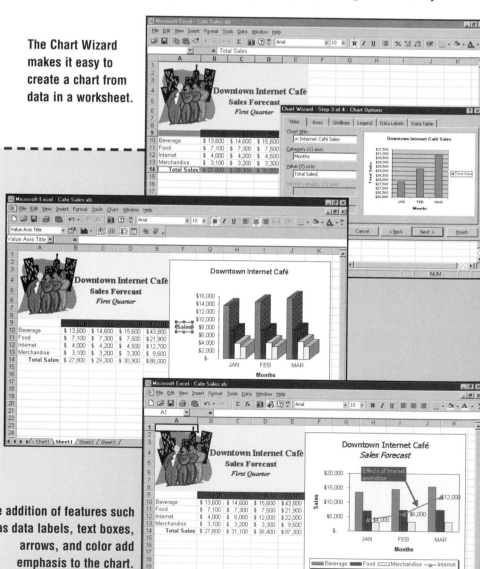

**The addition of features such as data labels, text boxes, arrows, and color add emphasis to the chart.**

You now believe that your initial sales estimates are too low. You too should be able to increase sales dramatically. In addition to sales of coffee and food items to customers, the Café also derives sales from charging for Internet connection time. In your discussions with other Internet café managers, you have found that Internet connection sales account for approximately 25 percent of their total sales. You would like to launch an aggressive advertising campaign to promote the new Internet aspect of the Downtown Internet Café. You believe that the campaign will lead to an increase in sales not only in Internet connection time but in food and beverage sales as well.

To convince Evan, you need an effective way to illustrate the sales growth you are forecasting. To do this, you decide to create charts of the sales projections as charts make it easy to visually understand numeric data. Excel 2000 can create many types of charts from data in a worksheet. In this tutorial, you will learn to use Excel 2000's chart-creating and formatting features to produce several different charts of your sales estimates, as shown below.

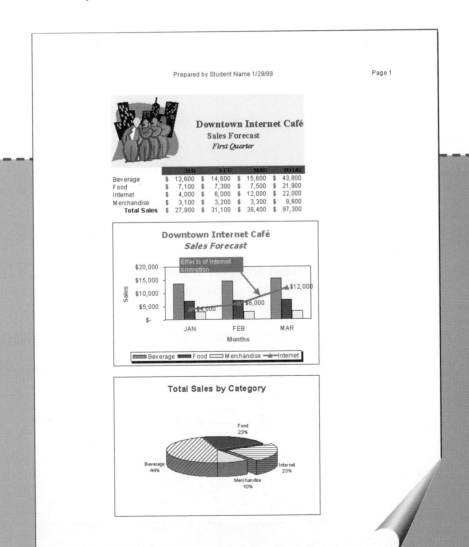

## Concept Overview

The following concepts will be introduced in this tutorial:

**1** **Chart Types**   Different types of charts are used to represent data in different ways. The type of chart you create depends on the type of data you are charting and the emphasis you want the chart to impart.

**2** **Chart Elements**   Chart elements consist of a number of parts that are used to graphically display the worksheet data.

**3** **Chart Objects**   A chart object is a graphic object that is created using charting features included in Excel. A chart object can be inserted into a worksheet or into a special chart sheet.

**4** **Group**   Because it consists of many separate objects a chart object is a group. A group is two or more objects that are treated as a single object.

**5** **Data Label**   Data labels provide additional information about a data marker.

**6** **Text Box**   A text box is a rectangular object in which you type text. Text boxes can be added to a sheet or an embedded chart.

**7** **Header and Footer**   Lines of text displayed below the top margin or above the bottom margin of each page are called headers and footers.

## Learning About Charts

- - - - - - - - - - - - - - - - - - - - - - - - - - - - - - - - - - - - - - - - - -

You have decided to chart the sales forecast data for the Downtown Internet Café to better see the sales trends. The sales data is in a separate workbook file named Café Sales.

**1** ■— ■ **Open the file Café Sales.**

Your screen should be similar to Figure 2–1.

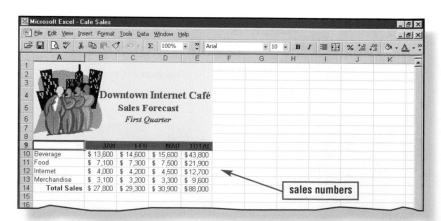

**Figure 2–1**

Although the worksheet shows the sales numbers for each category, it is hard to see how the different categories change over time. A visual representation of data in the form of a **chart** would convey that information in an easy-to-understand and attractive manner.

## Concept ① Chart Types

Different types of charts are used to represent data in different ways. The type of chart you create depends on the type of data you are charting and the emphasis you want the chart to impart. Excel 2000 can produce 14 standard types of graphs or charts, with many different sub-types for each standard type. In addition, Excel includes professionally designed built-in custom charts that include additional formatting and chart refinements. The basic chart types are:

| Type | Description |
|------|-------------|
|  | Area charts show the magnitude of change over time by emphasizing the area under the curve created by each data series. |
|  | Bar charts display data as evenly spaced bars. The categories are displayed along the Y axis and the values are displayed horizontally, placing more emphasis on comparisons and less on time. |
|  | Column charts display data as evenly spaced bars. They are similar to bar charts, except that categories are organized horizontally and values vertically to emphasize variation over time. |
|  | Line charts display data along a line. They are used to show changes in data over time, emphasizing time and rate of change rather than the amount of change. |
|  | Pie charts display data as slices of a circle or pie. They show the relationship of each value in a data series to the series as a whole. Each slice of the pie represents a single value in the series. |
|  | Doughnut charts are similar to pie charts except that they can show more than one data series. |

| Type | Description |
|------|-------------|
|  | Radar charts display a line or area chart wrapped around a central point. Each axis represents a set of data points. |
|  | XY (scatter) charts are used to show the relationship between two ranges of numeric data. |
|  | Surface charts display values as what appears to be a rubber sheet stretched over a 3-D column chart. These are useful for finding the best combination between sets of data. |
|  | Bubble charts compare sets of three values. It is like a scatter chart with the third value displayed as the size of bubble markers. |
|  | A stock chart is a high-low-close chart. It requires three series of values in this order. |
|  | Cylinder charts display values with a cylindrical shape. |
|  | Cone charts display values with a conical shape. |
|  | Pyramid charts display values with a pyramid shape. |

## Selecting the Data to Chart

------------------------------------------------

The first chart you want to create will show the total sales pattern over the three months. All charts are drawn from data contained in a worksheet. To create a new chart, you select the worksheet range containing the data you want displayed as a chart plus any row or column headings you want used in the chart. Excel then translates the selected data into a chart based upon the shape and contents of the worksheet selection.

A chart consists of a number of parts that are important to understand so that you can identify the appropriate data to select in the worksheet.

---

### Concept ② Chart Elements

A chart consists of a number of parts that are used to graphically display the worksheet data. The basic parts of a two-dimensional chart are shown in the figure below.

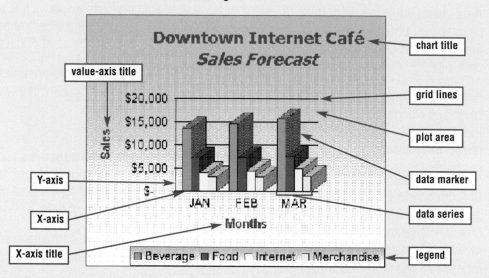

The bottom boundary line of the chart is the **X axis**. It is used to label the data being charted, such as a point in time or a category. The **category names** displayed along the X axis correspond to the headings for the worksheet data that is plotted along the X axis. The left boundary line of the chart is the **Y axis**, also called the **value axis**. This axis is a numbered scale whose numbers are determined by the data used in the chart. Typically the X-axis line is the horizontal line and the Y-axis line is the vertical line.

The selected worksheet data is visually displayed within the X- and Y-axis boundaries. This is called the **plot area**. Each group of related data, such as the numbers in a row or column of the selected area of the worksheet, is called a **data series**. Each number represented in a data series is identified by a **data marker**. A data marker can be a symbol, color, or pattern. To distinguish one data series from another, different data markers are used. In addition, chart gridlines are commonly displayed to make it easier to read the chart data. **Chart gridlines** extend from the Y-axis line across the plot area. A **legend** identifies the chart data series names and data markers that correspond to each data series.

A chart can also contain descriptive **titles** that explain the contents of the chart. The **chart title** is displayed centered above the charted data. Titles can also be used to describe the X and Y axes. The X-axis title line is called the **category-axis title**, and the Y-axis title is called the **value-axis title**.

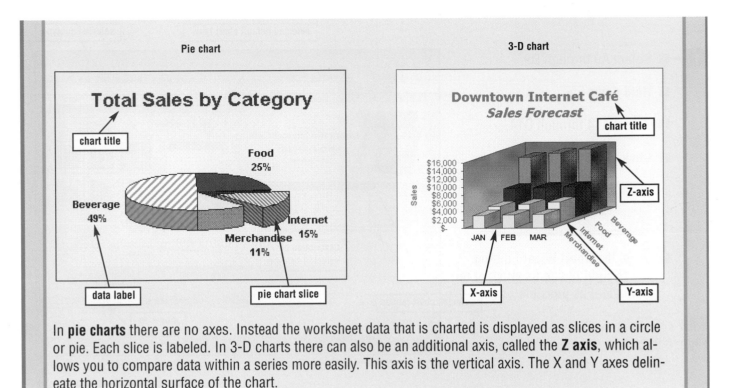

In **pie charts** there are no axes. Instead the worksheet data that is charted is displayed as slices in a circle or pie. Each slice is labeled. In 3-D charts there can also be an additional axis, called the **Z axis**, which allows you to compare data within a series more easily. This axis is the vertical axis. The X and Y axes delineate the horizontal surface of the chart.

The first chart you will create of the worksheet data will use the month labels in cells B9 through D9 to label the X-axis. The numbers to be charted are in cells B14 through D14. In addition, the label Total Sales in cell A14 will be used as the chart legend, making the entire range A14 through D14.

X-axis label

| | A | B | C | D | E |
|---|---|---|---|---|---|
| 9 | | JAN | FEB | MAR | TOTAL |
| 10 | Beverage | $ 13,600 | $ 14,600 | $ 15,600 | $43,800 |
| 11 | Food | $ 7,100 | $ 7,300 | $ 7,500 | $21,900 |
| 12 | Internet | $ 4,000 | $ 4,200 | $ 4,500 | $12,700 |
| 13 | Merchandise | $ 3,100 | $ 3,200 | $ 3,300 | $ 9,600 |
| 14 | Total Sales | $ 27,800 | $ 29,300 | $ 30,900 | $88,000 |

chart legend

data to chart

Notice that the two ranges, B9 through D9 and A14 through D14, are not adjacent and are not the same size. When plotting nonadjacent ranges in a chart, the selections must form a rectangular shape. To do this, the blank cell A9 will be included in the selection. To specify the range and create the chart,

**1** Select A9 through D9.

■ Hold down Ctrl.

■ Select A14 through D14.

■ Click 📊 Chart Wizard.

> The menu equivalent is Insert/Chart.

■ Move the Chart Wizard dialog box to right to see as much of the worksheet as possible.

Your screen should be similar to Figure 2-2.

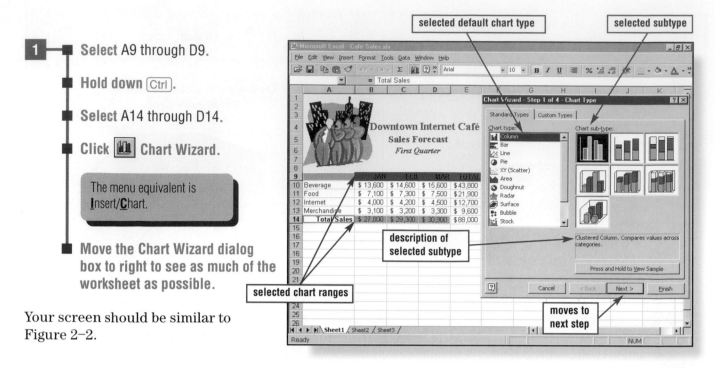

**Figure 2-2**

### Additional Information

Office 2000 includes many different wizards that provide step-by-step guidance to help you quickly perform many complicated tasks.

Chart Wizard is an interactive program that guides you through the steps to create a chart. The first step is to select the chart type from the Chart Type list box. The default chart type is a **column chart**. Each type of chart includes many variations. The variations associated with the column chart type are displayed as buttons in the Chart Sub-type section of the dialog box. The default column sub-type is a clustered column. A description of the selected sub-type is displayed in the area below the sub-type buttons. To use the default column chart type and move to the next step,

**2** Click Next >.

Your screen should be similar to Figure 2-3.

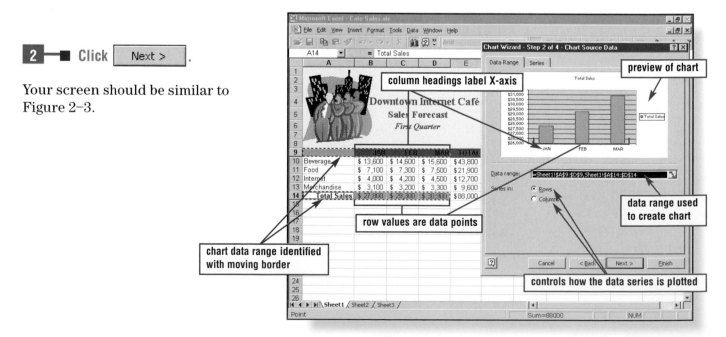

**Figure 2-3**

In the second Chart Wizard dialog box you specify the data range on the worksheet you want to plot. Because you selected the data range before starting the Chart Wizard, the range is correctly displayed in the Data range text box. In addition, the data range is identified with a moving border in the worksheet. The dialog box also displays a preview of the chart that will be created using the specified data and selected chart type.

The two Series In options change how Excel plots the data series from the rows or columns in the selected data range. The orientation Excel uses by default varies depending upon the type of chart selected and the number of rows and columns defined in a series. The worksheet data range that has the greater number of rows or columns appears along the X-axis and the smaller number is charted as the data series. When the data series is an equal number of rows and columns, as it is in this case, the default is to plot the rows. The first row defines the X-axis category labels and the second row the plotted data. The content of the first cell in the second row is used as the legend text. To accept the default settings,

**3** Click [ Next > ] .

■ If necessary, open the Titles tab.

Your screen should be similar to Figure 2–4.

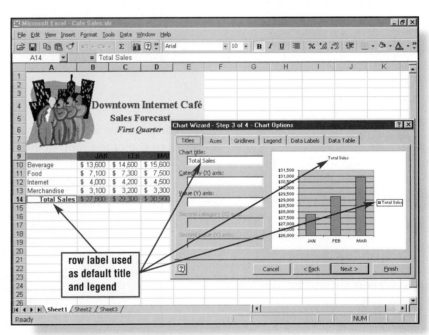

**Figure 2–4**

In the Step 3 dialog box, you can turn some standard options on and off and change the appearance of chart elements such as a legend and titles. To clarify the data in the chart, you will add a more descriptive chart title as well as titles along the X and Y axes. As you add the titles, the preview chart will update to display the new settings.

**4** ■ In the Chart Title text box, re-place the default title with **Downtown Internet Café Sales**

> Use ⎡Tab⎤, not ⎡Enter⎤, after typing the title text. Pressing ⎡Enter⎤ is the same as clicking ⎡ Next > ⎤.

■ In the Category (X) Axis text box, enter **Months**

■ In the Value (Y) Axis text box, enter **Total Sales**

Your screen should be similar to Figure 2–5.

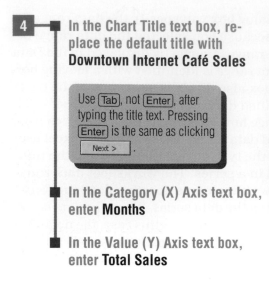
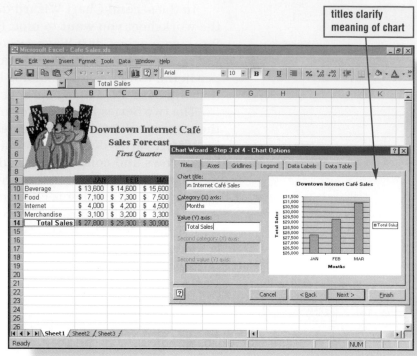

**Figure 2–5**

Because there is only one data range and the titles now fully explain the data in the chart, you decide to clear the display of the legend.

**5** ■ Open the Legend tab.

■ Click Show Legend to clear the checkmark.

Your screen should be similar to Figure 2–6.

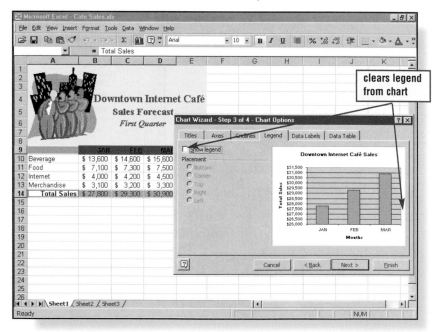

**Figure 2–6**

The legend is removed and the chart area resized to occupy the extra space.

**6** ■ Click [ Next > ] .

Your screen should be similar to Figure 2–7.

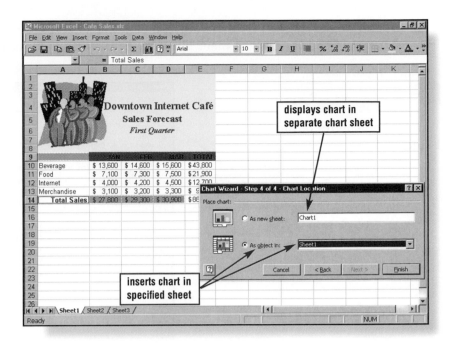

displays chart in separate chart sheet

inserts chart in specified sheet

**Figure 2–7**

In the last step, you specify where you want the chart displayed in the worksheet. A chart can be displayed in a separate chart sheet or as an object in an existing sheet.

---

**Concept ③ Chart Objects**

A **chart object** is a graphic object that is created using charting features included in Excel. A chart object can be inserted into a worksheet or into a special chart sheet.

Charts that are inserted into a worksheet are embedded objects. An **embedded chart** becomes part of the sheet in which it is inserted and is saved as part of the worksheet when you save the workbook file. Like all graphic objects, an embedded chart object can be sized and moved in a worksheet. A worksheet can contain multiple charts. As objects are added to the worksheet, they automatically **stack** in individual layers. The stacking order is apparent when objects overlap. Stacking allows you to create different effects by overlapping objects. Because you can rearrange the stacking order, you do not have to add or create the objects in the order in which you want them to appear.

**Triangle is on top of stack**

**Triangle is sent to the back**

**Square is brought to the front**

A chart that is inserted into a separate chart sheet is also saved with the workbook file. Only one chart can be added to a chart sheet and it cannot be sized and moved.

You would like this chart displayed as an object in the Sales worksheet. This is the default selection. To complete the chart,

**7** ━━■ Click [ Finish ] .

Your screen should be similar to
Figure 2–8.

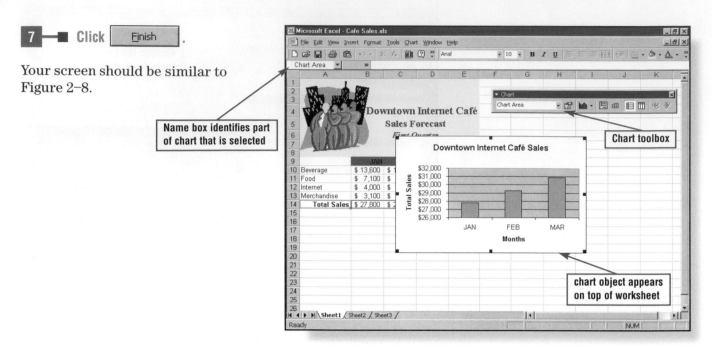

**Figure 2–8**

The chart with the settings you specified using the Chart Wizard is displayed on the worksheet. It covers some of the worksheet data because it
is a separate chart object that can be moved and sized within the worksheet.

Notice that the name box displays Chart Area. The Name box identifies the part of the chart that is selected, in this case the entire chart and
all its contents.

Also notice that the Chart toolbar is automatically displayed whenever a chart is selected. The Chart toolbar contains buttons for the most
frequently used chart editing and formatting features. These buttons are
identified below.

If your chart toolbar is not automatically displayed, open it by selecting
it from the toolbar shortcut menu.
It may also be docked already, depending on how it was last used.

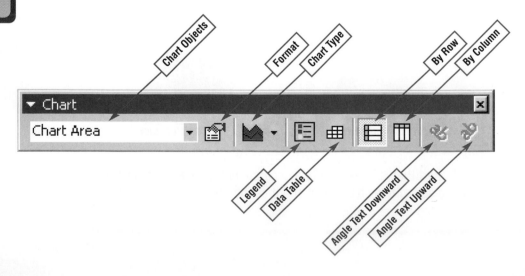

Move toolbars by dragging the title bar of the floating toolbar or move the handle ▯ of the docked toolbar.

**8** ■ If necessary, move the Chart toolbar to the row below the Standard and Formatting toolbars.

## Moving and Sizing a Chart

You want to move the chart so that it is displayed to the right of the worksheet data. In addition, you want to increase the size of the chart. A selected chart object is moved by pointing to it and dragging it to a new location. When you move the mouse pointer into the selected chart object, it will display a chart ScreenTip to advise you of the chart element that will be affected by your action. When moving the entire chart, the ScreenTip must display Chart Area.

**1** ■ Move the mouse pointer to different elements within the chart and note the different chart ScreenTips that appear.

■ With the chart ScreenTip displaying Chart Area, drag the chart object so that the upper-left corner is in cell F4.

The mouse pointer appears as a ✛ while dragging to move an object.

Your screen should be similar to Figure 2–9.

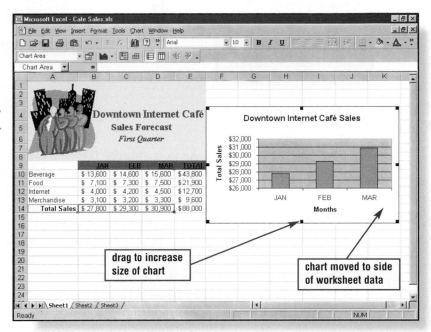

**Figure 2–9**

Next you will increase the size of the chart by dragging a **selection handle**. This is the same as sizing a graphic object.

**2** ■ **Point to the lower-center selection handle, hold down** Alt **, and drag the chart box down until it is displayed over cells F4 through K20.**

**Additional Information**

If you hold down Alt while dragging to move and size a chart object, the chart automatically snaps into position or aligns with the closest worksheet cell when you release the mouse button. Release the mouse button before you release Alt .

The mouse pointer appears as a ↕ while sizing an object.

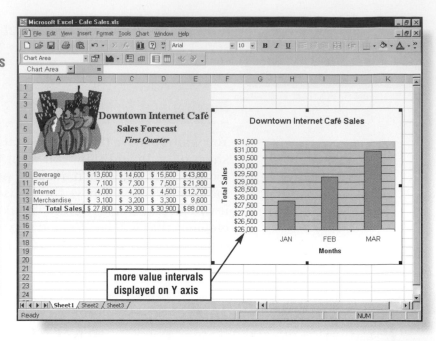

more value intervals displayed on Y axis

**Figure 2–10**

Your screen should be similar to Figure 2–10.

As you enlarge the chart, more value intervals are displayed along the Y axis, making the data in the chart easier to read. Additionally, the fonts in the chart scale proportionally as you resize the chart. The chart includes standard formats that are applied to the selected chart sub-type, such as a shaded background in the plot area and blue columns.

It is now easy to see how the worksheet data you selected is represented in the chart. Each column represents the total sales for that month in row 9. The month labels in row 3 have been used to label the X axis category labels. The range or scale of values along the Y axis is determined from the data in the worksheet. The upper limit is the maximum value in the worksheet rounded upward to the next highest interval.

## Changing the Type of Chart

The menu equivalent is **C**hart/Chart **T**ype.

Next you would like to see how the same data displayed in the column chart would look as a line chart. A **line chart** displays data as a line and is commonly used to show trends over time. This is easily done by changing the chart type using the ▥▾ Chart Type button on the Chart toolbar.

**1** Open the ◣▾ Chart Type drop-down list.

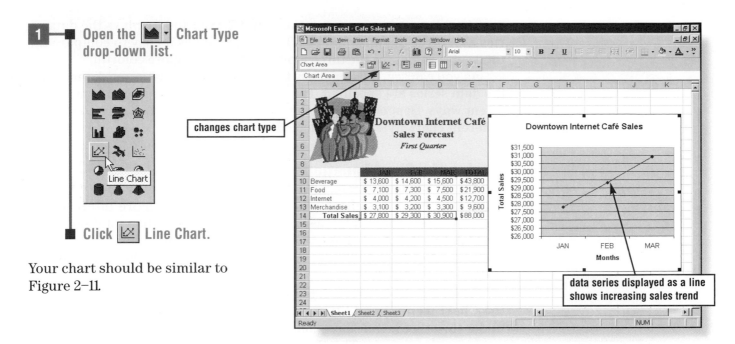

changes chart type

Click ◱ Line Chart.

Your chart should be similar to Figure 2–11.

**Figure 2–11**

The data for the total sales for the three months is now displayed as a line. Also notice the ◱▾ Chart type button displays a line chart, reflecting the last-selected chart type. The line shows the increasing sales trend from month to month. However, because the chart contains only one data series, a line chart is not very interesting or colorful. You will change it to a 3-D bar chart next.

**2** Click ◱▾ Chart Type.

Click ◢ 3-D Bar Chart.

Your chart should be similar to Figure 2–12.

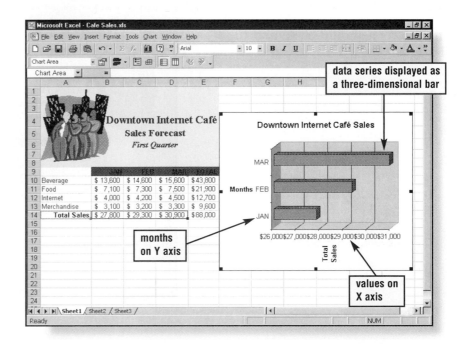

data series displayed as a three-dimensional bar

months on Y axis

values on X axis

**Figure 2–12**

The 3-D bar chart reverses the X and Y axes and displays the data series as a three-dimensional bar. This chart makes it easy to compare the total sales values for the three months and is a lot more colorful.

As you can see, it is very easy to change the chart type and format once the data series are specified. The same data can be displayed in many different ways. Depending upon the emphasis you want the chart to make, a different chart style can be selected.

## Moving the Chart Location

After modifying this chart, you decide that you are more interested in comparing the sales categories for each month rather than total sales. You could delete the chart simply by pressing [Delete] while it is selected; however, you decide just to move it to another location in the workbook for now.

When a chart is selected, the Data menu changes to the Chart menu. In addition, many of the commands under the other menus have changed to commands that apply to charts only. The Chart menu contains commands that can be used to modify the chart.

**1** ━━■ Choose Chart/Location

Your screen should be similar to Figure 2–13.

moves selected chart to specified location in workbook

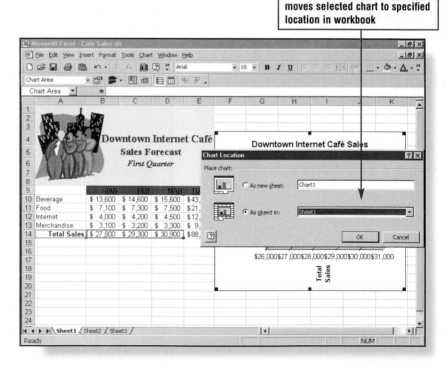

**Figure 2–13**

**2** ■ Choose As new <u>s</u>heet.

■ Click [ OK ] .

Your chart should be similar to
Figure 2–14.

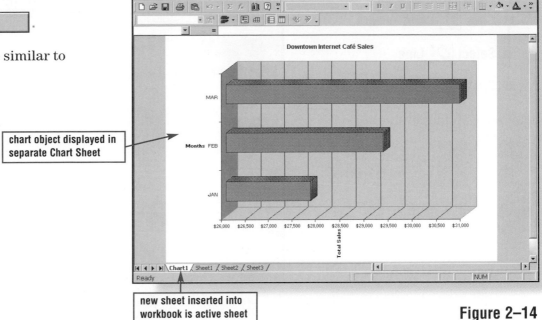

chart object displayed in
separate Chart Sheet

new sheet inserted into
workbook is active sheet

**Figure 2–14**

The bar chart is now an object displayed in a separate chart sheet.
Generally, you display a chart in a chart sheet when you want the chart
displayed separately from the associated worksheet data. The chart is still
automatically linked to the worksheet data from which it was created.

The new chart sheet named Chart1 was inserted to the left of the worksheet, Sheet1. The Chart sheet is the active sheet, or the sheet you are currently viewing and working in. To display Sheet1 containing the worksheet
data,

You can also press [Ctrl] + [Pg Up]
to move to the next sheet and [Ctrl]
+ [Pg Dn] to move to the previous
sheet.

**3** ■ Click the Sheet1 tab.

## Creating a Chart with Multiple Data Series

Now you are ready to continue your analysis of sales trends. You want to
create a second chart to display the sales data for each category for the
three months. You could create a separate chart for each category and
then compare the charts; however, to make the comparisons between the
categories easier, you will display all the categories on a single chart.

The data for the three months for the four categories is in cells B10
through D13. The month headings (X-axis data series) are in cells B9
through D9, and the legend text is in the range A10 through A13. To specify
the chart data series,

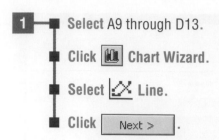

**1** ■ Select A9 through D13.

■ Click 📊 Chart Wizard.

■ Select 📈 Line.

■ Click [ Next > ].

Your screen should be similar to
Figure 2–15.

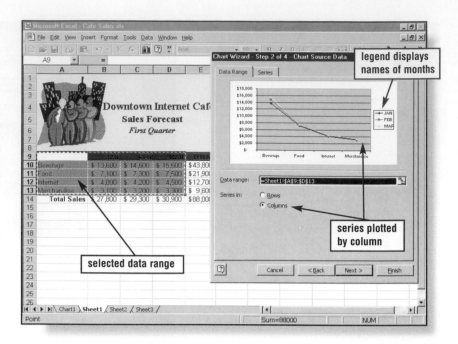

**Figure 2–15**

---

If you want to change the series orientation of an existing chart, you
can use ▤ By Row or ▥ By
Column in the Chart toolbar.

When plotting the data for this chart, Excel selected Columns as the
data series orientation because there are fewer columns than rows in the
data range. This time, however, you want to change the data series to
Rows so that the months are along the X axis.

---

**2** ■ Select Rows.

Your screen should be similar to
Figure 2–16.

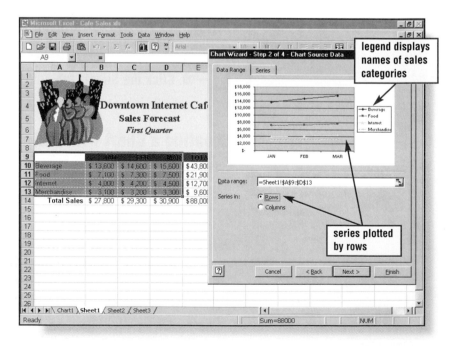

**Figure 2–16**

The sample chart is redrawn with the new orientation. The line chart
now compares the sales by month rather than by category. The Legend displays the names of the sales categories.

**3** Click  Next > .

Open the Titles tab.

Enter the following titles:

| Title | Entry |
|---|---|
| Chart title | **Downtown Internet Café Sales Forecast** |
| Category (X) axis | **Months** |
| Value (Y) axis | **Sales** |

Because you want this chart embedded in the worksheet, you can skip the next step, which accepts the default, and finish the chart.

**4** Click 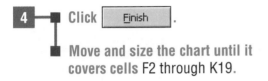 Finish .

Move and size the chart until it covers cells F2 through K19.

Your screen should be similar to Figure 2–17.

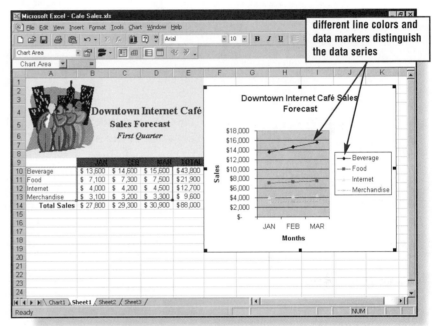

**Figure 2–17**

A different line color and data marker identify each data series and are reflected in the legend. The line chart shows that sales in all categories are increasing, with the sharpest increase occurring in beverage sales.

## Applying a Custom Chart Type

Although the line chart shows the sales trends for the three months for the sales categories, again it does not look very interesting. You decide to look at several other chart types to see if you can improve the appearance.

First you would like to see the data represented as an area chart. An **area chart** represents data the same as a line chart, but in addition, it shades the area below each line to emphasize the degree of change.

**1** ■ Click [icon] ▾ **Chart type.**

■ Click [icon] **Area Chart.**

Your chart should be similar to Figure 2–18.

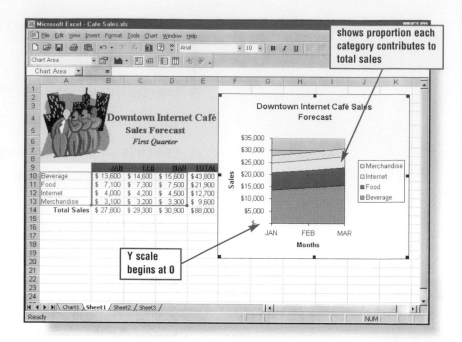

**Figure 2–18**

The Y-axis scale has changed to reflect the new range of data. The new Y-axis range is the sum of the five categories, or the same as the total number in the worksheet. Using this chart type, you can see the magnitude of change each category contributes to the total sales in each month.

Because this is not the emphasis you want to show, you decide to continue looking at other types of charts. Because not all chart types are available from the Chart Type drop-down list, you will use the Chart Type menu option in the Chart menu instead.

**2** ■ Choose <u>C</u>hart/Chart <u>T</u>ype.

Your screen should be similar to Figure 2–19.

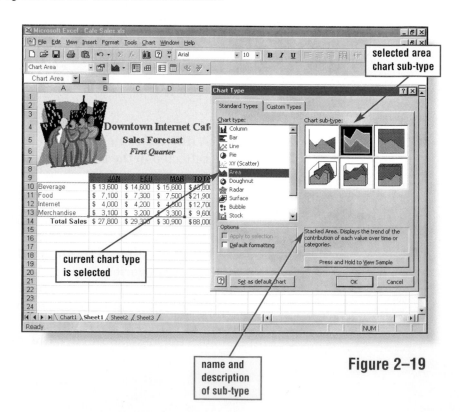

**Figure 2–19**

The Chart Type dialog box contains the same options as the Chart Wizard - Step 1 dialog box. The current chart type, Area, is the selected option. You want to see how this data will look as a stacked column chart.

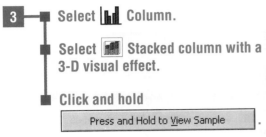

**3** ■ Select **∎∎** Column.

■ Select **∎∎** **Stacked column with a 3-D visual effect.**

■ Click and hold

> Press and Hold to View Sample

.

Your screen should be similar to Figure 2–20.

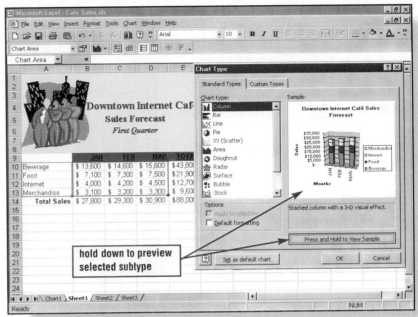

**Figure 2–20**

The sample chart is redrawn showing the data as a **stacked-column chart**. This type of chart also shows the proportion of each sales category to the total sales. To see what other types of charts are available,

**4** ■ Open the Custom Types tab.

■ Click **∎∎** **Area Blocks.**

Your screen should be similar to Figure 2–21.

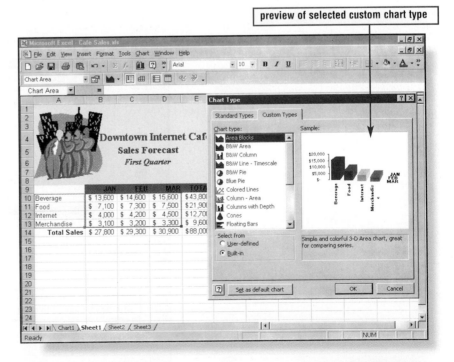

**Figure 2–21**

The sample area shows how the data you selected for the chart will appear in this style. Custom charts are based upon standard types that are enhanced with additional display settings and custom formatting. Although this is interesting, you feel the data is difficult to read.

**5** Select several other custom chart types to see how the data appears in the Sample area.

Select **▐▮▌** Columns with Depth.

Your screen should be similar to Figure 2–22.

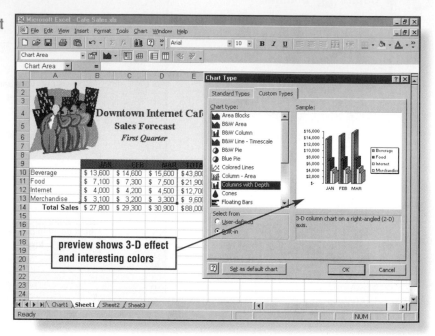

**preview shows 3-D effect and interesting colors**

**Figure 2–22**

This chart shows the sales for each category for each month with more interesting colors and three-dimensional depth.

**6** Click  OK .

Your screen should be similar to Figure 2–23.

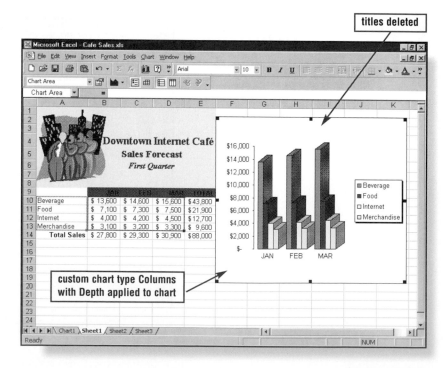

**titles deleted**

**custom chart type Columns with Depth applied to chart**

**Figure 2–23**

## Adding Chart Titles

Unfortunately, when applying a custom chart type, the chart titles are deleted and you need to add them again.

**1** — ■ Chart/Chart Options

■ In the Titles tab, enter the following titles:

| Title | Entry |
|---|---|
| Chart title | Downtown Internet Café |
| Category (X) axis | Months |
| Value (Z) axis | Sales |

Your screen should be similar to Figure 2–24.

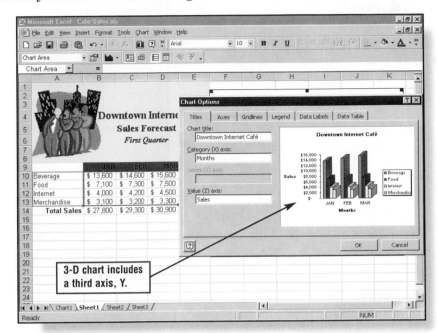

**Figure 2–24**

Notice that this time instead of entering the Value axis data in the Y axis, you entered it in the Z axis. This is because the Y axis is used as a Series axis on a three-dimensional chart. This three-dimensional chart only has one series of data so the Y axis is not used.

## Moving the Legend

While looking at the preview chart, you decide to move the legend below the X axis.

1 ■— Open the Legend tab.

■ Select Bottom.

■ Click [ OK ] .

Your screen should be similar to
Figure 2–25.

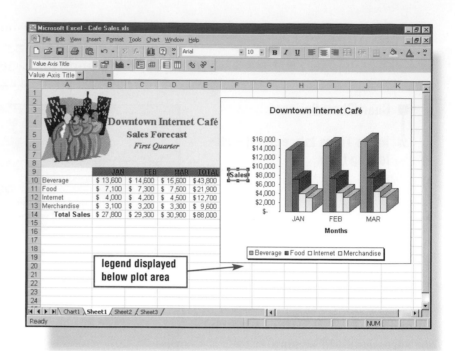

**Figure 2–25**

### Additional Information

You can also move the legend by
dragging it, and then you can resize
it to fit the new location.

The legend is centered below the plot area of the chart and resized to
fit the space.

## Formatting Chart Elements

Next you want to improve the appearance of the chart by applying formatting to the different chart parts. All the different parts of a chart are separate objects. Because a chart consists of many separate objects, it is a
group.

### Concept 4 Groups

Since a chart object consists of many separate objects, it is a group. A **group** is two
or more objects that are treated as a single object. The chart title is a single object
within the chart object. Some of the objects in a chart are also groups that consist of
other objects. For example, the legend is a group object consisting of separate items,
each identifying a different data series. Other chart objects are the axis lines, a data
series, a data marker, the entire plot area, or the entire chart.

An entire group or each object in a group can be individually selected and then
formatted or edited. By selecting the entire group, you can format all objects within the group at once.
Alternatively, you can select an object within a group and format it individually. For example, if you select
the legend group and apply a font format to it, all objects within the legend group are changed. If you select
a single object within the legend group, such as the legend for one data series, it can be formatted independently from the other objects in that group.

The first formatting change you want to make is to improve the appearance of the chart title.

**1** ◆— **Click on the chart title to select it.**

Your screen should be similar to Figure 2–26.

identifies selected object

title object selected inside chart object

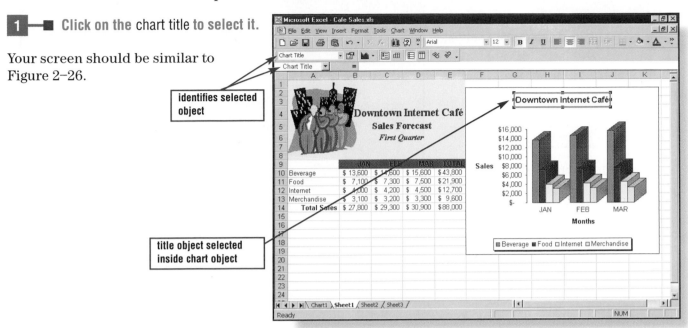

**Figure 2–26**

The title is surrounded by a dotted border and selection handles, indicating that it is the selected object and will be affected by any changes you make. In addition, the Name box and Chart Objects button display Chart Title as the selected chart object.

As different objects in the chart are selected, the commands on the Format menu change to commands that can be used on the selected object. In addition, the ⊞ Format Object button to the right of the Chart Object button can be used to format the selected object.

**2** ◆— **Click** ⊞ **Format Chart Title.**

> The menu equivalent is Format/**S**elected Chart Title and the shortcut is Ctrl+1.

◆ **Open the Font tab.**

Your screen should be similar to Figure 2–27.

formats selected object

changes formats associated with chart title

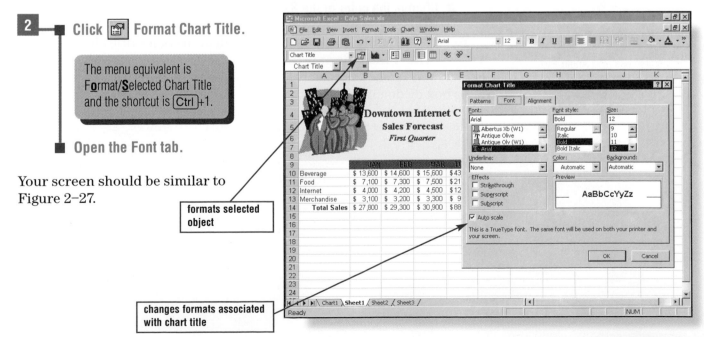

**Figure 2–27**

The Format Chart Title dialog box is used to change the patterns, font, and placement of the title.

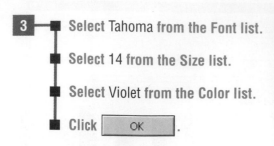

**3**

■ Select Tahoma from the Font list.

■ Select 14 from the Size list.

■ Select Violet from the Color list.

■ Click OK .

Your screen should be similar to Figure 2–28.

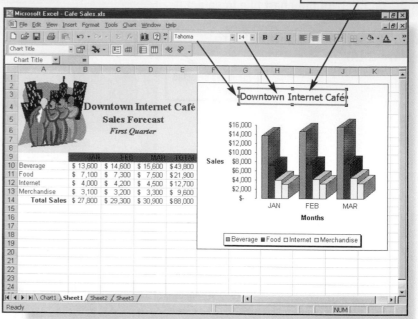

chart title formatted to new font, size and color

**Figure 2–28**

Next you want to change color of axis titles. A quicker way to make many formatting changes is to use the Formatting toolbar buttons.

**4**

■ Click the category-axis title Months.

■ Open the A ▾ Font Color palette and change the color to violet.

■ Change the color of the Sales title to violet in the same manner.

**Additional Information**

You can also use 🕮 Angle Text Downward or 🕮 Angle Text Upward to quickly change the angle of a label to 45 degrees.

You also want to change the orientation of the Sales title along the axis so it is parallel with the axis line. To do this, you will rotate the label 90 degrees. You can quickly select a chart object and open the related Format dialog box by double-clicking the object.

**5** ■ Double-click the border of the Sales title to open the Format dialog box.

■ Open the Alignment tab.

■ Drag the Orientation indicator arrow upward to rotate the text 90 degrees.

Your screen should be similar to Figure 2–29.

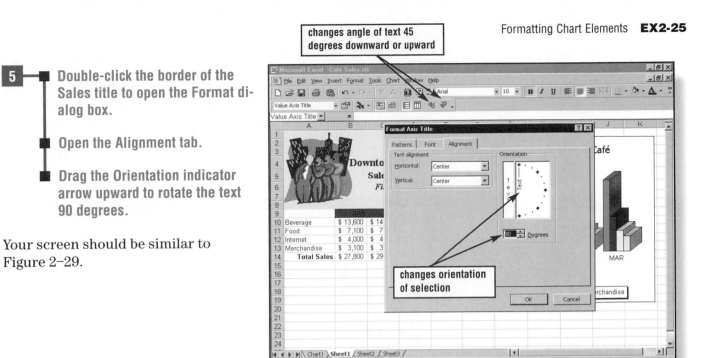

**Figure 2–29**

You could also enter a positive number in the degree box to rotate the selection from lower left to upper right or a negative number to rotate text in the opposite direction. Alternatively, you can use the degree scroll buttons to increase and decrease the degrees.

**6** ■ Click  .

The Sales label is now displayed parallel with the Y-axis line.

Finally, you want to add a second line to the chart title. You can select individual sections of text and apply formatting to them just as you would format any other text entry.

**7** ■ Select the chart title.

■ Click at the end of the title to place the insertion point.

■ Press Enter.

■ Type **Sales Forecast**.

■ Select (highlight) the words Sales Forecast.

■ Click *I* Italic.

■ Click in the title to clear the selection.

Your screen should be similar to Figure 2–30.

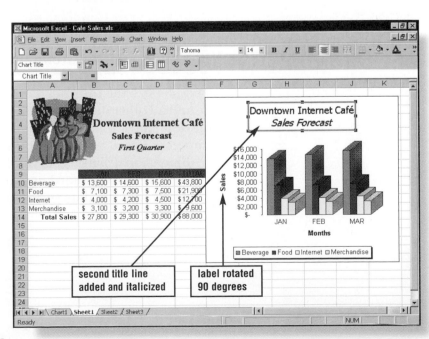

**Figure 2–30**

## Copying a Chart

Now you want to create another chart that will emphasize the sales trend for the Internet connection data series. This chart will use the same data series and titles as the current chart. Rather than recreate much of the same chart for the new chart, you will create a copy of the column chart and then modify it.

**1** Select the entire chart.

Click 🗎 Copy.

Move to A16.

Click 🗎 Paste.

**Additional Information**

You can also hold down (Ctrl) while clicking on the chart to create a copy of the chart at the current location in the worksheet.

Your screen should be similar to Figure 2–31.

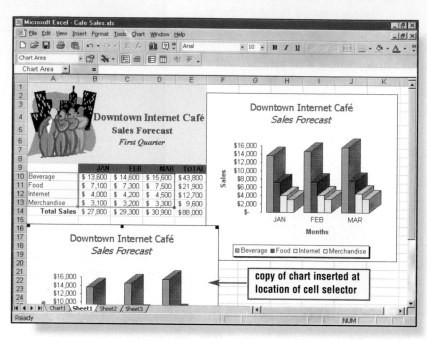

**Figure 2–31**

**2** Change the location of the copied chart to a new chart sheet (Chart2).

Move to Sheet1.

## Creating a Combination Chart

To emphasize the Internet data, you want to display the data series as a line and all other data series as columns. This type of chart is called a **combination chart**. It uses two or more chart types to emphasize different information. Because you cannot mix a three-dimensional chart type with a one-dimensional chart type, you first need to change the chart type for the entire chart to a standard one-dimensional column chart. Then you can change the Internet data series to a line.

**1** Select the chart and change the chart type to Column Chart.

Click on the Internet data series to select it.

> Sometimes when there are many objects close together, it is easier to select the object from the Chart Objects drop-down list.

From the 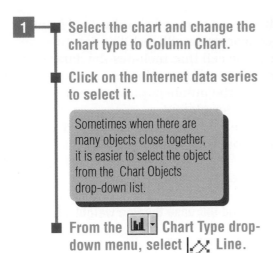 Chart Type drop-down menu, select 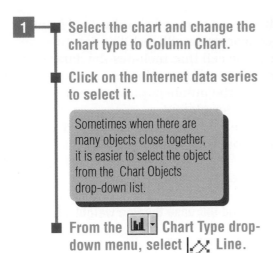 Line.

Your chart should be similar to Figure 2–32.

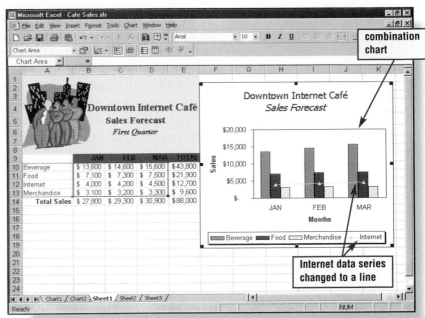

**Figure 2–32**

A combination chart makes it easy to see comparisons between groups of data or to show different types of data in a single chart. In this case, you can now easily pick out the Internet sales from the other sales categories.

## Changing Fill Colors

As the yellow line is difficult to see on a white background, you want to change the color of the line and add a fill color to the plot area to make the line more visible.

**1** Double-click on the line to select it and open the Format dialog box.

> Your ScreenTip should display Series "Internet" Point before you click.

Your screen should be similar to Figure 2–33.

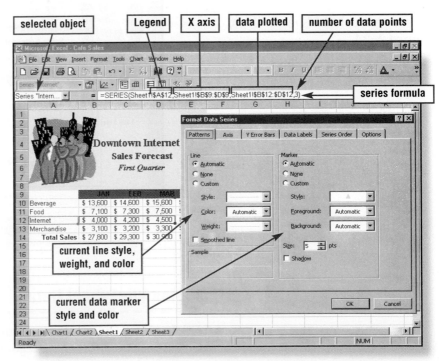

**Figure 2–33**

**EXCEL 2000**

Notice that the formula bar displays a **series formula**. This formula links the chart object to the source worksheet, Sheet1. The formula contains four arguments: a reference to the cell that includes the data series name (used in the legend), references to the cells that contain the categories (X-axis numbers), references to the numbers plotted, and an integer that specifies the number of data series plotted.

The current line and data marker settings are displayed in the Patterns tab. The Sample area shows how your selections will appear.

**2** ■ Open the Color palette and change the line color to sea green.

■ Open the Weight drop-down list and increase the line weight setting by one.

■ Change the Foreground and Background marker color to sea green.

■ Click   OK   .

Next you would like to change the plot area to ivory. You could use the Format Plot Area dialog box to change the color or the [fill color button] fill color button on the Formatting toolbar.

**3** ■ Select the plot area.

■ Click [Fill Color] Fill Color and select ivory.

Your screen should be similar to Figure 2–34.

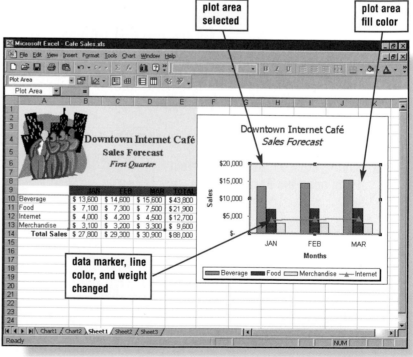

**Figure 2–34**

## Changing Worksheet Data

After checking the worksheet and reconsidering the amounts you have budgeted for the different categories, you now feel that you have underestimated the increase in Internet sales. You are planning to heavily promote the Internet aspect of the Café and anticipate that Internet usage will increase dramatically in February and March and then level off in the following months. You want to change the worksheet to reflect this increase.

**1** Change the February Internet sales value to **6000**.

Change the March Internet sales value to **12000**.

Your screen should be similar to Figure 2–35.

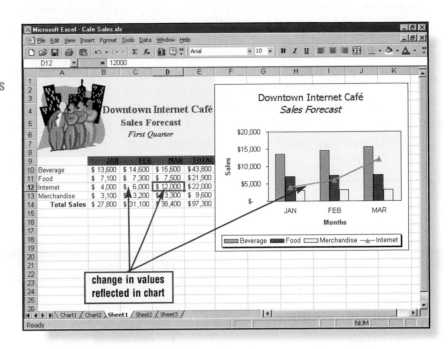

**Figure 2–35**

The worksheet has been recalculated and all charts that reference those worksheet cells have been redrawn to reflect the change in the data for the Internet sales. Since the chart document is linked to the source data, changes to the source data are automatically reflected in the chart.

**2** Look at the bar and column charts in the Chart1 and Chart2 sheets to see how they have changed to reflect the change in data.

Make the Sheet1 sheet active again.

## Adding Data Labels

You would also like to display data labels containing the actual numbers plotted for the Internet sales on the combination chart.

**Concept (5) Data Label**

**Data labels** provide additional information about a data marker. They can consist of the value of the marker, the name of the data series or category, a percent value, or a bubble size. The different types of data labels that are available depend on the type of chart and the data that is plotted.

Value data labels are helpful when the values are large and you want to know the exact value for one data series. Data labels that display a name are helpful when the size of the chart is large and it is hard to tell what value the data point is over. The percent data label is used when you want to display the percent of each series on charts that show parts to the whole. Bubble size is used on bubble charts to help the reader quickly see how the different bubbles vary in size.

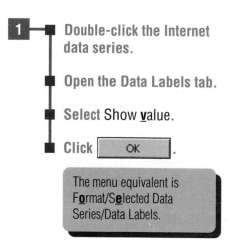

**1** — Double-click the Internet data series.

— Open the Data Labels tab.

— Select Show **v**alue.

— Click [ OK ] .

The menu equivalent is F**o**rmat/S**e**lected Data Series/Data Labels.

Your screen should be similar to Figure 2–36.

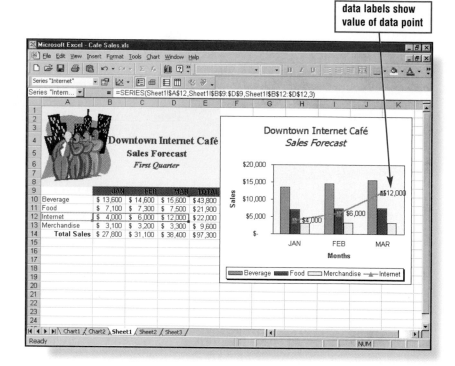

**Figure 2–36**

Data labels containing the actual values for Internet sales are displayed next to the data points on the line in the chart.

## Adding a Text Box

Because the chart reflects the Internet sales changes you made in the worksheet, you want to include a notation in the chart explaining the reason for the increase. This information can be entered in a text box.

## Concept ⑥ Text Box

A **text box** is a rectangular object in which you type text. Text boxes can be added to a sheet or an embedded chart. To add it to a chart, the chart object must be selected first, otherwise the text box is added to the worksheet. A text box that is part of a chart object can only be sized and moved within the chart object. If you move the chart object, the text box moves with it. If you do not add it to the chart, it will not move as part of the chart if you move the chart to another location.

Text that is entered in a text box wraps to fit within the boundaries of the text box. This feature is called **word wrap** and eliminates the need to press Enter to end a line. If you change the size and shape of the text box, the text automatically rewraps on the line to adjust to the new size.

You will add a text box containing the text **Internet Promotion** to the chart to draw attention to the Internet data. A text box is created using the 📰 Text Box button on the Drawing toolbar. To display the Drawing toolbar and create a text box,

**1**

■ Click 📰 Drawing (on the Standard toolbar).

■ Click 📰 Text Box.

■ Move the mouse pointer to the space above the February columns of data and drag to create a text box that is approximately 1½ inch by ½ inch.

> The mouse pointer appears as ╎ , indicating a text box will be created as you drag the mouse.

Your screen should be similar to Figure 2–37.

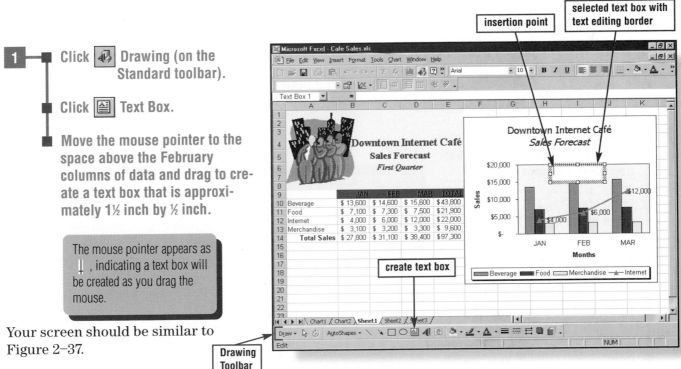

**Figure 2–37**

The text box is a selected object and is surrounded with a hatched border that indicates you can enter, delete, select, and format the text inside the box. It also displays an insertion point indicating that it is waiting for you to enter the text. As you type the text in the text box, do not be concerned if all the text is not visible within the text box. You will resize the box if needed to display the entire entry.

**2** ● Type **Effects of Internet promotion**

■ If necessary, adjust the size of the text box by dragging the sizing handles until it is just large enough to fully display the text on two lines.

Your screen should be similar to Figure 2–38.

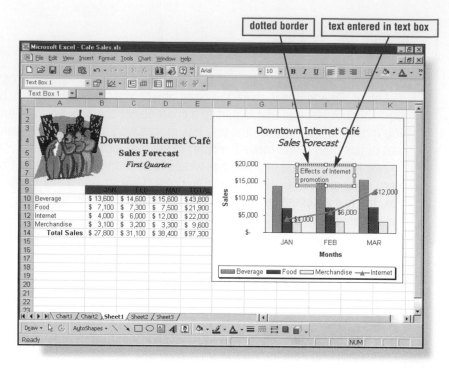

**Figure 2–38**

The text in the text box is difficult to read because it overlaps the plot area. To make it stand out better, you will add a fill color to the text box.

**3** ● Click the hatched text box border to turn off text editing (the insertion point disappears).

■ Open the ▨ ▾ Fill Color drop-down menu and select a color of your choice.

> You can use the ▨ ▾ and ▲ ▾ buttons on either the Formatting or Drawing toolbars.

■ Select a text color of your choice from the ▲ ▾ Font Color list.

> You can also choose Format/Text Box to format a text box.

■ Readjust the size of the text box and move it to the position displayed in Figure 2–39.

Your screen should be similar to Figure 2–39.

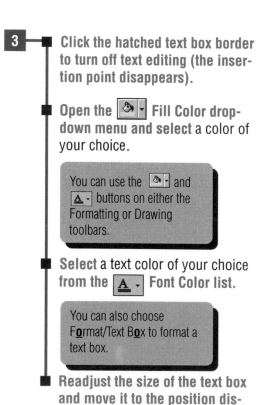
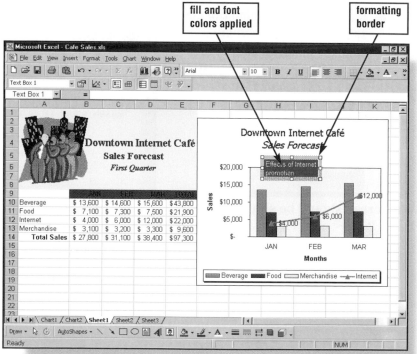

**Figure 2–39**

## Adding Arrows

Next you want to draw an arrow from the text box to the Internet line. Like a text box, an arrow is a separate object that can be added to a worksheet or a chart.

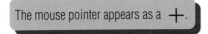

The mouse pointer appears as a ✛ .

If you hold down (Shift) while dragging, a straight horizontal line is drawn.

**1** • Click 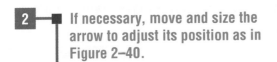 Arrow.

■ To draw the arrow, click on the right corner of the text box and drag to the Internet line. (See Figure 2–39)

A line with an arrowhead at the end is displayed. The arrow is automatically a selected object. The handles at both ends of the arrow let you adjust its size and location. You can also change the color and weight of the line to make it stand out more.

**2** ■ If necessary, move and size the arrow to adjust its position as in Figure 2–40.

■ Click  Line Color and select the same color for the arrow as you used for the text box.

■ Click ☰ Line Style and increase the line weight to 2¼ point.

■ Deselect the arrow.

Your screen should be similar to Figure 2–40.

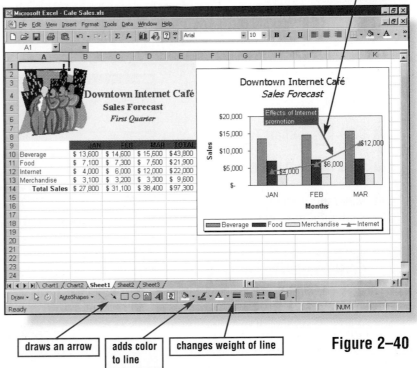

arrow with color
and heavier weight

draws an arrow | adds color to line | changes weight of line

**Figure 2–40**

## Creating a Pie Chart

The last chart you will make will use the Total worksheet data in column E. You want to see what proportion each type of sales are of all sales for the quarter. The best chart for this purpose is a pie chart. A pie chart compares parts to the whole in a similar manner to a stacked-column chart. However, each value in the range is a slice of the pie displayed as a percentage of the total.

**1 ■ Move the combination chart to top-align with cell A16 below the worksheet data.**

The use of X (category) and data series settings in a pie chart is different from their use in a column or line chart. The X series labels the slices of the pie rather than the X axis. The data series is used to create the slices in the pie. Only one data series can be specified in a pie chart.

**2 ■ Select** A10 through A13 **and** E10 through E13**.**

Another way to create a chart is to use the Chart Type toolbar button.

**Additional Information**

You can also create a chart using the default chart type (column) in a new chart sheet by selecting the data range and pressing F11.

**3 ■ If necessary, display the Chart toolbar.**

**■ Click** [☒ ▼] **Chart Type.**

**■ Click** [🍰] **3-D Pie Chart.**

**■ Move and expand the chart to be displayed over cells F2 through K18.**

Hold down Alt while moving to snap the chart to the cells.

Your screen should be similar to Figure 2–41.

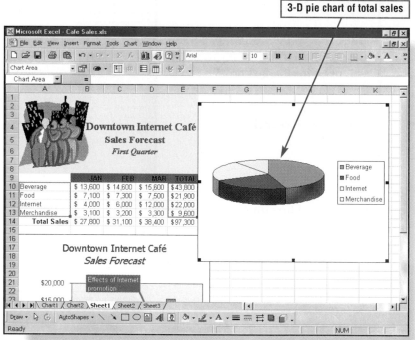

3-D pie chart of total sales

**Figure 2–41**

A three-dimensional pie chart is drawn in the worksheet. Each value in the data series is displayed as a slice of the pie chart. The size of the slice represents the proportion each sales category is of total sales. You need to add a chart title. In addition, you want to turn off the legend and display data labels instead to label the slices of the pie.

## Formatting the Pie Chart

To clarify the meaning of the chart, you will first add a chart title. A pie chart can have only a main title because it does not contain axis lines. Then you will add labels for the slices to identify the data in the chart.

**1** Choose **C**hart/Chart **O**ptions.

In the Chart Title text box of the Titles tab, enter the title **Total Sales by Category**

Open the Legend tab and clear the **S**how legend option.

You can also click 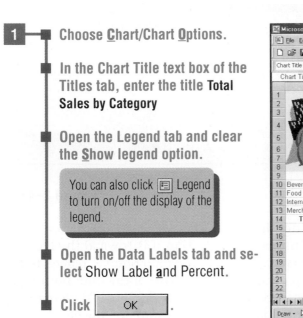 Legend to turn on/off the display of the legend.

Open the Data Labels tab and select Show Label **a**nd Percent.

Click [ OK ] .

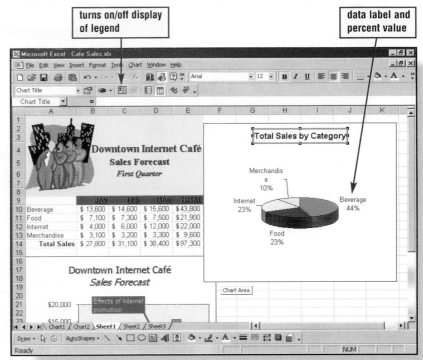

**Figure 2–42**

Your chart should be similar to Figure 2–42.

The pie chart is redrawn to show the data labels and percents. The data label text box size is based on the size of the chart and the text is appropriately sized to fit in the box. Because the default size of data labels is a little too large, the entire Merchandise label does not appear on one line. To fix this, you will reduce the size of the label text. You also want to enhance the appearance of the data labels and title.

**2** Select the data labels, reduce the font size by two points, and apply formatting of your choice.

Select the title and apply formatting of your choice.

## Exploding and Rotating the Pie

Next, you want to separate slightly or **explode** the Internet slice of the pie to emphasize the data.

**1** Select the Internet slice.

> To select an object within a group, select the group first and then select the object. Selection handles surround the selected object.

Drag the selected slice away from the pie.

> If all slices on the pie are selected, dragging one slice explodes all slices at the same time.

Your screen should be similar to Figure 2–43.

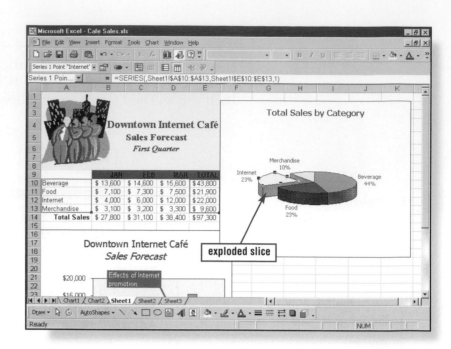

**Figure 2–43**

The slice is separated from the rest of the pie chart. You also want to change the position of the Internet slice so that it is toward the front of the pie. When Excel creates a pie chart, the first data point is placed to the right of the middle at the top of the chart. The rest of the data points are placed in order to the right until the circle is complete. To change the order in which the slices are displayed, you can rotate the pie chart.

**2** Double-click the Internet data series.

Open the Options tab.

Change the Angle of first slice setting to 180 degrees.

Your screen should be similar to Figure 2–44.

**3** Click OK.

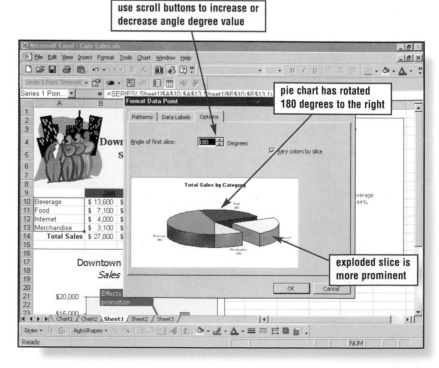

**Figure 2–44**

The entire pie chart has rotated 180 degrees to the right and now the Internet data slice appears toward the front of the chart.

## Applying Patterns and Color

The last change you would like to make is to add patterns to the pie chart data points. As you have seen, when Excel creates a chart each data series (or data point in the case of a pie chart) is automatically displayed in a different color. Although the data series are easy to distinguish from one another onscreen, if you do not have a color printer the colors are printed as shades of gray and may be difficult to distinguish. To make the data series more distinguishable on a black and white printer, you can apply a different pattern to each data series object.

**1** ■ **Double-click the Beverage data series slice.**

■ **Open the Pattern tab.**

Your screen should be similar to Figure 2–45.

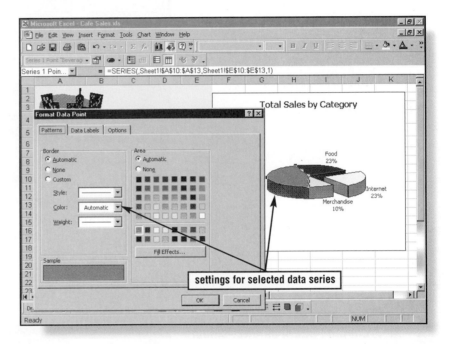

**Figure 2–45**

The options available in the Pattern tab vary depending upon the type of data marker that is selected. In this case, because the selected data marker is a pie slice, the options let you change the border and the background area. The current setting for the selected data marker is displayed in the sample area. This consists of a black border with a fill color of periwinkle blue. To add a pattern,

**2** ■ Click [ Fill Effects... ] .

■ **Open the Pattern tab.**

Your screen should be similar to
Figure 2–46.

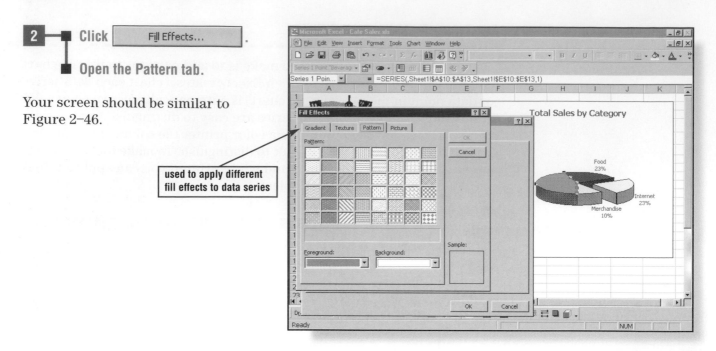

used to apply different
fill effects to data series

**Figure 2–46**

From the Fill Effects dialog box, you can change options for gradients,
textures, patterns, and pictures used in formatting the selected object. You
will add a pattern to the existing fill.

selected pattern is
applied to data series

**3** ■ **From the Pattern palette, select
a pattern of your choice.**

■ **Click [ OK ] (twice) to
close both dialog boxes.**

Your screen should be similar to
Figure 2–47.

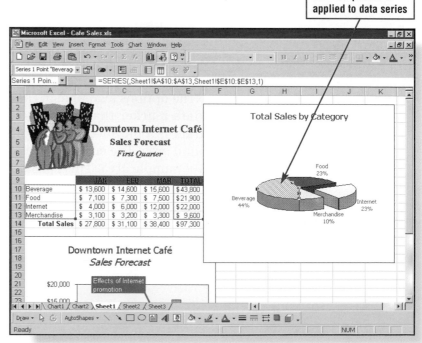

**Figure 2–47**

The pattern is applied to the selected data point. Next you will change
the color and add pattern to the Internet data series slice.

**4** ■ Double-click the Internet data series slice.

■ Click  Fill Effects... .

■ Open the Pattern tab.

Your screen should be similar to Figure 2–48.

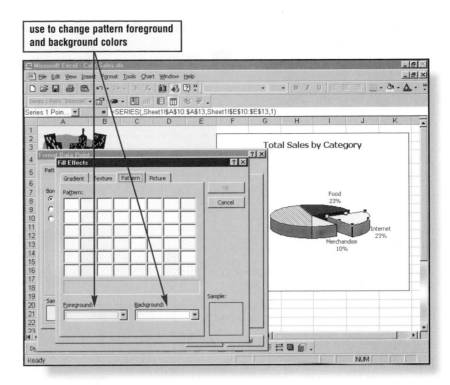

**Figure 2–48**

Because yellow is a light color, it is difficult to see the patterns in the Fill Effects dialog box. A pattern consists of a foreground color and a background color. The default foreground color is the same as the fill color and the background color is white. To increase the contrast, you can change the color selection of either.

**5** ■ From the Foreground color drop-down list, select a darker color of your choice.

■ Select a different pattern.

■ Click 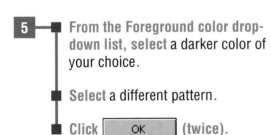 OK (twice).

Your chart should be similar to Figure 2–49.

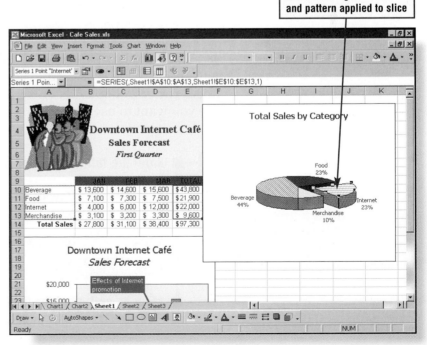

**Figure 2–49**

You will leave the other two data points without patterns.

**6** ━■ Move the pie chart below the column chart to top-align with cell A36.

## Documenting a Workbook

Now you are ready to save the changes you have made to the workbook file to your data disk. Before doing this, you want to document the workbook. Each workbook includes summary information that is associated with the file.

**1** ━■ Choose **F**ile/Proper**t**ies.

■ Select each tab in the Properties dialog box and look at the recorded information.

■ Open the Summary tab.

Your screen should be similar to Figure 2–50.

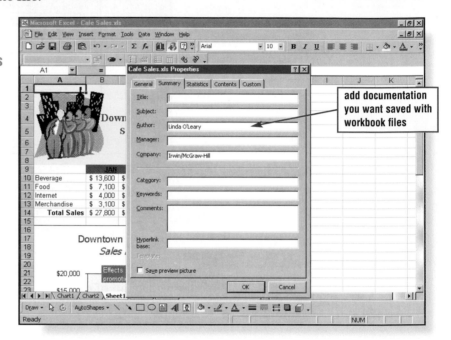

**Figure 2–50**

The Summary tab is used to specify information you want associated with the file such as a title, subject, author, keywords, and comments about the workbook file. This information helps you locate the workbook file you want to use as well as indicates the objectives and use of the workbook.

**2** ━■ Enter the following information in the Summary tab.

> The Author text box may be blank or may show your school or some other name. Clear the existing contents first if necessary.

| Title | **Downtown Internet Café** |
|-------|---------------------------|
| Subject | **Sales Forecast** |
| Author | **[your name]** |

■ Click    OK    .

■ Move to cell A9 of the worksheet and save the workbook file as Café Sales Charts to your data disk.

The updated documentation has been saved with the new file.

## Previewing the Workbook

It is very important before printing charts to preview how they will appear when printed. Formats that look good onscreen may not produce good printed results. Your workbook file includes two new chart sheets and a worksheet. To preview them all at once, you need to change the print setting to print the entire workbook first.

**1** — ■ Choose **F**ile/**P**rint/**E**ntire workbook

■ Click  Preview .

■ If necessary, reduce the zoom to see the full page.

Your screen should be similar to Figure 2–51.

changes settings associated with sheet you are previewing

preview of bar chart appears in shades of grey if you have a black-and-white printer

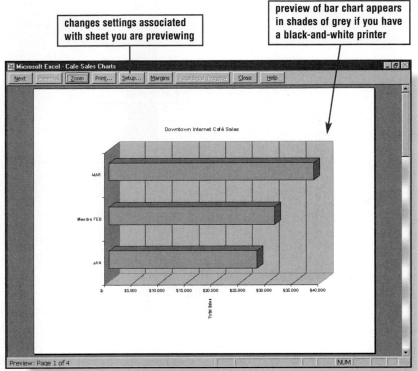

**Figure 2–51**

Because the bar chart is on a separate chart sheet, it is displayed on a page by itself. In addition, if you are not using a color printer, the preview displays the chart as it will appear when printed on a black-and-white printer. The colors appear as shades of gray by default. Since this chart has a dark-gray plot area fill, the bars do not stand out well. You will change the print setting associated with this chart sheet to fix this problem. The Print Preview toolbar buttons are used to access many print and page layout changes while you are previewing a document.

**2** ■ Click  .

■ **Open the Chart tab.**

Your screen should be similar to Figure 2–52.

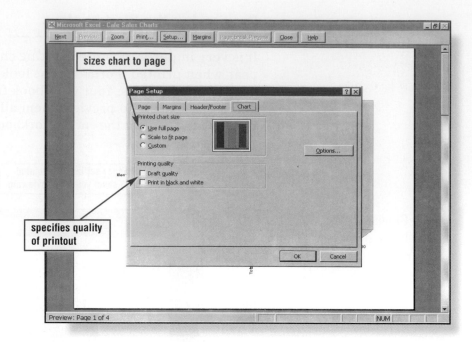

**Figure 2–52**

Because chart sheets print only one chart on a page, the default setting is to size the chart to fill the entire page. The Draft Quality setting suppresses the printing of graphics and gridlines thereby reducing printing time. The black-and-white option applies patterns to data series in place of colors while leaving other areas in shades of gray. On a color printer, all other areas are still printed in color when this option is selected.

**3** ■ **Select Print in black and white.**

■ **Click**  .

Your screen should be similar to Figure 2–53.

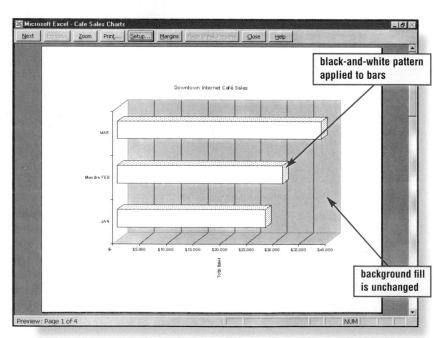

**Figure 2–53**

A black-and-white pattern has been applied to the bars and the background fill has not changed.

**4** ⬛━■ Click Next to see the column chart in the next Chart sheet.

This chart looks as if it will print satisfactorily using the default print settings.

**5** ⬛━■ Click Next to see the worksheet and charts in Sheet 1.

Your screen should be similar to Figure 2–54.

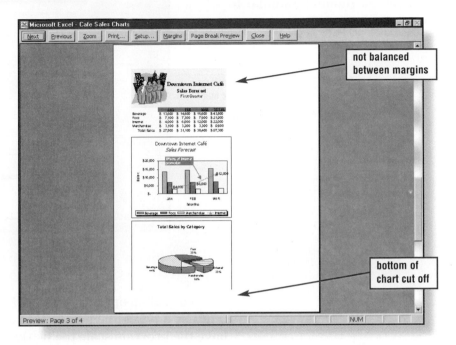

**Figure 2–54**

You can now see that the bottom of the pie chart exceeds the page margins and will not print on the page. You can also see that the printout will not appear balanced between the page margins. Finally, you want to include a header on each page. You will make several changes to the layout of the page to correct these problems.

## Sizing the Worksheet

First you will reduce the worksheet and chart sizes so that they will fit on one page.

**1** ▪ Click [Setup...] .

▪ If necessary, open the Page tab.

Your screen should be similar to
Figure 2–55.

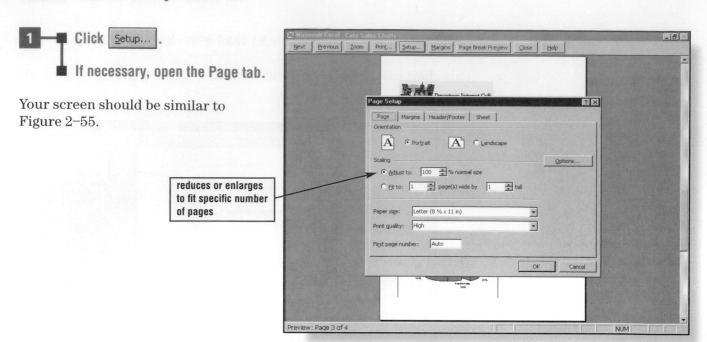

reduces or enlarges
to fit specific number
of pages

**Figure 2–55**

The scaling options allow you to reduce or enlarge the worksheet contents by a percentage or fit it to a specific number of pages. You want to
have the program scale the worksheet to fit on one page.

**2** ▪ Select **F**it to

The default of 1 page is appropriate.

## Aligning a Sheet on a Page

You would also like to center the worksheet horizontally on the page. To
make this change,

**1** ━■ Open the Margins tab.

Your screen should be similar to Figure 2–56.

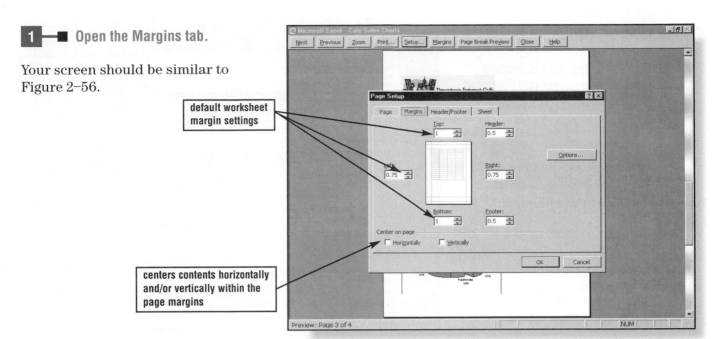

default worksheet margin settings

centers contents horizontally and/or vertically within the page margins

**Figure 2–56**

The default worksheet margin settings are displayed. They can be changed individually by adjusting the size of the settings. You want to center the worksheet data horizontally within the existing margins.

**2** ━■ Select Hori̱zontally.

## Adding Predefined Headers and Footers

You would like to include your name and the date in a header.

---

**Concept ⑦ Header and Footer**

A **header** is a line or several lines of text that appears at the top of each page just below the top margin. A **footer** is a line or several lines of text that appears at the bottom of each page just above the bottom margin.

You can select from predefined header and footer text or enter your own custom text. The information contained in the predefined header and footer text is taken from the document properties associated with the worksheet and from the program and system settings. Header and footer text can be formatted like any other text. In addition, you can control the placement of the header and footer text by specifying where it should appear: left-aligned, centered, or right-aligned in the header or footer space. Information that is commonly placed in a header or footer includes the date and page number.

**1** ■ **Open the Header/Footer tab.**

■ **Open the He_a_der drop-down list box and select the** Prepared By [your name] [date], Page 3 **option.**

> The menu equivalent is _F_ile/ Page Set_u_p/Header/Footer.

Your screen should be similar to Figure 2–57.

**Additional Information**

Predefined footers can be added by selecting the footer option from the _F_ooter drop-down list.

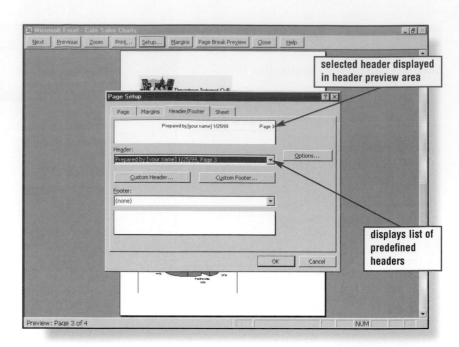

selected header displayed in header preview area

displays list of predefined headers

**Figure 2–57**

The selected header is displayed in the header area of the dialog box.

**2** ■ **Click**  .

Your screen should be similar to Figure 2–58.

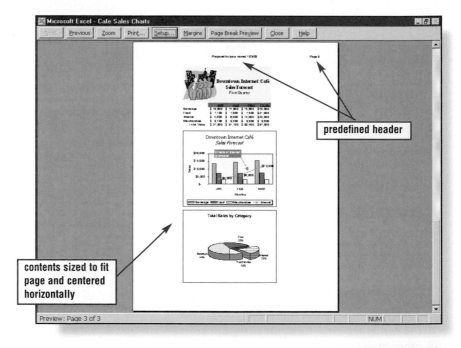

predefined header

contents sized to fit page and centered horizontally

**Figure 2–58**

The worksheet layout settings you specified are reflected in the preview window. It now appears the way you want it to look when printed.

> Click Previous to display previous sheets.

**3** ■ **Add a predefined footer to the two chart sheets that displays your name, page number, and date.**

## Printing the Workbook

Printing a worksheet that includes charts requires a printer with graphics capability. However, the actual procedure to print is the same as printing a worksheet that does not include charts.

**1** — ■ Click 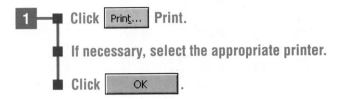 Print.

■ If necessary, select the appropriate printer.

■ Click 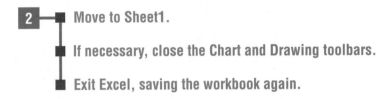 .

Your printer should be printing all three sheets in the workbook.

**2** — ■ Move to Sheet1.

■ If necessary, close the Chart and Drawing toolbars.

■ Exit Excel, saving the workbook again.

# Concept Summary

## Tutorial 2: Charting Worksheet Data

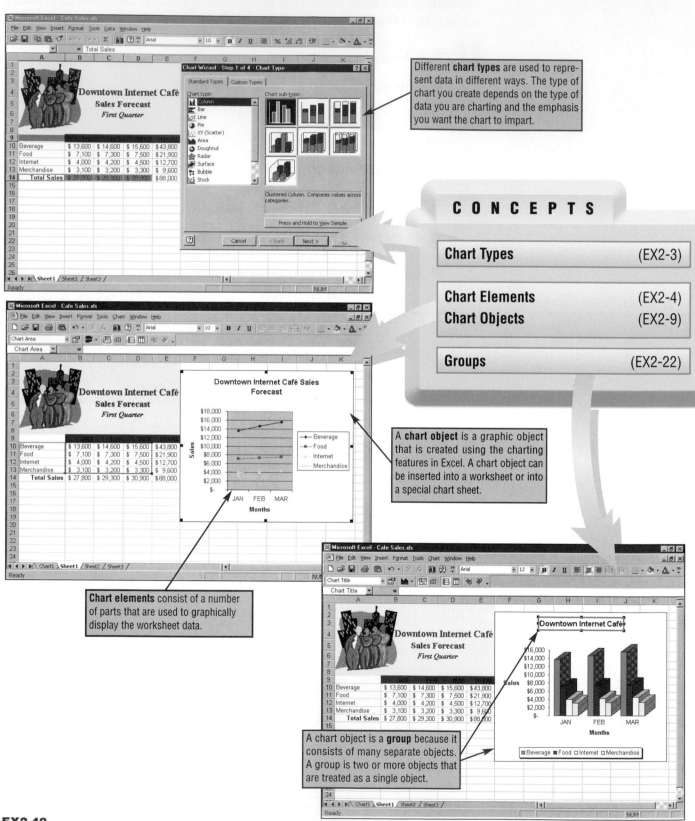

Different **chart types** are used to represent data in different ways. The type of chart you create depends on the type of data you are charting and the emphasis you want the chart to impart.

### CONCEPTS

| | |
|---|---|
| **Chart Types** | (EX2-3) |
| **Chart Elements** | (EX2-4) |
| **Chart Objects** | (EX2-9) |
| **Groups** | (EX2-22) |

A **chart object** is a graphic object that is created using the charting features in Excel. A chart object can be inserted into a worksheet or into a special chart sheet.

**Chart elements** consist of a number of parts that are used to graphically display the worksheet data.

A chart object is a **group** because it consists of many separate objects. A group is two or more objects that are treated as a single object.

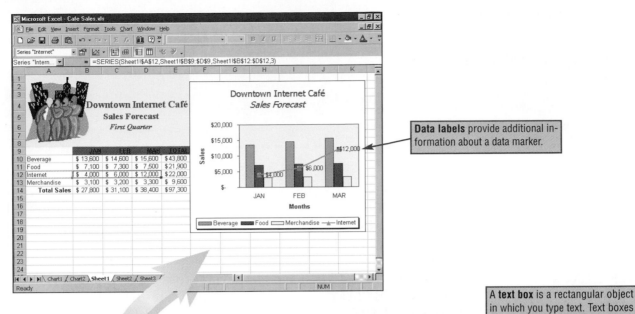

**Data labels** provide additional information about a data marker.

A **text box** is a rectangular object in which you type text. Text boxes can be added to a sheet or an embedded chart.

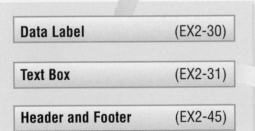

| Data Label | (EX2-30) |
| Text Box | (EX2-31) |
| Header and Footer | (EX2-45) |

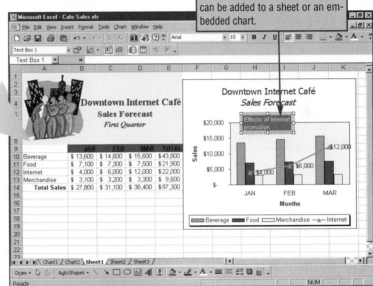

Lines of text displayed below the top margin or above the bottom margin of each page are called **headers and footers**.

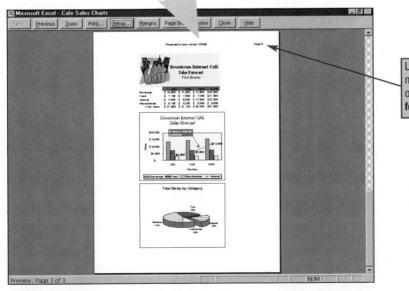

# Tutorial Review

## Key Terms

area chart   EX2-17
category-axis title   EX2-4
category name   EX2-4
chart   EX2-3
chart gridlines   EX2-4
chart object   EX2-9
chart title   EX2-4
column chart   EX2-6
combination chart   EX2-26
data label   EX2-30
data marker   EX2-4

data series   EX2-4
embedded chart   EX2-9
explode   EX2-35
footer   EX2-45
group   EX2-22
header   EX2-45
legend   EX2-4
line chart   EX2-12
pie chart   EX2-5
plot area   EX2-4
selection handle   EX2-11

series formula   EX2-28
stack   EX2-9
stacked-column chart   EX2-19
text box   EX2-31
title   EX2-4
value axis   EX2-4
value-axis title   EX2-4
word wrap   EX2-31
X axis   EX2-4
Y axis   EX2-4
Z axis   EX2-5

## Command Summary

| Command | Shortcut Keys | Button | Action |
|---|---|---|---|
| **F**ile/**P**rint/**E**ntire Workbook | | | Prints all the sheets in a workbook |
| **F**ile/Propert**i**es | | | Displays information about a file |
| **F**ile/Page Set**u**p/Header/Footer | | | Adds header and/or footer |
| **I**nsert/C**h**art | | | Inserts chart into worksheet |
| F**o**rmat/S**e**lected Data Series/Data Labels | Ctrl + 1 | | Inserts data labels into chart |
| F**o**rmat/S**e**lected Legend | Ctrl + 1 | | Changes legend |
| F**o**rmat/S**e**lected Chart Title | Ctrl + 1 | | Changes format of selected chart title |
| F**o**rmat/S**e**lected Data Series | Ctrl + 1 | | Changes format of selected data series |
| F**o**rmat/S**e**lected Object | | | Changes format of embedded objects |
| **C**hart/Chart **T**ype | | | Changes type of chart |
| **C**hart/Chart **O**ptions | | | Adds options to chart |
| **C**hart/**L**ocation | | | Moves chart from worksheet to chart sheet |

# Screen Identification

1. In the following worksheet and chart, letters identify important elements. Enter the correct term for each screen element in the space provided.

a. _____     f. _____

b. _____     g. _____

c. _____     h. _____

d. _____     i. _____

e. _____

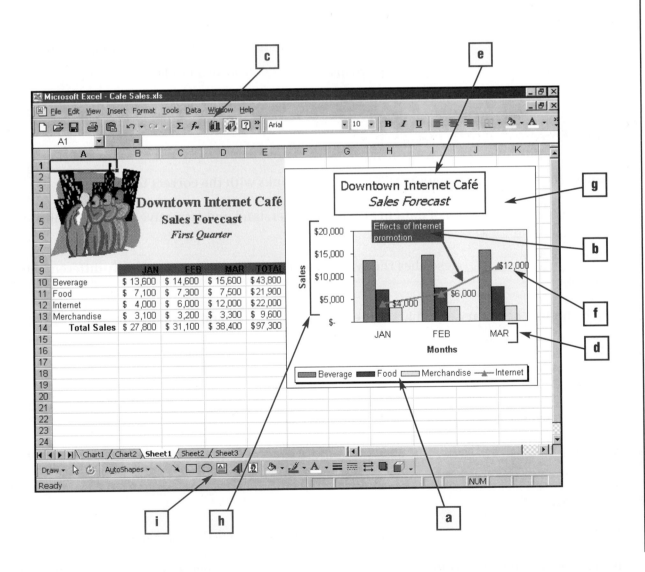

# Matching

Match the lettered item on the right with the numbered item on the left.

| | | |
|---|---|---|
| 1. chart gridlines | _____ a. | left boundary line of the chart |
| 2. data marker | _____ b. | bottom boundary line of the chart |
| 3. stacked-column | _____ c. | identifies each number represented in a data series |
| 4. X axis | _____ d. | area of chart bounded by X and Y axes |
| 5. explode | _____ e. | extend from the Y-axis line across the plot area |
| 6. plot area | _____ f. | identifies the chart data series names and data markers |
| 7. category-axis | _____ g. | X-axis title line |
| 8. Y axis | _____ h. | shows proportion of each value |
| 9. legend | _____ i. | to separate wedge slightly from other wedges of pie |
| 10. pie chart | _____ j. | displays data as slices of a circle |

# Fill-In

Complete the following statements by filling in the blanks with the correct terms.

1. A visual representation of data in an easy-to-understand and attractive manner is called a(n) _____.

2. A(n) _____ describes the symbols used within the chart to identify different data series.

3. The bottom boundary of a chart is the _____ and the left boundary is the _____.

4. A chart that is inserted into a worksheet is a(n) _____ object.

5. A(n) _____ chart and a(n) _____ chart both display data as a set of evenly spaced bars.

6. A(n) _____ and a(n) _____ compare parts to the whole.

7. The _____ toolbar contains buttons for the most frequently used chart editing and formatting features.

8. The _____ title is displayed centered above the charted data.

9. The black-and-white option applies _____ to data series in place of colors while leaving other areas in shades of gray.

10. When a wedge of a pie chart is separated from the other wedges, the wedge has been _____.

# Multiple-Choice

Circle the correct response to the questions below.

1. _____ charts are used to show changes in data over time, emphasizing time and rate of change rather than the amount of change.

    **a.** bar
    **b.** line
    **c.** column
    **d.** area

2. The _____ names displayed along the X axis correspond to the headings for the worksheet data that is plotted along the X axis.

    **a.** variable
    **b.** category
    **c.** value
    **d.** option

3. A _____ identifies the chart data series names and data markers that correspond to each data series.

    **a.** category
    **b.** value axis
    **c.** legend
    **d.** data label

4. Charts that are inserted into a worksheet are called:

    **a.** embedded objects
    **b.** attached objects
    **c.** inserted objects
    **d.** active objects

5. A _____ is two or more objects that are treated as a single object.

    **a.** group
    **b.** embedded object
    **c.** category
    **d.** combined object

6. _____ can consist of the value of the marker, the name of the data series or category, a percent value, or a bubble size.

    **a.** legends
    **b.** X axis
    **c.** Y axis
    **d.** data labels

7. A _____ is a rectangular object in which you type text.

   **a.** text box

   **b.** label

   **c.** input box

   **d.** embedded object

8. A _____ is a line or several lines of text that appears at the bottom of each page just above the bottom margin.

   **a.** footer

   **b.** header

   **c.** footing

   **d.** heading

9. Charts that display data as slices of a circle and show the relationship of each value in a data series to the series as a whole are called:

   **a.** area charts

   **b.** value charts

   **c.** pie charts

   **d.** bar charts

10. A chart that uses two or more chart types to emphasize different information is called a(n):

   **a.** area chart

   **b.** pie chart

   **c.** bar chart

   **d.** combination chart

# True/False

Circle the correct answer to the following questions.

| | | | |
|---|---|---|---|
| 1. | The plot area is visually displayed within the X- and Y-axis boundaries. | True | False |
| 2. | A bar chart displays data as a line and is commonly used to show trends over time. | True | False |
| 3. | The Y-axis title line is called the category-axis title. | True | False |
| 4. | An entire group or each object in a group can be individually selected and then formatted or edited. | True | False |
| 5. | A series formula links the chart object to the source worksheet. | True | False |
| 6. | Value data labels are helpful when the values are large and you want to know the exact value for one data series. | True | False |
| 7. | Text that is entered in a text box wraps to fit within the boundaries of the text box. | True | False |
| 8. | Separating slightly or exploding a slice of a pie chart emphasizes the data. | True | False |

9. Patterns can be added to slices of a pie chart to make it easier to read.  True  False

10. A header is a line or several lines of text that appears at the bottom of each page just below the top margin.  True  False

# Discussion Questions

1. Define each of the following terms and discuss how they are related to one another: chart type, chart element, and chart object.

2. Discuss how column and bar charts represent data. How do they differ from pie charts?

3. What type of information would best be represented by a line chart?

4. Describe how a 3-D column chart differs from a 2–D column chart.

# Hands-On Practice Exercises

**Step by Step**

Rating System  ☆ Easy
☆ ☆ Moderate
☆ ☆ ☆ Difficult

**1.** Jennifer's environmental studies paper is on the endangered Bengal tiger. She has some data saved in a worksheet on the estimated number of tigers in 1997. She has asked you to help her chart the data and make the worksheet look more attractive. The completed worksheet with charts is shown here.

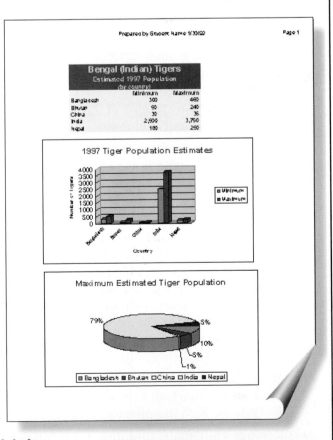

a. Open the worksheet Tiger Data on your data disk.

b. Create a clustered column with 3-D effect chart of the data in cells B6 through D11. Enter the Chart title **1997 Tiger Population Estimates**. Enter the Category (X) axis title **County** and the Value (Z) axis **Number of Tigers**. Include the chart in the worksheet.

c. Size the chart over cells A13 through F30.

d. Rotate the Z-axis label 90 degrees. Angle the X-axis labels 45 degrees upward. Reduce the font size for the axis titles and legend by 2 points.

e. Create a 3-D pie chart in the worksheet showing the maximum tiger population estimates. Include the title **Maximum Estimated Tiger Population** and display percents as data labels.

f.  Display the legend below the chart. Rotate the chart 90 degrees.

g.  Move the pie chart below the column chart and size it appropriately.

h.  Document the workbook file by adding your name as author.

i.  Preview the worksheet. Add a predefined header to the worksheet that displays your name, page number, and date. Center the worksheet horizontally on the page.

j.  If necessary, adjust the size and placement of the charts on the sheet so that they print on a single page. Print the worksheet.

k.  Save the workbook as Tiger Charts.

☆

2.  To complete this problem, you must have completed problem 3 in Tutorial 1. Mark Ernster works for a real estate company and has been collecting information on sales prices for existing homes across the country. Mark wants to graph some of the data in the worksheet for his upcoming presentation. The completed worksheet with charts is shown here.

a.  Open the workbook file Real Estate Prices on your data disk.

b.  Create a line chart on a separate sheet showing the housing prices for the four years for the U.S. only. Remove the legend. Title the chart appropriately. Make the line heavier and change the line and data marker color. Change the fill of the plot area to a gradient effect with two colors. Add data labels that display the values. Increase the size of the chart title and add color.

c.  Create a column chart in the worksheet showing housing prices for the four regions for the four years. The X axis will display the regions and the years will be the legend. Title the chart appropriately. Move the legend to the bottom of the chart. Increase the size of the chart title and add color. Position the chart below the worksheet data and size it appropriately.

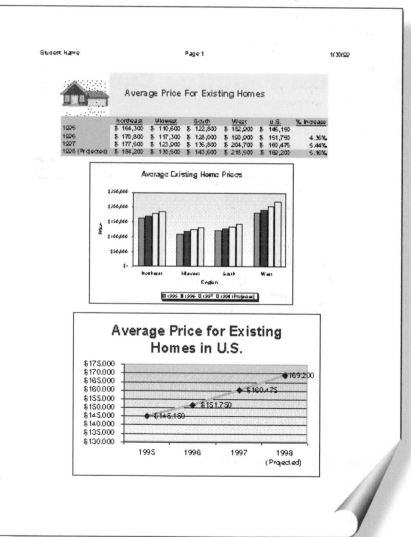

d.  Move the line chart to below the column chart on the worksheet. Size the chart appropriately.

e.  Remove your name and date from the worksheet. Document the workbook file by adding your name as author.

**f.** Preview the workbook. Add a predefined header to the worksheet that displays your name, page number, and date. Center the worksheet horizontally on the page. Size the sheet to print on one page. Print the worksheet.

**g.** Save the workbook as Real Estate Charts.

**3.** Tyler Johnson works for Books Online. He has compiled a list of the 10 best-selling children's books. He would like a chart that shows management how the list price differs from the selling price of the books. The completed worksheet with charts is shown here.

**a.** Open the file Book List on your data disk.

**b.** Chart the data in column A, C, and D by rows as a 3-D clustered bar chart.

**c.** Enter the Chart title **Top 10 Best Selling Books**, the Category (X) axis as **Books by Ranking** and the Value (Y) axis as **Price**.

**d.** Position the chart over cells A17 through E35.

**e.** Add color and font refinements to the chart as you like.

**f.** Document the workbook file by adding your name as author.

**g.** Preview the worksheet. Add a predefined header to the worksheet that displays your name, page number, and date. Center the worksheet horizontally on the page. Print the worksheet.

**h.** Save the workbook file as Book List Chart.

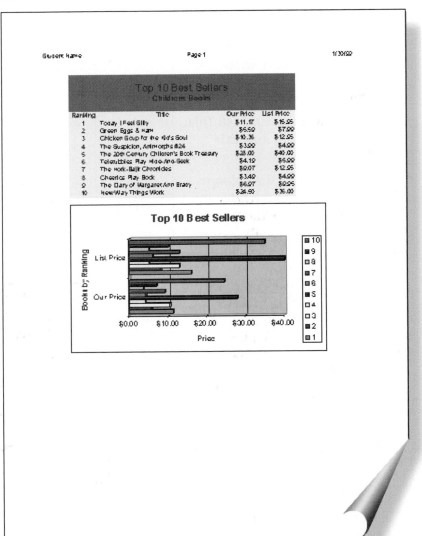

☆ ☆

**4.** To complete this problem, you must have completed problem 2 in Tutorial 1. Lisa Sutton is still working on her worksheets for jobs in New Jersey for her upcoming seminar. The completed chart is ishown here.

a.  Open the workbook file Highest Paying Jobs Revised on your data disk.

b.  Create a custom type Column-Area chart of the data for Physicians and Surgeons, Podiatrists, Dentists, and Lawyers on a separate chart sheet.

c.  Enter the chart title **Hourly Wages- N.J. vs U.S.**, the Category (X) axis title **Job Title** and the Value (Y) axis title **Hourly Wage**.

d.  Add a pattern to the columns. Change the plot area fill color to ivory.

e.  Increase the font size of the chart title to 16. Add color to the title.

f.  Position the legend at the bottom of the chart. Increase the font size of the legend to 12.

g.  Document the workbook file by adding your name as author.

h.  Preview the chart. Add a predefined header to the chart sheet that displays your name, page number, and date. Print the chart.

i.  Save the file as Highest Paying Jobs Chart.

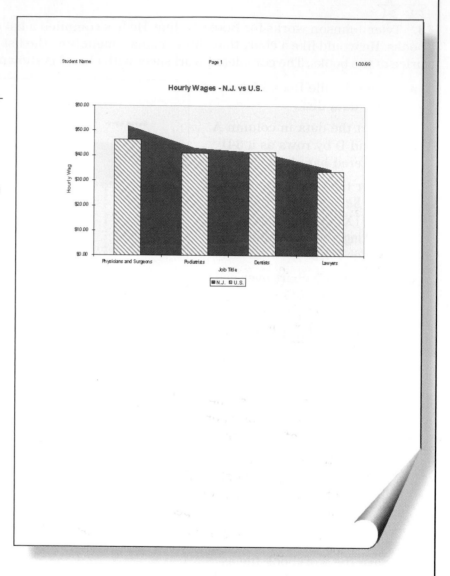

☆ ☆ ☆

**5.** To complete this problem, you must have completed problem 4 in Tutorial 1. Will Bloomquist is still working on the data for his article on student athletes. The completed worksheet with charts is shown here.

a.  Open the workbook Athlete Data Revised on your data disk. Delete the picture inserted at the right of the worksheet.

b.  Create an embedded line chart of the data in cells A4 through C7. Enter the chart title **High School Athletes**, the Category (X) axis title **Years** and the Value (Y) axis title **Number of Athletes**.

**c.** Position the chart over cells D2 through I18.

**d.** Edit the chart title to include the subtitle (in millions) on a second line. Add a color of your choice to the title.

**e.** Display the values for the girls next to the data points. Increase the weight of both lines.

**f.** Move the legend to the lower-right corner of the chart.

**g.** Add a text box and an arrow pointing to the girls' data line. Include the text Steady Increase. Format the text box and arrow as you like.

**h.** Add a gradient fill color to the plot area and make other chart enhancements as you like.

**i.** Create a 3-D pie chart on the same worksheet of the data in cells A11 through C12. Edit the chart title to College Athletes in 1990–1991.

**j.** Rotate the chart so that the female slice is positioned on the right side of the chart.

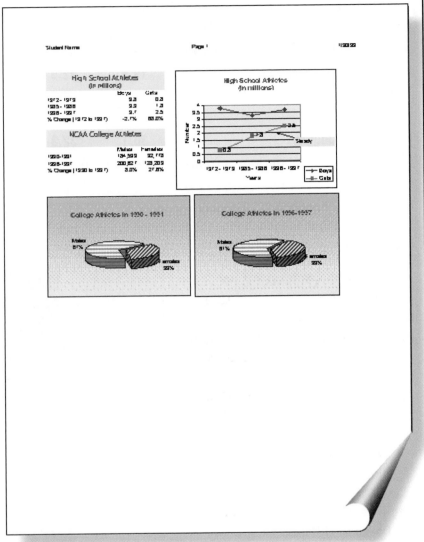

**k.** Remove the legend and display data labels that show the label and percent. Increase the size of the title to 18. Explode the female slice. Add a pattern to both slices of the pie. Add other formatting of your choice to improve the appearance of the chart.

**l.** Create a second 3-D pie chart on the same worksheet of the data for college athletes in 1996–1997. Format this chart to look like the chart for 1990–1991.

**m.** Document the workbook file by adding your name as author.

**n.** Preview the workbook. Add a predefined header to the worksheet that displays your name, page number, and date. Size the worksheet to fit on one page. Print the worksheet.

**o.** Save the workbook file as Student Athlete Charts.

**6.** Carol Hayes is the program coordinator for Fitness Lifestyles, a physical conditioning and health center. She is proposing to management that they increase their emphasis on fitness activities by expanding their exercise equipment area. To reinforce the need for this type of investment, she has found some recent data about growth in the use of exercise equipment in the last decade. She wants to create several charts of this data to emphasize the demand.

**a.** Create a worksheet of the following data.

|  | 1987 | 1993 | 1997 |
|---|---|---|---|
| Free Weights | 24.5 | 31 | 43.2 |
| Resistance Machines | 15.3 | 19.4 | 22.5 |
| Stationary Cycling | 33.4 | 39.1 | 34.8 |
| Treadmill | 4.4 | 19.7 | 36.1 |
| Running/Jogging | 32.9 | 30.1 | 32.3 |

*Source*: American Sports Analysis study conducted by American Sports Data, Inc.

**b.** Add an appropriate title over the data and format the numbers to show two decimal places. Enhance the worksheet as you like to improve its appearance.

**c.** Create an embedded combination chart of the worksheet data showing the free weight and treadmill data as lines. Enter a chart title and appropriate X and Y axis titles. Include a text box and arrows pointing out the sharp increase in free weight and treadmill participation. Enhance the chart using features presented in the tutorial.

**d.** Position the chart below the worksheet. Size the chart appropriately.

**e.** Create a 3-D pie chart in the worksheet showing the 1997 data for the four types of equipment. Include the title **Most Used Fitness Equipment**. Remove the legend and display labels and percents as data labels. Add a pattern to two of the pie slices. Enhance the chart using features presented in the tutorial.

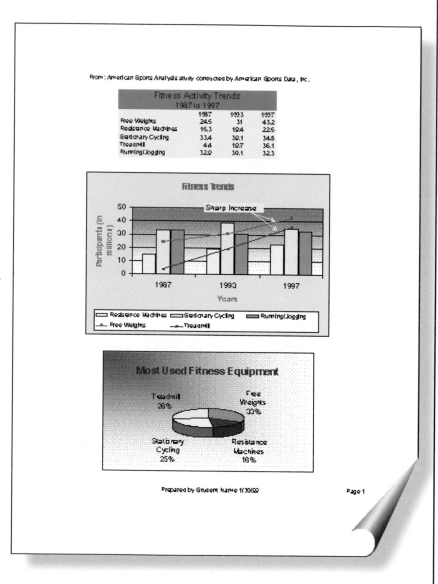

**f.** Move the pie chart below the combination chart and size it appropriately.

**g.** Document the workbook file by adding your name as author.

**h.** Preview the worksheet. Add a predefined footer to the worksheet that displays your name, page number, and date. Center the worksheet horizontally on the page. Print the worksheet.

**i.** Save the workbook file as Fitness Activity Charts.

## On Your Own

**7.** Create a worksheet that tracks your grades. It can be a record of the test scores you received this semester, or it can be a record of your GPA each semester. Create an embedded chart that best represents your grade trends. Use the formatting techniques you have learned to change the appearance of the worksheet and the chart. Save the workbook as Grades. Include a header or footer that displays your name and the current date in the worksheet. Print the worksheet with the chart.

**8.** Andrew Beinbrink is learning about the stock market. Use Help to learn more about the Stock chart type. Pick four related stocks and create an embedded Stock chart of the data. Save the worksheet with the chart as Stocks. Include a header or footer that displays your name and the current date in the worksheet. Print the worksheet with the chart.

**9.** Kevin Tillman has started a new job with Baseball Statistics, Inc. He would like some help creating a worksheet that contains team win/loss records for the last five years. He asks you to search the Web for records. Choose a MLB team of your choice and locate the win/loss record for the last five years. Enter the data into a worksheet. Enhance the worksheet using the features you have learned. Create an embedded chart that displays the information over the five years. Include a header or footer that displays your name and the current date in the worksheet. Save and print the worksheet with the chart.

**10.** Karen Blake is thinking about purchasing a new sports utility vehicle. However, she is also concerned about the mileage per gallon ratings for the vehicles. She wants to find out the base price on several different models and the MPG rate. Use the Web or visit several local car dealerships to get this information. Create a worksheet that contains the models, base selling price, and MPG rate for each vehicle. Create an embedded combination chart of the data that shows the models along the X axis, price as the Y axis value, and MPG rate as a secondary value Y axis. The line should represent the MPG data. Use Help for information about plotting a secondary value axis. Enhance the chart appropriately. Include a header or footer that displays your name and the current date in the worksheet. Save and print the worksheet and chart.

# Managing and Analyzing a Workbook

## Competencies

After completing this tutorial, you will know how to:

1. Spell-check a sheet.
2. Use Paste Function.
3. Use absolute references.
4. Apply styles.
5. Copy, move and name sheets.
6. Use AutoFill.
7. Reference multiple sheets.
8. Zoom the worksheet.
9. Split windows and freeze panes.
10. Use What-If analysis and Goal Seek.
11. Change page orientation.
12. Add custom headers and footers.
13. Print selected sheets.

**Case Study** You present your new, more optimistic, first quarter forecast for the Downtown Internet Café to Evan, who has made several formatting and design changes. In addition he asks you to include an Average calculation and to extend the forecast for the next three quarters. Moreover, he wants to hold back on your idea of an aggressive Internet sales promotion. The Café's

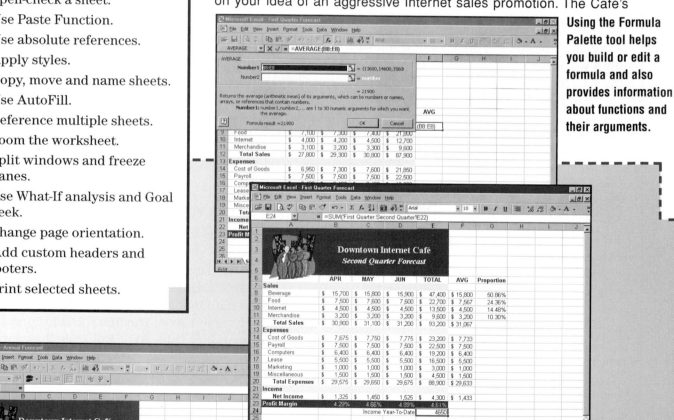

**Using the Formula Palette tool helps you build or edit a formula and also provides information about functions and their arguments.**

**Multiple sheets in a workbook make it easy to edit several sheets simultaneously and to perform calculations based on data from multiple sheets.**

**Forecasting values using what-if analysis and using charts to visually represent the change are powerful features of Excel.**

funds are low due to the cost of the recent renovations. Evan feels, therefore, that you should stick with a more conservative forecast of income derived from Internet sales.

After discussing the situation, you agree that the Café will likely lose money during the first month of operations. Then the café should start to show increasing profitability. Evan stresses that the monthly profit margin should reach 5 per cent in the second quarter.

As you develop the Café's financial forecast, the worksheet grows in size and complexity. You will learn about features of Excel 2000 that help you manage a large workbook efficiently. You will also learn how you can manipulate the data in a worksheet to reach a goal using the what-if analysis capabilities of Excel. The completed annual forecast is shown here.

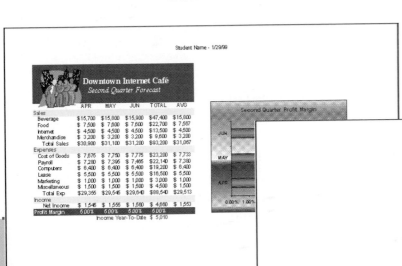

## Concept Overview

The following concepts will be introduced in this tutorial:

**1** **Spell Checking**   The spell-checking feature locates all misspelled words, duplicate words, and capitalization irregularities in the active worksheet and proposes the correct spelling.

**2** **Absolute References**   An absolute reference is a cell or range reference in a formula whose location does not change when the formula is copied.

**3** **Styles**   A style consists of a combination of formats that have been named and that can be quickly applied to a selection.

**4** **Sheet Names**   Each sheet in a workbook can be assigned a descriptive name to identify the contents of the sheet.

**5** **AutoFill**   The AutoFill feature makes entering long or complicated headings easier by logically repeating and extending the series.

**6** **Sheet and 3-D References**   A formula containing sheet and 3-D references to cells in different worksheets in a workbook allows you to use data from other worksheets and to calculate new values based on this data.

**7** **Split Windows**   A sheet window can be split into sections called panes to make it easier to view different parts of the sheet at the same time.

**8** **Freeze Panes**   Freezing panes prevents the data in the panes from scrolling as you move to different areas in the worksheet.

**9** **What-If Analysis**   What-if analysis is a technique used to evaluate the effects of changing selected factors in a worksheet.

**10** **Goal Seek**   Goal Seek is a tool that is used to find the value needed in one cell to attain a result you want in another cell.

## Spell-Checking a Sheet

Evan, the owner of the Café, has made several changes to the first quarter forecast file. To see the file with these changes,

**1** ■ Load Excel.

■ Open the worksheet file First Quarter Forecast.

Your screen should be similar to Figure 3–1.

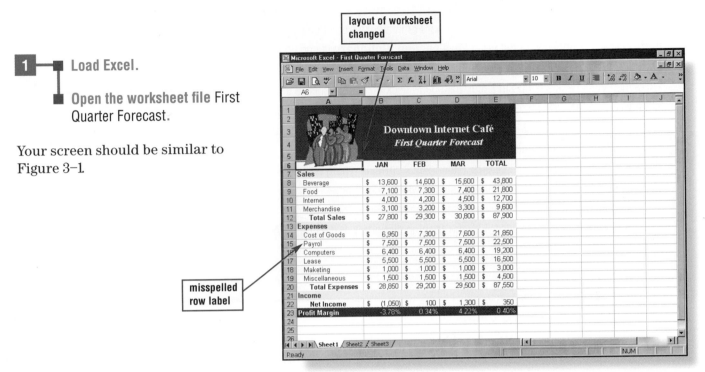

**Figure 3–1**

The owner changed the layout of the worksheet by moving the graphic into the title area. Additionally, several changes were made to the row labels. For example, the Salary label has been replaced with Payroll. However, the new label is misspelled. Just to make sure there are no other spelling errors, you will check the spelling of all text entries in this worksheet.

## Concept ① Spell Checking

The **spell-checking** feature locates all misspelled words, duplicate words, and capitalization irregularities in the active worksheet and proposes the correct spelling. This feature works by comparing each word to a dictionary of words. If the word does not appear in the main dictionary or in a custom dictionary, it is identified as misspelled. The **main dictionary** is supplied with the program; a **custom dictionary** is one you can create to hold words you commonly use but that are not included in the main dictionary.

When you check spelling in Excel, the spell-checking feature checks the entire active worksheet including cell values, text boxes, headers and footers, and text in embedded charts. It does not check spelling in formulas or text that results from formulas. You can also restrict the area to be checked by first selecting a range. If the formula bar is active when you check spelling, only the contents of the formula bar are checked.

Excel also includes an AutoCorrect feature that corrects typing errors automatically as you type by comparing each completed word to a list of commonly mistyped words and phrases. You can also add words and phrases you commonly mistype to the list and they will be corrected automatically as you type.

If you have Microsoft Office 2000, the spelling dictionary and listing of AutoCorrect entries is shared with the other Office applications.

Excel begins checking all worksheet entries from the active cell forward. To check the spelling in the worksheet,

**2** ■ Click 📝 Spelling.

> The menu equivalent is **T**ools/**S**pelling and the keyboard shortcut is ⌨ F7 .

Your screen should be similar to Figure 3–2.

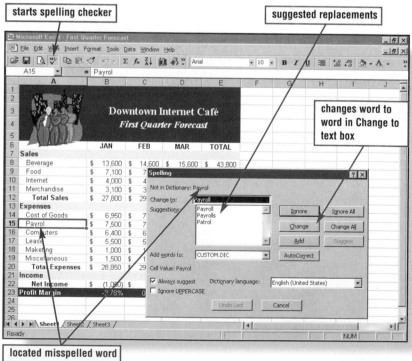

**Figure 3–2**

**Additional Information**

Spell Checking operates the same way in all Office 2000 programs.

Excel 2000 immediately begins checking the worksheet for words that it cannot locate in its main dictionary. The cell selector moves to the first cell containing a misspelled word and the Spelling dialog box is displayed. The word it cannot locate in the dictionary is displayed in the first line of the dialog box. The Change to text box displays the suggested replacement. A list of other possible replacements is displayed in the Suggestions list box. If the Change to replacement is not correct, you can select from the suggestions list or type the correct word in the Change to text box.

The option buttons shown in the table below have the following effects:

| Option | Effect |
|---|---|
| **Ignore** | Leaves selected word unchanged |
| **Ignore All** | Leaves this word and all identical words in worksheet unchanged |
| **Change** | Changes selected word to word displayed in Change to text box |
| **Change All** | Changes this word and all identical words in worksheet to word displayed in Change to text box |
| **Add** | Adds selected word to a custom dictionary so Excel will not question this word during subsequent spell checks |
| **Suggest** | Turns on the display of proposed alternatives for a misspelled word |
| **AutoCorrect** | Adds a word to the AutoCorrect list so the word will be corrected as you type |

To accept the suggested replacement,

**3** ━■ Click  .

The correction is made in the worksheet, and the program continues checking the worksheet and locates another error, "Maketing."

**4** ━■ Change this word to Marketing.

The program continues checking the worksheet. When it reaches the end of the sheet, because the cell selector was not at the beginning of the sheet when checking started, the program asks if you want to continue checking at the beginning of the sheet.

**5** ━■ Click  .

The program continues checking the worksheet and does not locate any other errors. A dialog box is displayed, informing you that the entire worksheet has been checked. To end spell-checking,

**6** ━■ Click  .

## Using Paste Function

Next you need to add a column showing the average values for the first quarter.

**1** ▪ Enter the heading **AVG** in cell F6.

▪ Move to F8.

Notice the new heading is already appropriately formatted to bold and centered. This is because Excel automatically extends formats to new cells if the format of at least three of the last five preceding columns appear that way.

You could enter a function in cell F8 to calculate the average beverage sales. However, another way is to use the Paste Function feature. This feature simplifies entering functions by prompting you to select a function from a list and then helps you enter the arguments correctly.

**2** ▪ Click [$f_x$] Paste Function.

> The menu equivalent is **I**nsert/**F**unction and the keyboard shortcut is [⇧ Shift] + [F3].

Your screen should be similar to Figure 3–3.

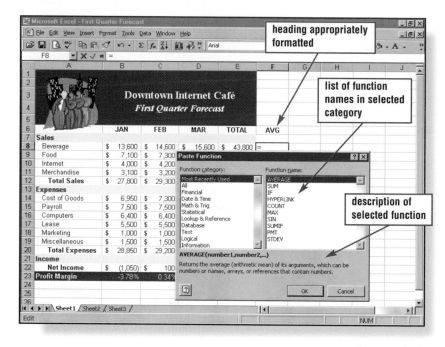

**Figure 3–3**

> The Most Recently Used function category initially displays 10 of the most common functions.

First you select the type of function you want to use. The Function Category list box displays the names of the function categories, and the Function Name list box displays the names of the functions in the selected category. The currently selected category is Most Recently Used. This category displays the names of the last 10 functions used.

**3** ■ **Select** AVERAGE **from the Function Name list box.**

If Average is not displayed in the list box, select it from the Statistical category.

■ **Click** OK .

Your screen should be similar to Figure 3-4.

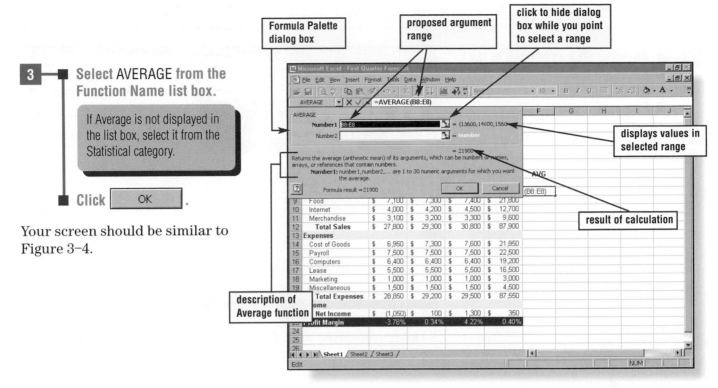

**Figure 3-4**

You can also display the Formula Palette by clicking = Edit Formula in the Formula bar.

**Additional Information**

When the Formula Palette is open, the name box changes to a drop-down function list, allowing you to change the selected type of function.

Next, the Formula Palette dialog box is displayed to help you enter the arguments required for the selected function. The upper section displays the proposed argument range in the Number1 text box. Also notice the actual numbers in the selected range are displayed to the right of the textbox. The lower section describes the Average function and what the function requires for arguments. Because the proposed argument range (B8:E8) is incorrect, you need to specify the correct range (B8:D8) in the Number1 text box. The numbers or the cell references containing the numbers can be entered in the text box directly, or can be entered by selecting the cell or range from the worksheet. Selecting the range is usually faster, and it avoids the accidental entry of incorrect references. To select the range B8 through D8 from the worksheet,

**4** ■ **Click the** 🔲 **at the end of the Number1 text box.**

■ **Select B8 through D8.**

Your screen should be similar to Figure 3–5.

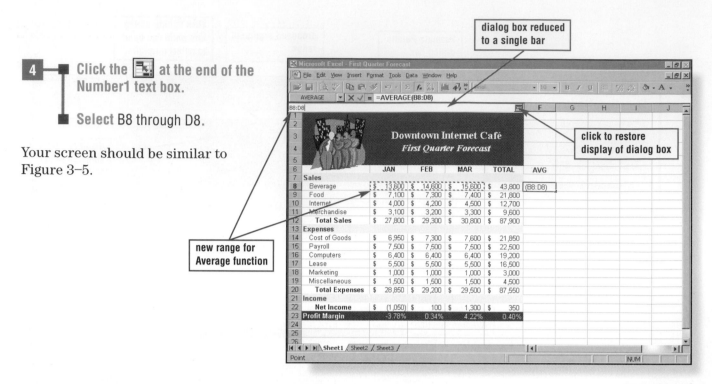

**Figure 3–5**

The dialog box is reduced to a single bar to allow easy access to the worksheet. The new range appears in the formula bar and the cell, as well as in the Formula Palette dialog box bar. To redisplay the dialog box and complete the function,

**5** ■ **Click** 🔲 .

You can also press ⏎Enter to redisplay the dialog box.

■ **Click** ☐ OK ☐ .

Your screen should be similar to Figure 3–6.

**Figure 3–6**

The average of the beverage sales for the quarter, 14,600, is calculated and displayed in cell F8. Notice that Excel again extended the format to the new cell, saving you the step of applying the Accounting format.

## Using the Fill Handle to Delete Cell Contents

Next you need to copy the function down column F.

**1** ━■ Copy the function into cells F9
through F22.

Your screen should be similar to
Figure 3–7.

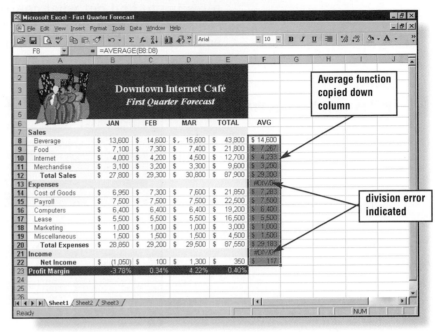

**Figure 3–7**

The average value has been correctly calculated for each row. Notice, however, that two cells display #DIV/0!. This indicates a division error occurred because the formula divides by zero. You will clear the formulas
from these cells using the fill handle.

**2** ━■ Move to cell F13.

■ Point to the fill handle and when
the mouse pointer changes to
**+**, drag upward until the cell is
gray.

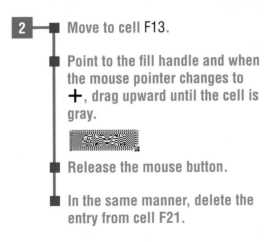

■ Release the mouse button.

■ In the same manner, delete the
entry from cell F21.

Your screen should be similar to
Figure 3–8.

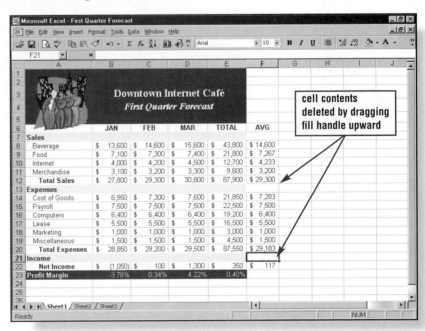

**Figure 3–8**

To avoid unintentionally deleting cell contents when using the fill handle,
drag the fill handle out of the selected area before releasing.

## Using Absolute References

While looking at the sales data in the worksheet, you decide it may be interesting to find out what contribution each sales item makes to total sales. To find out, you will enter a formula to calculate the proportion of sales by each in column G. The formula to calculate the proportion for beverage sales is Total Beverage Sales/Total Sales.

**1** Enter the heading **Proportion** in cell G6.

■ Enter the formula **=E8/E12** in cell G8.

■ Move to G8.

Your screen should be similar to Figure 3–9.

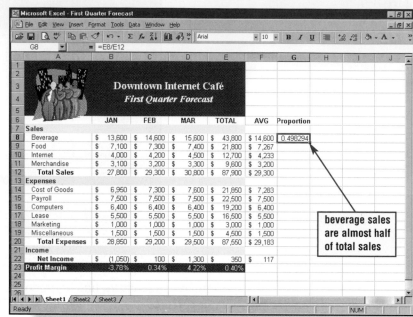

**Figure 3–9**

The value 0.498294 is displayed in cell G8. This shows that the beverage sales are approximately 50 percent of total sales.

Next, to calculate the proportion for Food Sales, you will copy the formula from G8 to G9. Another quick way to copy cell contents is to drag the cell border while holding down Ctrl. This method is most useful when the distance between cells is short and they are both visible in the window. It cannot be used if you are copying to a larger range than the source range.

**2** ■ Point to the border of cell G8 and when the mouse pointer shape is ⬚ , hold down Ctrl and drag the mouse pointer to cell G9.

Your screen should be similar to Figure 3–10.

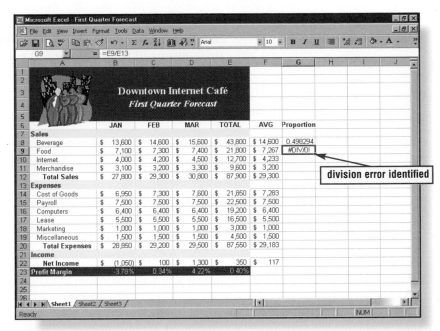

Figure 3–10

You see a #DIV/0! error is displayed in cell G9. To check the formula in that cell,

**3** ■ Double-click cell G9.

Your screen should be similar to Figure 3–11.

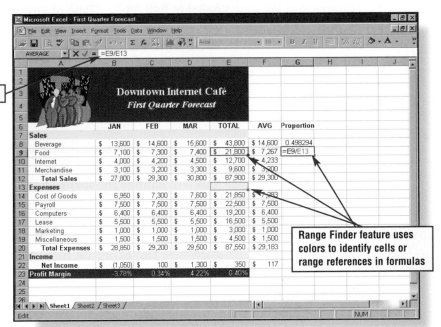

Figure 3–11

Notice that the cell references in the formula are color coded to match the borders Excel displays around the referenced worksheet cells. This is Excel's Range Finder feature. It is designed to provide visual cues to the relationships between the cells that provide values to the formulas or the cells that depend on the formulas. You can now see the error occurred because the relative reference to cell E12 adjusted correctly to the new location when the formula was copied and now references cell E13, a blank cell.

The formula in G8 needs to be entered so that the reference to the Total Sales value in cell E12 does not change when the formula is copied. To do this, you need to make the cell reference absolute.

## Concept ② Absolute References

An **absolute reference** is a cell or range reference in a formula whose location does not change when the formula is copied.

To stop the relative adjustment of cell references, enter a $ (dollar sign) character before the column letter and row number. This changes the cell reference to absolute. When a formula containing an absolute cell reference is copied to another row and column location in the worksheet, the cell reference does not change. It is an exact duplicate of the cell reference in the original formula.

A cell reference can also be a **mixed reference**. In this type of reference, either the column letter or the row number is preceded with the $. This makes only the row or column absolute. When a formula containing a mixed cell reference is copied to another location in the worksheet, only the part of the cell reference that is not absolute changes relative to its new location in the worksheet.

The table below shows examples of relative and absolute references and the results when a reference in cell G8 to cell E8 is copied to cell H9.

| Cell Contents of G8 | Copied to Cell H9 | Type of Reference |
| --- | --- | --- |
| $G$8 | $G$8 | Absolute reference |
| G$8 | H$8 | Mixed reference |
| $G8 | $G9 | Mixed reference |
| G8 | H9 | Relative reference |

You will change the formula in cell G8 to include an absolute reference for cell E12. Then you will copy the formula to cells G9 through G11.

You can change a cell reference to absolute or mixed by typing in the dollar sign directly or by using the ABS (Absolute) key, F4. To use the ABS key, the program must be in the Edit mode and the cell reference that you want to change must be selected.

**4** ■ Press Esc to exit from edit mode.

■ Move to G8.

■ Click on the reference to E12 in the formula bar to enter Edit mode and select the reference.

■ Press F4.

Your screen should be similar to Figure 3–12.

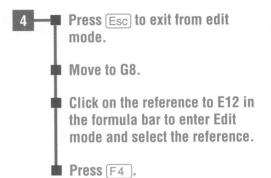

**Figure 3–12**

The cell reference now displays $ characters before the column letter and row number, making this cell reference absolute. If you continue to press F4, the cell reference will cycle through all possible combinations of cell reference types. Leaving the cell reference absolute, as it is now, will stop the relative adjustment of the cell reference when you copy it again.

**5** ■ Click ✓.

■ Copy the revised formula to cells G9 through G11.

■ Move to cell G9.

Your screen should be similar to Figure 3–13.

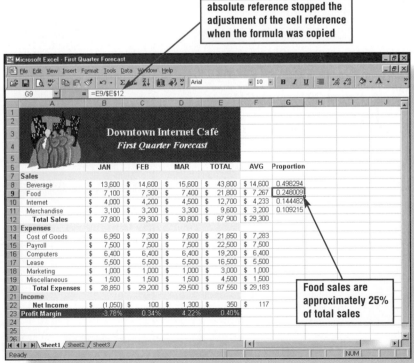

**Figure 3–13**

The formula has correctly adjusted the relative cell reference to Food sales in cell E9 and not adjusted the reference to E12 because it is an absolute reference.

**6** ■ Move to cells G10 and G11 and confirm that the formulas were adjusted appropriately.

### Applying Styles

Next you want to format the proportion values in cells G8 through G11 and the profit margin to display as a percent. You could apply the Percent format using the Format/Cells menu command as you did in Tutorial 1. Another way, however, is to select a predefined format style.

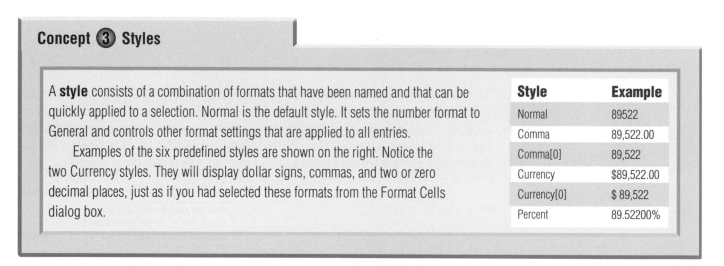

**Concept 3  Styles**

A **style** consists of a combination of formats that have been named and that can be quickly applied to a selection. Normal is the default style. It sets the number format to General and controls other format settings that are applied to all entries.

Examples of the six predefined styles are shown on the right. Notice the two Currency styles. They will display dollar signs, commas, and two or zero decimal places, just as if you had selected these formats from the Format Cells dialog box.

| Style | Example |
|---|---|
| Normal | 89522 |
| Comma | 89,522.00 |
| Comma[0] | 89,522 |
| Currency | $89,522.00 |
| Currency[0] | $ 89,522 |
| Percent | 89.52200% |

**1** ■ Select G8 through G11.

■ Choose Format/Style.

Your screen should be similar to Figure 3–14.

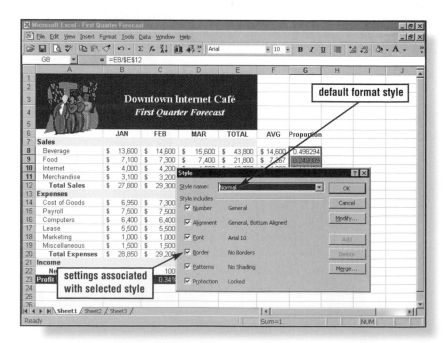

**Figure 3–14**

The Style dialog box displays the name of the default worksheet style, Normal, in the Style Name list box. The check boxes in the Style Includes area of the dialog box show the options that are included in this style and a description or sample. You want to use the Percent style.

**2** ■ Open the Style Name drop-down list box.

■ Select Percent.

■ Click [ OK ] .

The toolbar shortcut for Percent Style is %.

Your screen should be similar to Figure 3–15.

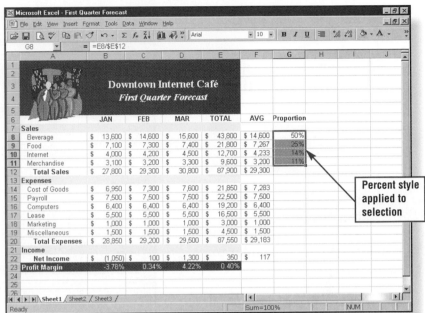

**Figure 3–15**

**Additional Information**

You can also quickly apply the Accounting format by selecting the Currency style or $.

The Percent style setting automatically displays the value as a percent with no decimal places. To make the percentage more accurate, you will increase the decimal place setting to 2.

**3** ■ Click [+.0/.00] Increase Decimal twice.

■ Clear the selection.

■ Size column G to fit the contents.

The calculated proportion shows the same values that a pie chart of this data would show.

## Copying a Sheet

Next you want to add the second quarter forecast to the workbook. You want this data in a separate sheet in the same workbook file. To make it easier to enter the forecast for the next quarter, you will copy the contents of the first quarter forecast in Sheet1 into another sheet in the workbook. Then you will change the month headings, the title, and the number data. Although the workbook already includes two extra blank sheets, if you pasted the data into an existing sheet, the column width settings would not be copied and you would need to reset the widths. To retain column widths and to duplicate an existing sheet with all its formats, you need to create a new sheet.

To copy the active sheet into a new sheet, you hold down Ctrl while dragging the sheet tab to where you want the new sheet inserted. The mouse pointer changes to a ▯ as you drag the mouse from one tab to another. The + indicates that the sheet is being copied. A black triangle ▼ also appears, indicating where the sheet will be inserted.

**1** ▪ **Hold down** Ctrl **and click on the Sheet1 tab.**

▪ **When the mouse pointer is a ▯, drag the Sheet1 tab to the Sheet2 tab.**

> The ▼ appears at the right side of the Sheet1 tab.

▪ **Release the mouse button and then release** Ctrl**.**

Your screen should be similar to Figure 3–16.

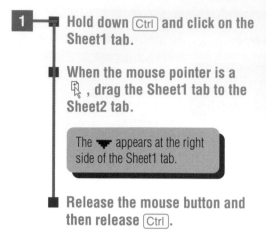

new sheet tab inserted between Sheet1 and Sheet 2

copied worksheet is an exact duplicate of Sheet1

**Figure 3–16**

Excel 2000 names the copy of the sheet Sheet1(2) and inserts it before Sheet2. The new sheet is the active sheet and contains a duplicate of the first quarter budget in Sheet1.

## Naming Sheets

As more sheets are added to a workbook, remembering what information is in each sheet becomes more difficult. To help clarify the contents of the sheets, you can rename the sheets.

**Concept ④ Sheet Names**

Each sheet in a workbook can be assigned a descriptive name to help identify the contents of the sheet. The following guidelines should be followed when naming a sheet. A sheet name:

- ▪ Can be up to 31 characters
- ▪ Can be entered in uppercase or lowercase letters or a combination (it will appear as entered)
- ▪ Can contain any combination of letters, numbers, and spaces
- ▪ Cannot contain the characters : ? * / \
- ▪ Cannot be enclosed in square brackets [ ]

Double-clicking the sheet tab activates the tab and highlights the existing sheet name. The existing name is cleared as soon as you begin to type the new name. You will change the name of Sheet1 to First Quarter and Sheet1(2) to Second Quarter.

**1** — ■ Double-click the Sheet1 tab.

■ Type **First Quarter**.

■ Press ⏎Enter.

■ Change the name of the Sheet1(2) tab to **Second Quarter**.

> The menu equivalent is F**o**rmat/S**h**eet/**R**ename.

Your screen should be similar to Figure 3–17.

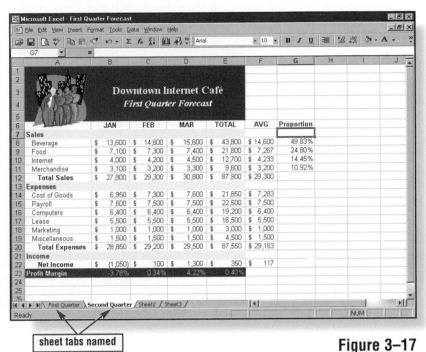

sheet tabs named

**Figure 3–17**

## Using AutoFill

- - - - - - - - - - - - - - - - - - - - - - - - - - - - - - - - - - -

Now you can change the worksheet title and data in the second quarter sheet.

**1** — ■ Change the title in cell B4 to **Second Quarter Forecast**.

■ Change the month heading in cell B6 to **APR**.

Now you need to change the remaining month headings to MAY and JUN. You will use the AutoFill feature to enter the month headings.

## Concept ⑤ AutoFill

The **AutoFill** feature makes entering a series of headings easier by logically repeating and extending the series. AutoFill recognizes trends and automatically extends data and alphanumeric headings as far as you specify.

Dragging the fill handle activates the AutoFill feature if Excel recognizes the entry in the cell as an entry that can be incremented. When AutoFill extends the entries, it uses the same style as the original entry. For example, if you enter the heading for July as JUL (abbreviated with all letters uppercase), all the extended entries in the series will be abbreviated and uppercase. Dragging down or right increments in increasing order, and up or left increments in decreasing order. A linear series increases or decreases values by a constant value, and a growth series multiplies values by a constant factor.

| Initial Selection | Extended series |
|---|---|
| Qtr1 | Qtr2, Qtr3, Qtr4 |
| Mon | Tue Wed Thu |
| Jan, Apr | Jul, Oct, Jan |

A starting value of a series may contain more than one item that can be incremented, such as JAN-02, in which both the month and year can increment. If you want only one value to increment, hold down the right mouse button as you drag, and then click the appropriate command on the AutoFill shortcut menu to specify which value to increment.

The entry in cell B6, APR, is the starting value of a series of months.

**2** ■ To automatically complete the month entries, drag the fill handle to extend the range from cell B6 through cell D6.

The mouse pointer displays the entry that will appear in each cell as you drag.

### Additional Information

If a series is created when you drag the fill handle that you do not want incremented, select the original values again and hold down (Ctrl) as you drag the fill handle. The entries will be copied, not incremented.

Your screen should be similar to Figure 3–18.

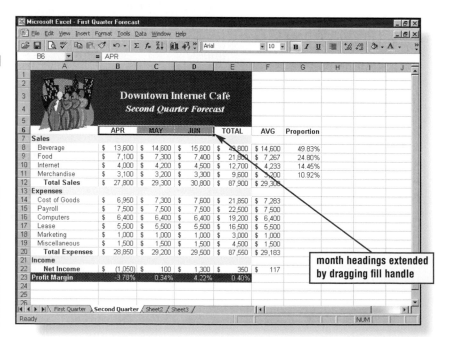

month headings extended by dragging fill handle

**Figure 3–18**

**3** Finally, to update the budget for April through June beverage, food, Internet, and merchandise sales, enter the new numbers as shown in the table below.

| Sales | Cell | Number |
|-------|------|--------|
| Beverage | B8 | 15700 |
| | C8 | 15800 |
| | D8 | 15900 |
| Food | B9 | 7500 |
| | C9 | 7600 |
| | D9 | 7600 |
| Internet | B10 | 4500 |
| | C10 | 4500 |
| | D10 | 4500 |
| Merchandise | B11 | 3200 |
| | C11 | 3200 |
| | D11 | 3200 |

Your screen should be similar to Figure 3–19.

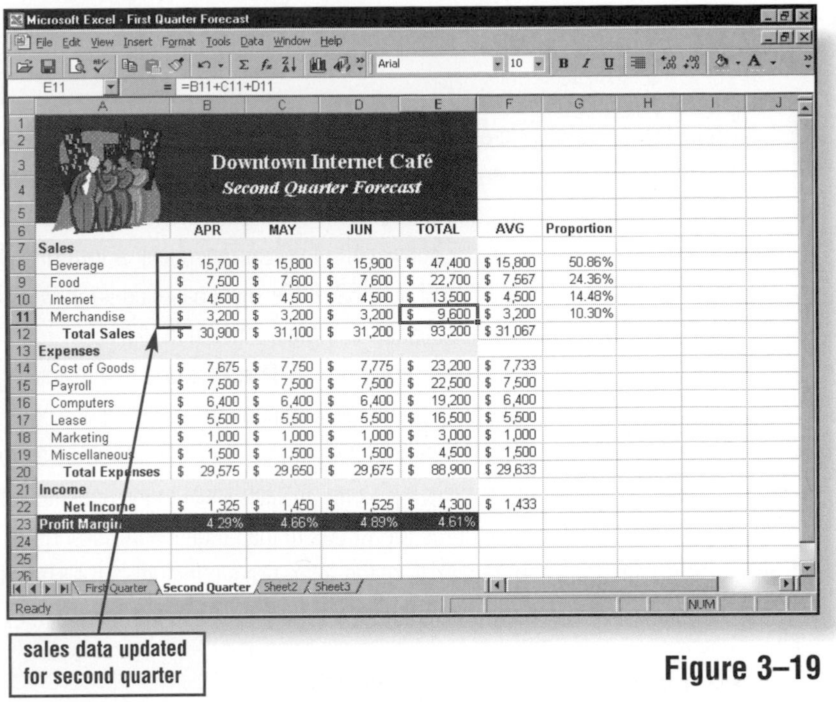

sales data updated for second quarter

**Figure 3–19**

The worksheet has been recalculated and now contains the data for the second quarter.

## Referencing Multiple Sheets

You also want to display a year-to-date income total in cell E24. The formula to make this calculation will sum the total income numbers from First Quarter cell E22 and Second Quarter cell E22. To reference data in another sheet in the same workbook, you enter a formula that references cells in other worksheets.

## Concept ⑥ Sheet and 3-D References

A formula that contains references to cells in other sheets of a workbook allows you to use data from multiple sheets and to calculate new values based on this data. The formula contains a **sheet reference** consisting of the name of the sheet, followed by an exclamation point and the cell or range reference. For example, the formula =Sheet2!B17 would display the entry in cell B17 of Sheet2 in the active cell of the current sheet. A formula can be created using references on multiple sheets; for example, =Sheet1!A1+Sheet2!B2. If the sheet name contains nonalphabetic characters, such as a space, the sheet name (or path) must be enclosed in single quotation marks.

The link can also be created by entering a **3-D reference** in a formula. A 3-D reference is a reference to the same cell or range on multiple sheets in the same workbook. A 3-D reference consists of the names of the beginning and ending sheets enclosed in quotes and separated by a colon. This is followed by an exclamation point and the cell or range reference. The cell or range reference is the same on each sheet in the specified sheet range. For example, the formula =SUM(Sheet1:Sheet4!H6:K6) sums the values in the range H6 through K6 of sheets 1 through 4. Any sheets stored between the starting and ending names of the reference are included. If a sheet is inserted or deleted, the range is automatically updated. 3-D references make it easy to analyze data in the same cell or range of cells on multiple worksheets.

| 3-D reference | Description |
|---|---|
| =SUM(Sheet1:Sheet4!H6:K6) | Sums the values in cells H6 through K6 in sheets 1, 2, 3, and 4. |
| =SUM(Sheet1!H6:K6) | Sums the values in cells H6 through K6 in sheet 1. |
| =SUM(Sheet1:Sheet4!H6) | Sums the values in cell H6 of Sheets 1, 2, 3 and 4. |

Just like a formula that references cells within a sheet, a formula that references cells in multiple sheets is automatically recalculated when data in a referenced cell changes.

You will enter a 3-D reference formula in cell E24 and a descriptive text entry in cell D24.

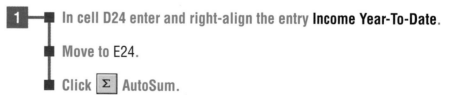

**1** ■ In cell D24 enter and right-align the entry **Income Year-To-Date**.

■ Move to E24.

■ Click Σ AutoSum.

The SUM function argument will consist of a 3-D reference to cell E22 in the First and Second Quarter sheets. Although a 3-D reference can be entered by typing it using the proper syntax, it is much easier to enter it by pointing to the cells on the sheets. To enter a 3-D reference, select the cell or range in the beginning sheet and then hold down Shift and click on the sheet tab of the last sheet in the range. This will include the indicated cell range on all sheets between and including the first and last sheet specified.

**2** ■ Click cell E22.

■ Hold down ⇧Shift and click the First Quarter tab.

■ Release ⇧Shift.

■ Press ←Enter.

■ Move to E24.

Your screen should be similar to Figure 3–20.

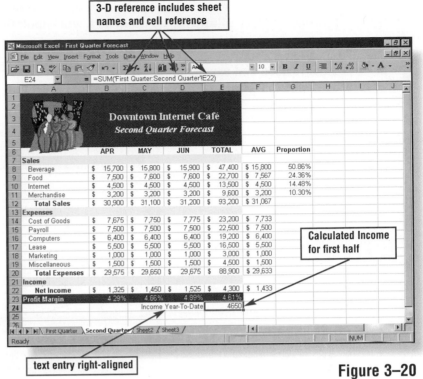

Figure 3–20

The calculated number 4650 appears in cell E24 and the function containing a 3-D reference appears in the formula bar.

You have now completed the forecast for the first half of the year.

**3** ■ Change the format of cell E24 to Accounting with zero decimal places.

■ Save the workbook file as **First Half Forecast**.

■ Enter your name in the workbook file documentation as the author.

■ Preview the entire workbook.

■ Add a predefined footer containing your name to both sheets.

■ Print both worksheets.

■ Close the workbook file, saving it again.

*Note:* If you are running short on lab time, this is an appropriate place to end this session and begin again at a later time.

## Zooming the Worksheet

You presented the completed first and second quarterly forecasts to Evan who now wants you to create worksheets for the third and fourth quarters and a combined annual forecast. Evan also wants you to show a profit margin of 5 percent at the end of the second quarter and 6 percent by the end of the year. You have already made several of the changes requested and saved them as a workbook file named Annual Forecast.

**1** To see the revised and expanded forecast, open the workbook file Annual Forecast.

Your screen should be similar to Figure 3–21.

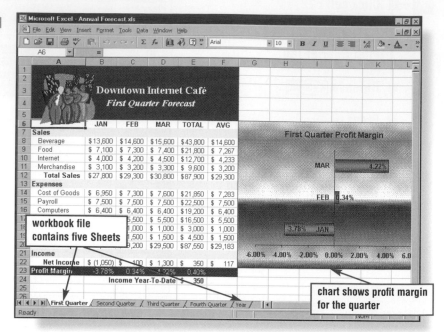

**Figure 3–21**

The workbook file now contains five sheets: First Quarter, Second Quarter, Third Quarter, Fourth Quarter, and Year. The Year sheet contains the forecast data for the entire 12 months. Each quarter sheet also includes a chart of the profit margin for that quarter. As you can now easily see, the profit margin by the end of the first quarter is showing a profit.

**2** Click on each of the Quarter sheet tabs to view the quarterly data and profit margin chart.

Make the Year sheet active.

Your screen should be similar to Figure 3–22.

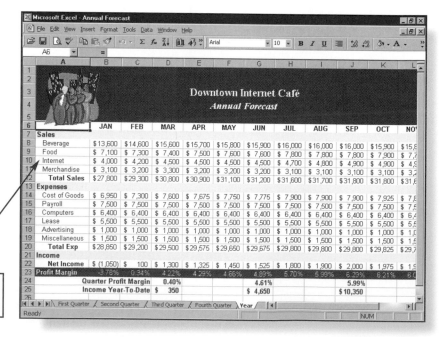

**Figure 3–22**

The Year sheet displays all of the quarterly data. The entire sheet, however, is not visible in the window. You can change how much information is displayed in the window to make it easier to navigate, view, and select the worksheet data by adjusting the zoom percentage. The default zoom setting is 100 percent. This setting displays data onscreen the same size that it will appear on the printed page. You can reduce or enlarge the amount of information displayed onscreen by changing the magnification from between 10 to 400 percent. You want to decrease the zoom percent to display more information in the window.

> The Zoom feature is common in all Office 2000 programs.

**3** ■ Open the `100%` Zoom drop-down menu.

■ Select **75%**.

> The menu equivalent is **V**iew/**Z**oom.

> The Selection option adjusts the percentage to fit the selected range in the current window size.

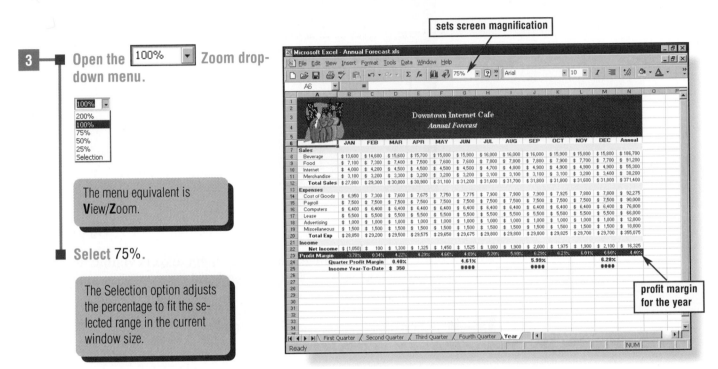

**Figure 3–23**

Your screen should be similar to Figure 3–23.

You can now see the entire worksheet and note that the total profit margin for the year is 4.4%.

**4** ▬■ Reduce the zoom percent to 50%.

Your screen should be similar to Figure 3–24.

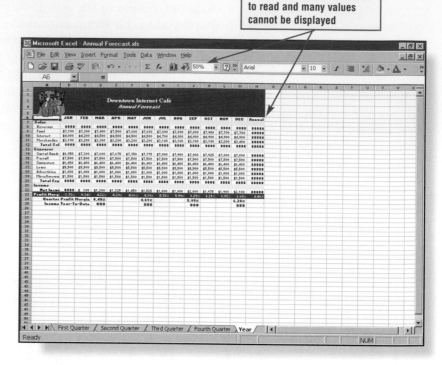

at 50% worksheet is difficult to read and many values cannot be displayed

**Figure 3–24**

As you reduce the percentage, more worksheet area is visible in the window. However, it gets more difficult to read and many of the values can no longer be displayed.

**5** ▬■ Return the zoom percent back to 100%.

## Moving a Sheet

Next you want to move the Annual sheet from the last position in the workbook to the first. You can quickly rearrange sheets in a workbook by dragging the sheet tab to the new location. Just as when copying a sheet, the symbol ▼ indicates where the sheet will appear.

**1**━━■ Drag the Year tab to the left end of the First Quarter tab.

Your screen should be similar to Figure 3–25.

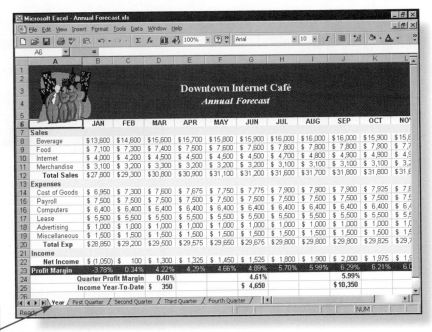

Year sheet moved to beginning of workbook file

**Figure 3–25**

## Splitting Windows

Most of the monthly values in the Year sheet, such as cell B8, contain linking formulas that reference the appropriate cells in the appropriate quarter sheets. Others, such as the total formulas and the formula to calculate the income, do not reference cells outside the Year worksheet.

　　To see several of the formulas in cells that reference the quarter sheets,

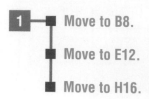

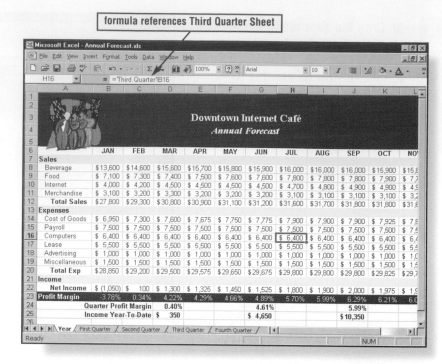

**Figure 3–26**

Each of these cells contained a formula that referenced a cell in the appropriate quarter sheet. To see the total formulas for the year in column N, you will move to cell N16 using the Goto feature.

Your screen should be similar to Figure 3–27.

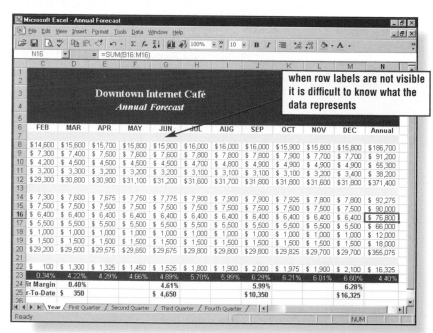

**Figure 3–27**

The cell pointer is now in cell N16 in the total column. The formula in this cell calculates the total of the values in row 16 and does not reference another sheet. However, it is difficult to know what the numbers represent in this row because the row headings are not visible. For example, is this number the total for the lease expenses, advertising expenses, or miscellaneous expenses? Without scrolling back to see the row headings, it is difficult to know.

Whenever you scroll a large worksheet, you will find that information you may need to view in one area scrolls out of view as you move to another area. Although you could reduce the zoom percent to view more of a worksheet in the window, you still may not be able to see the entire worksheet if it is very large. And as you saw, continuing to reduce the zoom makes the worksheet difficult to read and prevents some values from fully displaying. To view different areas of the same sheet at the same time, you can split the window into panes.

## Concept ⑦ Split Windows

A sheet window can be split into sections called **panes** to make it easier to view different parts of the sheet at the same time. The panes can consist of any number of columns or rows along the top or left edge of the window. You can divide the sheet into two panes either horizontally or vertically, or into four panes if you split the window both vertically and horizontally.

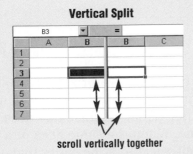

**Vertical Split**

scroll vertically together

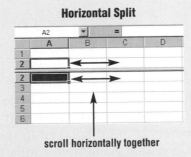

**Horizontal Split**

scroll horizontally together

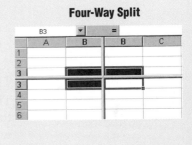

**Four-Way Split**

Each pane can be scrolled independently to display different areas of the sheet. When split vertically, the panes scroll together when you scroll vertically, but scroll independently when you scroll horizontally. Horizontal panes scroll together when you scroll horizontally, but independently when you scroll vertically.

Dragging the split box at the top of the vertical scroll bar downward creates a horizontal split, and dragging the split box at the right end of the horizontal scroll bar leftward creates a vertical split. The Window/Split command can be used to quickly create a four-way split at the active cell.

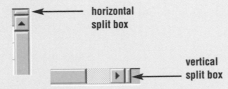

horizontal split box

vertical split box

Panes are most useful for viewing a worksheet that consists of different areas or sections. Creating panes allows you to display the different sections of the worksheet in separate panes and then to quickly switch between panes to access the data in the different sections without having to repeatedly scroll to the areas.

You will split the window into two vertical panes. This will allow you to view the titles in column A at the same time as you are viewing data in column N. Pointing to the vertical split box and dragging the split bar to the left creates a vertical pane.

**1** ▪ Point to the split box in the horizontal scroll bar.

The mouse pointer changes to a ←‖→ to show you can drag to create a split.

▪ Drag to the left and position the bar between columns D and E.

Your screen should be similar to Figure 3–28.

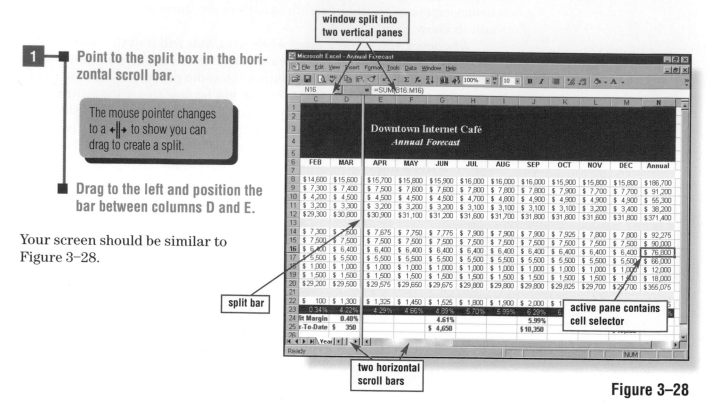

**Figure 3–28**

There are now two vertical panes with two separate horizontal scroll bars. The highlighted cell selector is visible in the right pane. The left pane also has a cell selector in cell N16, but it is not visible because that area of the worksheet is not displayed in the pane. When the same area of a worksheet is visible in multiple panes, the cell selector in the panes that are not active is highlighted whereas the cell selector in the **active pane** is clear. The active pane will be affected by your movement horizontally. The cell selector moves in both panes, but only the active pane scrolls.

You will scroll the left pane horizontally to display the month headings and then scroll horizontally to display the row headings.

**2** Click C16 in the left pane to display the active cell selector in the pane.

■ Press ← twice.

Your screen should be similar to Figure 3–29.

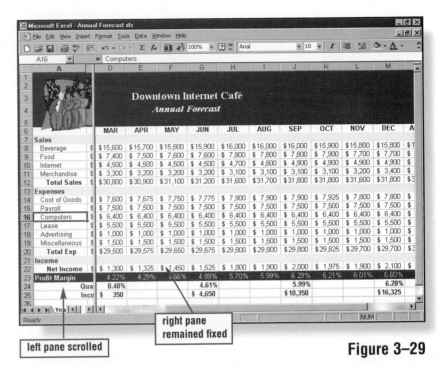

**left pane scrolled**

**right pane remained fixed**

**Figure 3–29**

The right pane did not scroll when you moved horizontally through the left pane to display the row headings. The cell selector in the right pane is in the same cell location as in the left pane (A16), although it is not visible.

**3** Drag the split bar to the right three columns.

Now you can see the data for the first quarter. To quickly compare the first quarter data to the last quarter data, you will scroll the right pane.

**4** Click cell E16 in the right pane.

■ Press End →.

■ Press → three times.

Your screen should be similar to Figure 3–30.

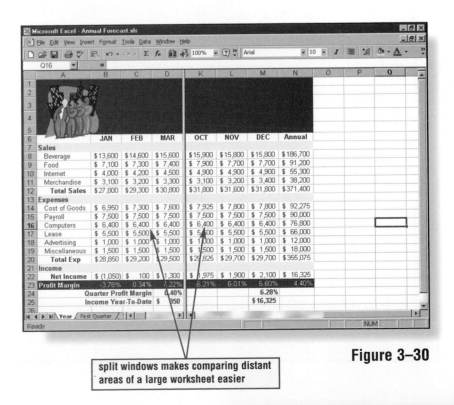

**split windows makes comparing distant areas of a large worksheet easier**

**Figure 3–30**

Now the first and last quarter data are side by side. As you can see, creating panes is helpful when you want to display and access distant areas of a worksheet quickly. After scrolling the data in the panes to display the appropriate worksheet area, you can then quickly switch between panes to make changes to the data that is visible in the pane. This saves you the time of scrolling to the area each time you want to view it or make changes to it. To clear the horizontal split from the window,

> The menu equivalent is **W**indow/Remove **S**plit.

**5** ■ **Double-click anywhere on the split bar.**

## Freezing Panes

Another way to manage a large worksheet is to freeze panes.

### Concept ⑧ Freeze Panes

**Freezing** panes prevents the data in the pane from scrolling as you move to different areas in a worksheet. You can freeze the information in the top and left panes of a window only. The Freeze command on the Window menu is used to freeze panes.

To create two horizontal panes with the top pane frozen, move the cell selector in the leftmost column in the window to the row below where you want the split to appear before choosing the command.

**Top Pane Frozen**

| | A | B | C |
|---|---|---|---|
| 9 | Total Sales | $234,000 | $224,000 |
| 10 | | | |
| 19 | Total Expenses | $232,080 | $225,880 |
| 20 | | | |
| 21 | INCOME | $  1,920 | $  (1,880) |
| 22 | | | |

To create two vertical panes with the left pane frozen, move the cell selector in the top row of the window and select the column to the right of where you want the split to appear.

**Left Pane Frozen**

| | A | M | N |
|---|---|---|---|
| 9 | Total Sales | $670,000 | $3,883,000 |
| 10 | | | |
| 11 | EXPENSES | | |
| 12 | | | |
| 13 | Advertising | $  26,800 | $  155,320 |
| 14 | Cost of Goods | $388,600 | $2,252,140 |

To create four panes with the top and left panes frozen, click the cell below and to the right of where you want the split to appear.

**Top and Left Pane Frozen**

| | A | B | C |
|---|---|---|---|
| 3 | | | |
| 4 | | JAN | FEB |
| 11 | EXPENSES | | |
| 12 | | | |
| 13 | Advertising | $  9,360 | $  8,960 |
| 14 | Cost of Goods | $135,720 | $129,920 |

This feature is most useful when your worksheet is organized using row and column headings. It allows you to keep the titles on the top and left edge of your worksheet in view as you scroll horizontally and vertically through the worksheet data.

You want to keep the month headings in row 6 and the row headings in column A visible in the window at all times while looking at the Income and Profit Margin data beginning in row 21. To do this, you will create four panes and freeze the headings in the upper and left panes. When creating frozen panes, first position the sheet in the window to display the information you want to appear in the top and left panes. This is because data in the frozen panes cannot be scrolled like data in regular panes. The worksheet is already positioned appropriately in the window.

**1** ■ **Move to B7.**

■ **Choose Window/Freeze Panes.**

Your screen should be similar to Figure 3-31.

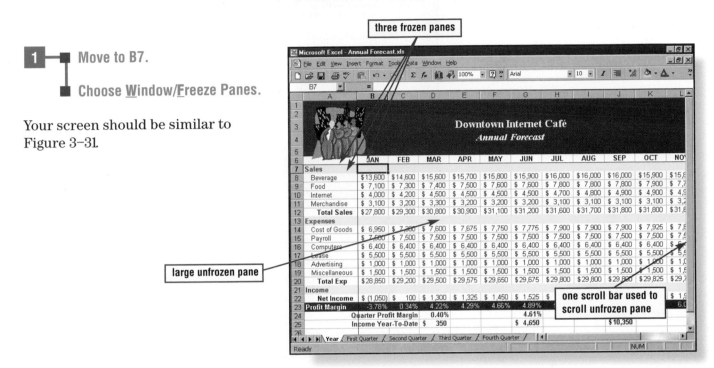

**Figure 3-31**

The window is divided into four panes at the cell selector location. Only one scroll bar is displayed because the only pane that can be scrolled is the larger lower-right pane. You can move the cell selector into a frozen pane, but the data in the frozen panes will not scroll. Also, there is only one cell selector that moves from one pane to another over the pane divider, making it unnecessary to click on the pane to make it active before moving the cell selector in it.

**2** ■ Use the ↓ key to move the cell pointer down column B to row 39.

Your screen should be similar to Figure 3–32.

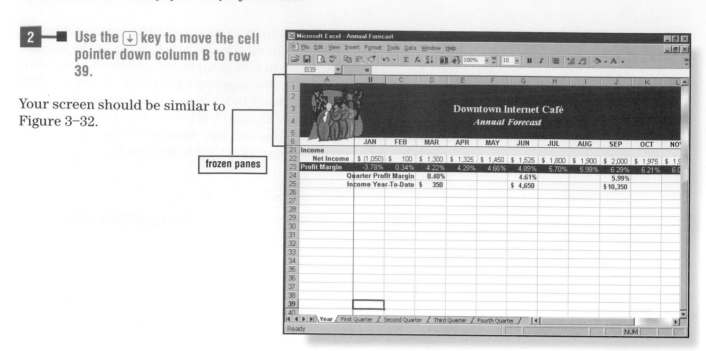

**Figure 3–32**

Now the only information visible is the title and month headings and Income data. All data in rows 7 through 20 is no longer visible, allowing you to concentrate on the Income area of the worksheet.

The company owner wants you to adjust the forecast for the second quarter to show a profit margin of at least 5 percent for each month.

## Using What-If Analysis

To increase the profit margin for the second quarter, you will need to adjust the values in the second quarter sheet.

**1** ■ Make the Second Quarter sheet active.

Your screen should be similar to Figure 3–33.

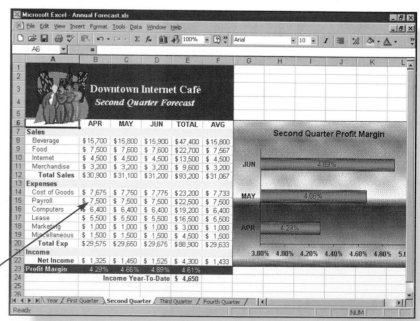

you will reduce payroll expenses to increase the profit margin

**Figure 3–33**

After some consideration, you decide you can most easily reduce monthly payroll expenses by carefully scheduling employee work during these three months. Reducing the monthly expense will increase the profit margin for the quarter. You want to find out what the maximum payroll value you can spend during that period is for each month to accomplish this goal.

To do this, you will enter different payroll expense values for each month and see what the effect is on that month's profit margin. The process of evaluating what effect reducing the payroll expenses will have on the profit margin is called what-if analysis.

**Concept (9) What-If Analysis**

**What-if analysis** is a technique used to evaluate the effects of changing selected factors in a worksheet. This technique is a common accounting function that has been made much easier with the introduction of spreadsheet programs. By substituting different values in cells that are referenced by formulas, you can quickly see the effect of the changes when the formulas are recalculated.

You will adjust the May payroll value first.

**2** ■ Enter **7300** in cell C15.

Your screen should be similar to Figure 3–34.

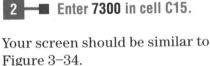
decreasing May payroll value increased May profit margin

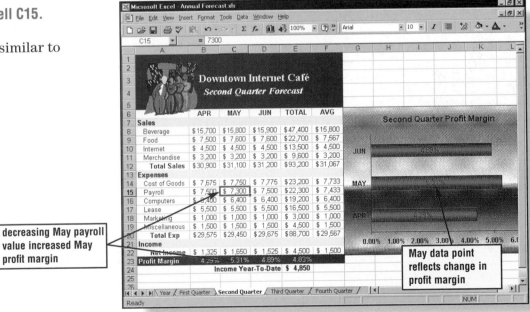

**Figure 3–34**

Now by looking in cell C23 you can see that decreasing the payroll expenses has increased the profit margin for the month to 5.31 percent. Also notice the chart has changed to reflect the change in May's profit margin. This is more than you need.

**3** ■ Enter **7400** in cell C15.

The profit margin is now 4.98 percent. That's closer—you just need to reduce the payroll value slightly.

**4** ■ Enter **7390** in cell C15.

■ Enter **7395** in cell C15.

Your screen should be similar to Figure 3–35.

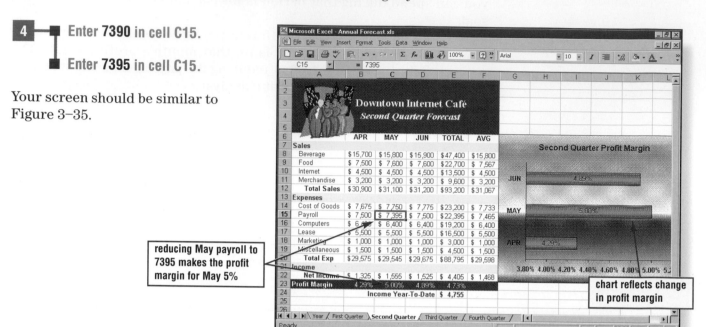

reducing May payroll to 7395 makes the profit margin for May 5%

chart reflects change in profit margin

**Figure 3–35**

That's it! Reducing the payroll value from 7500 to 7395 will achieve the 5% profit margin goal for the month.

## Using Goal Seek

It took you several tries to find the payroll value that would achieve the profit margin objective. A quicker way to find the payroll value that will achieve the desired result is to use the Goal Seek tool.

## Concept ⑩ Goal Seek

The **Goal Seek** tool is used to find the value needed in one cell to attain a result you want in another cell. Goal Seek varies the value in the cell you specify until a formula that is dependent on that cell returns the desired result. The value of only one cell can be changed.

You will use this method to find the payroll value for April that will produce a 5 percent profit margin for that month. The current profit margin value is 4.29 percent in cell B23.

**1** ■ Move to B23.

■ Choose **T**ools/**G**oal Seek.

Your screen should be similar to Figure 3–36.

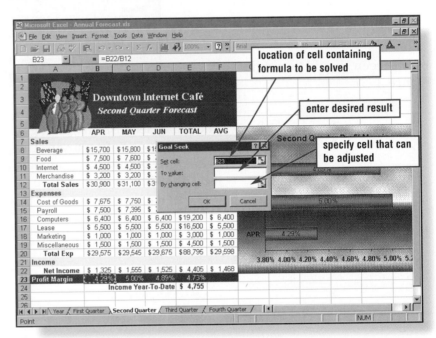

**Figure 3–36**

In the Goal Seek dialog box, you need to specify the location of the cell containing the formula to be solved, the desired calculated value, and the cell containing the number that can be adjusted to achieve the result. You want the formula in cell B23 to calculate a result of 5 percent by changing the payroll number in cell B15. The Set Cell text box correctly displays the current cell as the location of the formula to be solved. To complete the information needed in the Goal Seek dialog box,

**2** ■ Click in the To Value text box and enter the value **5.00%**.

■ Click in the By Changing Cell text box and then click on cell B15 in the worksheet to enter the cell reference to cell B15 in the text box.

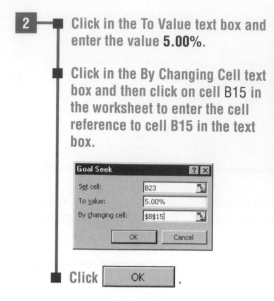

■ Click [ OK ] .

Your screen should be similar to Figure 3–37.

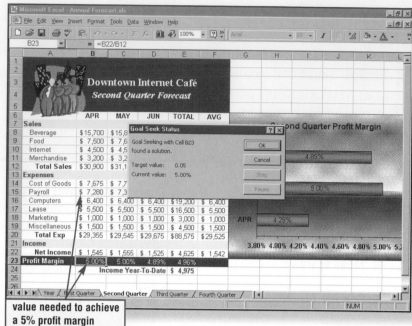

**Figure 3–37**

The Goal Seek Status dialog box tells you it found a solution that will achieve the 5 profit margin. The payroll value of 7280 that will achieve the desired result has been temporarily entered in the worksheet. You can reject the solution and restore the original value by choosing [ Cancel ] . In this case, however, you want to accept the solution.

**3** ━■ Click OK

Your screen should be similar to
Figure 3–38.

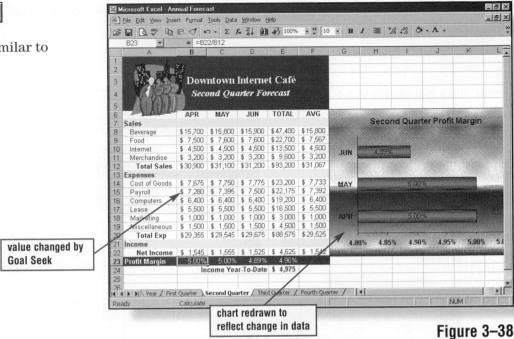

value changed by
Goal Seek

chart redrawn to
reflect change in data

**Figure 3–38**

The payroll value is permanently updated and the chart redrawn to reflect
the change in profit margin.

Finally, you need to adjust the June payroll value. This time you will
find the value by dragging the June chart data marker to the 5% position
on the chart. As you drag the data marker, a dotted bar line will show the
new bar length and a ChartTip will display the new profit margin value.
An indicator on the X axis also marks your location. Releasing the mouse
button with the bar at the new position specifies the new value and opens
the Goal Seek dialog box.

The bar is surrounded by eight selection handles.

**4** ▬ Click on the June data series bar twice (slowly) to select the individual bar.

**5** ▬ Drag the middle selection handle on the right end of the bar to increase the length of the bar. When the bar ChartTip value is 0.05 or as close as your mouse will allow, release the mouse button.

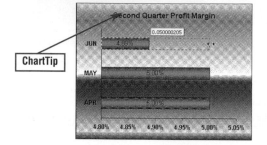

ChartTip

Your screen should be similar to Figure 3-39.

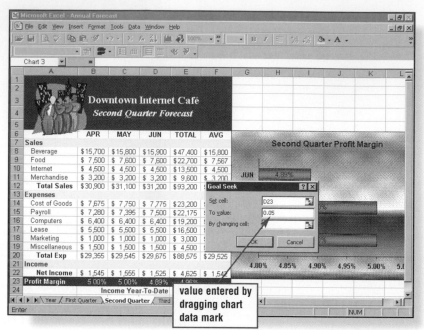

**Figure 3-39**

Dragging the data marker specifies the value you want to change to and the location of the cell containing the formula. The Goal Seek dialog box is displayed. The Set Cell location and value to attain are entered. Depending on the value you were able to attain by dragging the data mark, you may still need to adjust the value to the exact value of .05. You also need to specify the cell location of the value to change.

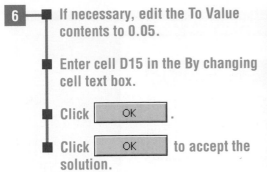

**6**
- If necessary, edit the To Value contents to 0.05.
- Enter cell D15 in the By changing cell text box.
- Click [ OK ] .
- Click [ OK ] to accept the solution.

Your screen should be similar to Figure 3–40.

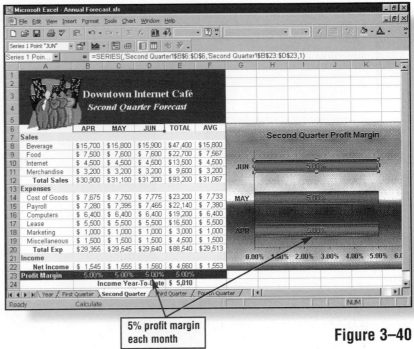

5% profit margin each month

**Figure 3–40**

The second quarter values are now at the 5 percent profit margin objective.

**7**
- Make the Year sheet active and verify that the profit margin values for the second quarter have changed.
- Choose Window/Unfreeze Panes.
- Update the workbook documentation by entering your name as author.
- Save the revised forecast as **Annual Forecast Revised**.

## Changing Page Orientation

Now you are ready to print the workbook. To preview all the sheets in the workbook,

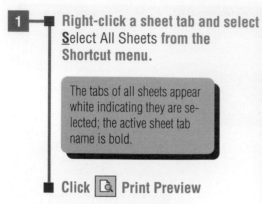

**1** ▪ **Right-click a sheet tab and select <u>S</u>elect All Sheets from the Shortcut menu.**

> The tabs of all sheets appear white indicating they are selected; the active sheet tab name is bold.

▪ **Click**  **Print Preview**

Your screen should be similar to Figure 3–41.

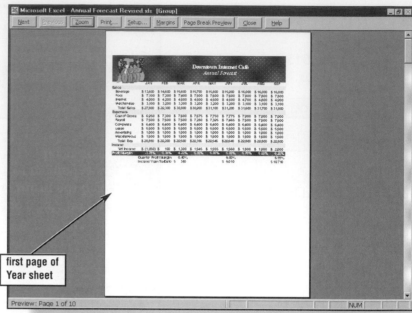

first page of Year sheet

**Figure 3–41**

The first page of the Year worksheet is displayed in the Preview window. Notice that the entire sheet does not fit across the width of the page. To see the second page,

**2** ▪ **Click** Next .

The last three columns of data appear on the second page. Although you could use the Fit To feature to compress the worksheet to a single page, this would make the data small and difficult to read. Instead you can change the orientation or the direction the output is printed on a page. The default orientation is **portrait.** This setting prints across the width of the page. You will change the orientation to **landscape** so that the worksheet prints across the length of the paper. Then you will use the Fit To feature to make sure it fits on one page with the new orientation.

**3** Click [Previous].

Click [Setup...].

If necessary, open the Page tab.

Select Landscape.

Select Fit to.

Click [ OK ].

Your screen should be similar to
Figure 3-42.

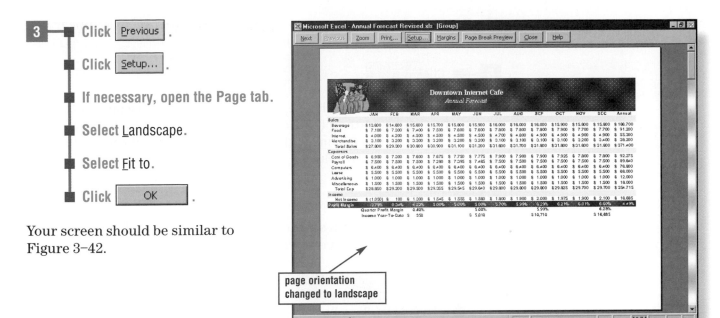

page orientation
changed to landscape

**Figure 3-42**

The entire worksheet now easily fits across the length of the page.
Because the worksheet is large, you also feel the worksheet may be easier
to read if the row and column grid lines were printed. In addition, you
want the worksheet to be centered horizontally on the page. To make
these changes,

**4** Click [Setup...].

From the Sheet tab, select
Gridlines.

From the Margins tab, select
Horizontally.

Click [ OK ].

Your screen should be similar to
Figure 3-43.

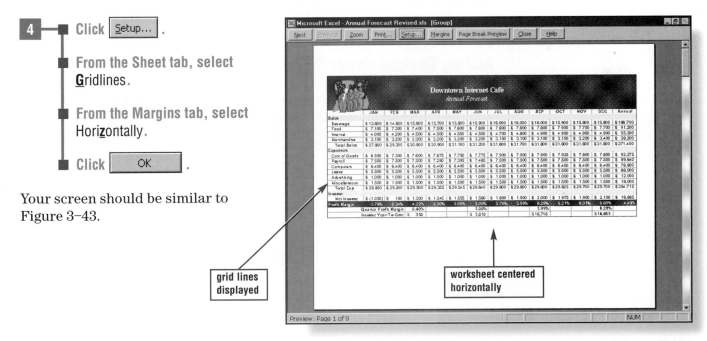

grid lines
displayed

worksheet centered
horizontally

**Figure 3-43**

The Preview screen is recreated showing how the sheet will appear centered horizontally and with gridlines.

**5** ── ■ Click  .

You would also like to change the orientation to landscape for the four quarterly sheets. Rather than change each sheet individually in the Preview window, you can make this change to the four sheets at the same time in the worksheet window.

**6** ── ■ Click  .

The five sheet tabs are still selected. To deselect the Year sheet and change the orientation to landscape for the four selected sheets,

**7** ── ■ Hold down Ctrl and click the Year tab.

■ Choose **F**ile/Page Set**u**p

■ Select **L**andscape from the Page tab.

■ Click [ Print Preview ] .

■ Look at the four sheets.

The four sheets are displayed in landscape orientation in the Preview window. With landscape orientation, there is more white space to the right of the chart. Before printing, you will move the chart slightly away from the worksheet data to make it look more balanced on the page.

## Adding Custom Headers and Footers

You would also like to add a custom footer to all the sheets. It is faster to add the footer to all sheets at the same time. If you make changes to the active sheet when multiple sheets are selected, the changes are made to all other selected sheets. These changes may replace data on other sheets.

**1** Click Close .

■ Hold down Ctrl and click the Year sheet tab again to add it to the selection.

■ Choose File/Page Setup.

■ Open the Header/Footer tab.

■ Click Custom Footer... .

Your screen should be similar to Figure 3–44.

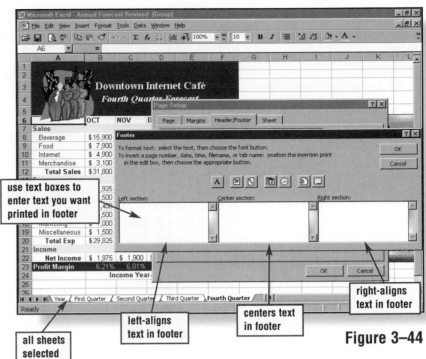

**Figure 3–44**

The Left Section text box will display the footer text you entered aligned with the left margin, the Center Section will center the text, and the Right Section will right-align the text. The insertion point is currently positioned in the Left Section text box. You want to enter your name, class, and the date in this box. You will enter your name and class by typing it directly in the box. Instead of typing the date, however, you will enter a code that will automatically insert the current date whenever the worksheet is printed. The buttons above the section boxes are used to enter the codes for common header and footer information. They are identified below.

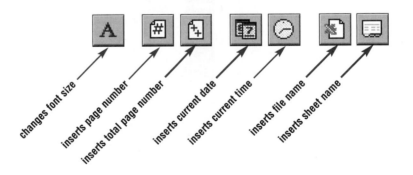

**2** ■ Type **Created by [your name]**.

■ Press Tab.

■ Enter the name of your class and the section or time.

■ Press Tab.

■ Click 📅 Date.

Your screen should be similar to Figure 3–45.

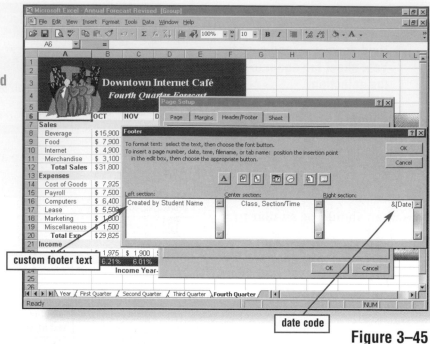

Figure 3–45

**3** ■ Click OK.

■ Click Print Preview.

Your screen should be similar to Figure 3–46.

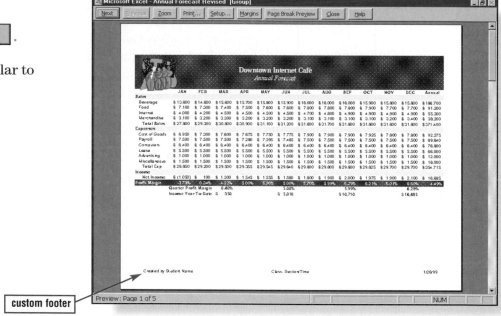

Figure 3–46

The footer as you entered it appears on the preview page for the Year sheet.

**4** ■ Look at the other sheets to confirm that the footer was added to them as well.

■ Close the Preview window.

## Printing Selected Sheets

You want to print the Year and Second Quarter worksheets only. First you want to adjust the placement of the chart in the Second Quarter sheet. Then you will select the two sheets you want to print.

**1** Make the Second Quarter sheet active.

Move the chart so that it is evenly balanced between the right edge of the worksheet and the right page break line.

Make the Year sheet active and save the file again.

Hold down Ctrl and click the Second Quarter Sheet tab to add it to the selection of sheets to print.

Click Print.

> If you need to specify print settings that are different from the default settings on your system, use the Print command on the File menu to print the worksheet.

Your printed output should look like that shown in the Case Study at the beginning of this tutorial.

# Concept Summary

## Tutorial 3: Managing and Analyzing a Workbook

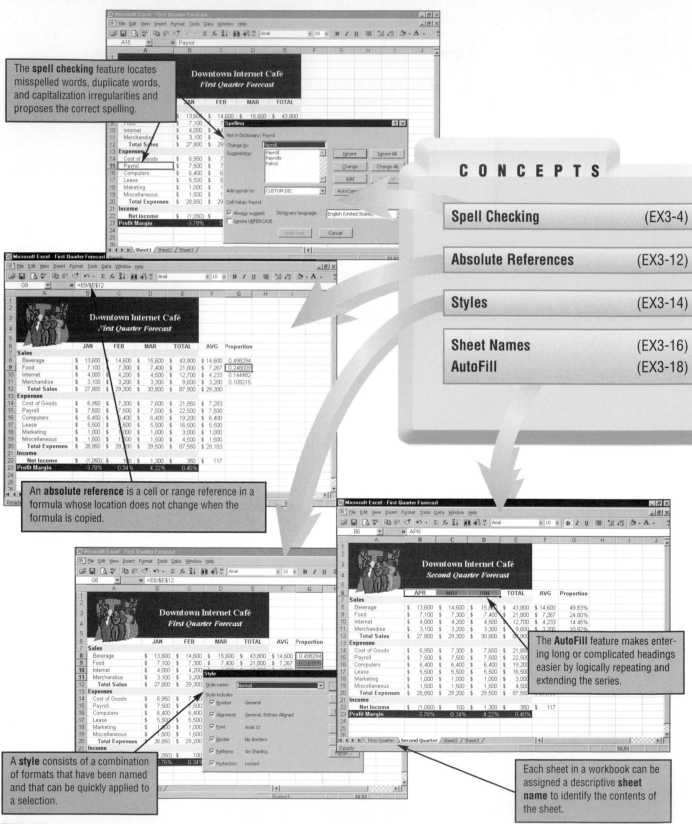

The **spell checking** feature locates misspelled words, duplicate words, and capitalization irregularities and proposes the correct spelling.

### CONCEPTS

| Spell Checking | (EX3-4) |
| Absolute References | (EX3-12) |
| Styles | (EX3-14) |
| Sheet Names | (EX3-16) |
| AutoFill | (EX3-18) |

An **absolute reference** is a cell or range reference in a formula whose location does not change when the formula is copied.

The **AutoFill** feature makes entering long or complicated headings easier by logically repeating and extending the series.

A **style** consists of a combination of formats that have been named and that can be quickly applied to a selection.

Each sheet in a workbook can be assigned a descriptive **sheet name** to identify the contents of the sheet.

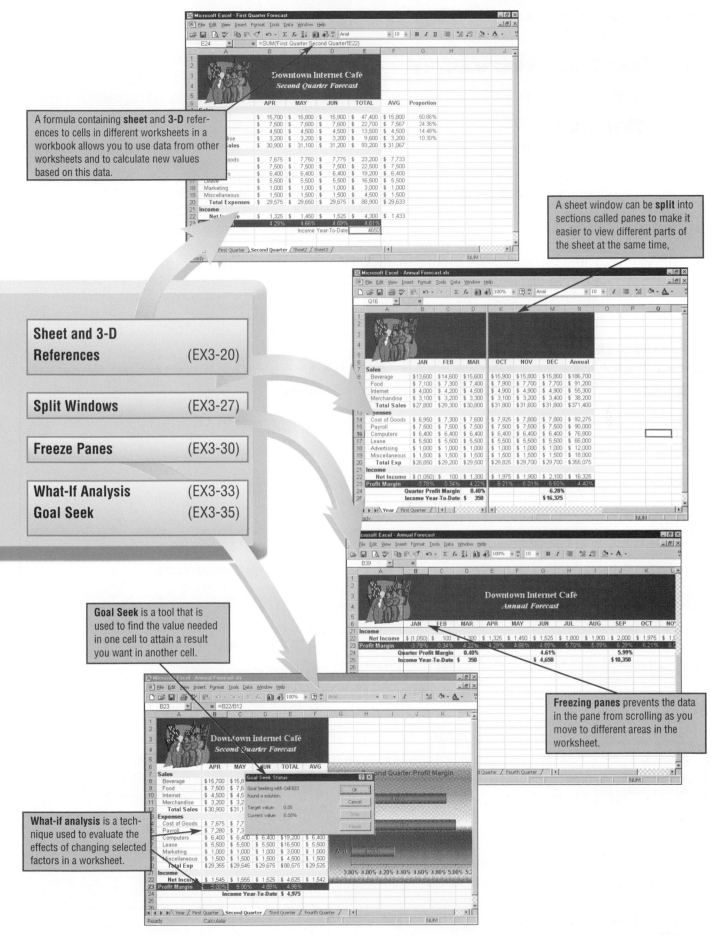

A formula containing **sheet** and **3-D** references to cells in different worksheets in a workbook allows you to use data from other worksheets and to calculate new values based on this data.

A sheet window can be **split** into sections called panes to make it easier to view different parts of the sheet at the same time.

| Sheet and 3-D References | (EX3-20) |
| Split Windows | (EX3-27) |
| Freeze Panes | (EX3-30) |
| What-If Analysis | (EX3-33) |
| Goal Seek | (EX3-35) |

**Goal Seek** is a tool that is used to find the value needed in one cell to attain a result you want in another cell.

**Freezing panes** prevents the data in the pane from scrolling as you move to different areas in the worksheet.

**What-if analysis** is a technique used to evaluate the effects of changing selected factors in a worksheet.

# Tutorial Review

## Key Terms

3-D reference   EX3-20
absolute reference   EX3-12
active pane   EX3-28
AutoFill   EX3-18
custom dictionary   EX3-4
freeze   EX3-30

Goal Seek   EX3-35
landscape   EX3-40
main dictionary   EX3-4
mixed reference   EX3-12
pane   EX3-27
portrait   EX3-40

sheet reference   EX3-20
spell-checking   EX3-4
style   EX3-14
what-if analysis   EX3-33

## Command Summary

| Command | Shortcut Keys | Button | Action |
|---|---|---|---|
| **E**dit/**M**ove or Copy Sheet | | | Moves or copies selected sheet |
| **F**ile/Page Set**u**p/Page/**L**andscape | | | Changes orientation to landscape |
| **I**nsert/**F**unction | ⇧Shift + F3 | $f_x$ | Inserts a function |
| F**o**rmat/S**h**eet/**R**ename | | | Renames sheet |
| F**o**rmat/**S**tyle/**S**tyle name/Currency | | \$ | Applies currency style to selection |
| F**o**rmat/**S**tyle/**S**tyle name/Percent | | ± | Changes cell style to display percentage |
| **T**ools/**S**pelling | F7 | | Spell-checks worksheet |
| **T**ools/**G**oal Seek | | | Adjusts value in specified cell until a formula dependent on that cell reaches specified result |
| **V**iew/**Z**oom | | 100% ▾ | Changes magnification of window |
| **W**indow/Un**f**reeze | | | Unfreezes window panes |
| **W**indow/**F**reeze Panes | | | Freezes top and/or leftmost panes |
| **W**indow/**S**plit | | | Divides window into four panes at active cell |
| **W**indow/Remove **S**plit | | | Removes split bar from active worksheet |

# Screen Identification

In the following worksheet and chart, several items are identified by letters. Enter the correct term for each item in the space provided.

a. _____

b. _____

c. _____

d. _____

# Matching

Match the lettered item on the right with the numbered item on the left.

| | | |
|---|---|---|
| 1. 'Second Quarter!'A13 | _____ | **a.** prevents scrolling of information in upper and left panes of a window |
| 2. pane | _____ | **b.** spell-checks worksheet |
| 3. freeze | _____ | **c.** tool to find the value needed in one cell to attain a desired result in another cell |
| 4. F7 | _____ | **d.** the sections of a divided window |
| 5. Sheet1:Sheet3!H3:K5 | _____ | **e.** sheet reference |
| 6. #DIV/0! | _____ | **f.** mixed cell reference |
| 7. landscape | _____ | **g.** 3-D reference |
| 8. $M$34 | _____ | **h.** indicates division by zero error |
| 9. Goal Seek | _____ | **i.** prints across the length of the paper |
| 10. $B12 | _____ | **j.** absolute cell reference |

**EXCEL 2000**

# Fill-In

------------------------------------------------------------

Complete the following statements by filling in the blanks with the correct terms.

1. Excel checks spelling by comparing text entries to words in a(n) _____.

2. You can create a _____ dictionary to hold words you use that are not included in the main dictionary.

3. A worksheet window can be divided into four _____.

4. A(n) _____ reference is a cell or range reference in a formula whose location does not change when the formula is copied.

5. _____ _____ varies the value in a specified cell until a formula that is dependent on that cell returns a desired result.

6. _____ panes prevents the data in the pane from scrolling as you move to different areas in a worksheet.

7. _____ analysis is a technique used to evaluate the effects of changing selected factors in a worksheet.

8. When a window is split, the _____ pane is affected by your movements.

9. Use _____ to make entering long or complicated headings easier by logically repeating and extending the series.

10. Use _____ to find the value in a single cell to achieve the result you want in another cell.

# Multiple-Choice

------------------------------------------------------------

Circle the correct response to the questions below.

1. The spell-checking feature locates:

   **a.** misspelled words

   **b.** duplicate words

   **c.** capitalization irregularities

   **d.** all of the above

2. The cell reference to adjust row 4 without adjusting column C is:

   **a.** $C$4

   **b.** C4

   **c.** $C4

   **d.** C$4

3. The number 32534 displayed with the Currency[0] style would appear as _____ in a cell.

   **a.** 32,534

   **b.** $32534

   **c.** $32,534

   **d.** $32,534.00

4. Each sheet in a workbook can be assigned a descriptive name called a:

   **a.** sheet name

   **b.** reference name

   **c.** content name

   **d.** label name

5. A(n) _____ consists of a combination of formats that have been named and that can be quickly applied to a selection.

   **a.** copy reference

   **b.** relative reference

   **c.** style

   **d.** sheet

6. A _____ reference is a reference to the same cell or range on multiple sheets in the same workbook.

   **a.** copied

   **b.** 3-D

   **c.** sheet

   **d.** workbook

7. To make it easier to view different parts of the sheet at the same time, a sheet window can be split into _____.

   **a.** windows

   **b.** parts

   **c.** panes

   **d.** sections

8. The information in the worksheet can be _____ in the top and left panes of a window only.

   **a.** frozen

   **b.** fixed

   **c.** aligned

   **d.** adjusted

9. A common accounting function that helps evaluate data by allowing the user to adjust values to see the effect is called:

   **a.** auto calculate

   **b.** what-if analysis

   **c.** auto fill

   **d.** value analysis

10. The _____ tool is used to find the value needed in one cell to attain a result you want in another cell.

    **a.** AutoFill

    **b.** function

    **c.** value analysis

    **d.** Goal Seek

# True/False

Circle the correct answer to the following questions.

| | | | |
|---|---|---|---|
| **1.** | The main dictionary supplied with the program allows the user to add words. | True | False |
| **2.** | An absolute reference is a cell or range reference in a formula whose location does not change when the formula is copied. | True | False |
| **3.** | A style consists of a combination of formats that have been named and that can be quickly applied to a selection. | True | False |
| **4.** | A sheet name can be up to 255 characters in length. | True | False |
| **5.** | Dragging the fill handle activates the AutoFill feature if Excel recognizes the entry in the cell as an entry that can be incremented. | True | False |
| **6.** | The sheet reference consists of the name of the sheet separated from the cell reference by an exclamation point. | True | False |
| **7.** | When split horizontally, the panes scroll together when you scroll vertically. | True | False |
| **8.** | To create two horizontal panes with the left pane frozen, move the cell selector in the top row of the window and select the column to the left of where you want the split to appear. | True | False |
| **9.** | What-if analysis is a technique used to evaluate the effects of changing selected factors in a worksheet. | True | False |
| **10.** | Goal Seek varies the value in the cell you specify until a formula that is dependent on that cell returns the desired result. | True | False |

# Discussion Questions

1. Define, compare, and contrast relative references, sheet references, and 3-D references. Provide a brief example of each.

2. Discuss how absolute and mixed cell references can be used in a worksheet. What is an advantage of using these types of references over a relative cell reference?

3. Discuss the differences between splitting a window and freezing a window. When would it be appropriate to split a window? When would it be appropriate to freeze a window?

4. Discuss the differences between what-if analysis and Goal Seek. Under what conditions would it be more appropriate to use what-if analysis. When would it be more appropriate to use Goal Seek?

# Hands-On Practice Exercises

**Step by Step**

Rating System
☆ Easy
☆ ☆ Moderate
☆ ☆ ☆ Difficult

☆

1. John Walsh owns the Gourmet Cookie Shop. He has created a worksheet to record the shop's first quarter sales. John would like you to extend this first quarter sales worksheet to another worksheet that provides a sales forecast for the second quarter. The completed worksheets are shown here.

   a. Open the workbook file Gourmet Cookie. Insert a copy of Sheet1 before Sheet2. Rename the Sheet1 tab to **1st Quarter Sales** and then rename Sheet1(2) tab to **2nd Quarter Sales**.

   b. In the 2nd Quarter Sales sheet, change the monthly labels to **Apr, May,** and **June** using AutoFill.

   c. Enter the following projected April sales figures:

| Type | Number |
|------|--------|
| Chocolate Chip | 1900 |
| Chocolate Chip w/Nuts | 1425 |
| White Chocolate Macadamia | 1300 |
| Butterscotch | 780 |
| Peanut Butter | 950 |
| Oatmeal Raisin | 350 |
| Gingerbread | 525 |

   d. A new advertising campaign for May and June is expected to increase monthly sales. May sales for each type of cookie is expected to be 10 percent more than April sales and June sales are expected to be 15 percent more than May. Enter formulas to calculate May and June sales for chocolate chip cookies and then copy these formulas into the other appropriate cells.

e. Enter and bold the heading Projected Sales in cell C2. Center the heading over columns C and D.

f. Enter, bold, italicize, and right-align the heading Sales Year-To-Date: in cell D14. In cell E14 enter a formula to calculate the total sales for the first six months by summing cells E12 on both sheets. Format the value to currency with two decimal places.

g. Make the following changes in both sheets:

■ format the numbers to currency with two decimal places.

■ format the column headings to centered, bold, and underlined.

■ format the worksheet title to 14 pt, with a color and font of your choice.

■ indent, bold, and italicize the Total row heading.

■ bold and italicize the Total row values.

■ add a custom header that contains your name and the date right-aligned.

h. Preview the workbook. Save the workbook file as Gourmet Cookie Revised. Print the workbook.

2. Lang's is an office supply company located in the Midwest. Their accountant, Ron, has just completed the budgeted income statement for the first quarter. You are going to use this statement to test the sensitivity of Sales to Net Income. The completed worksheet is shown here.

a. Open the file Lang's Income Statement. Examine the contents of the cells under Jan. You will notice that Sales and Fixed Costs are values while the other entries are formulas. This is also the case for the cells under Feb and Mar.

b. Ron has been told there may be a rent increase beginning in February that will increase fixed costs to 1000. Update the February and March fixed expense values to see the effect of this increase.

c. Next Ron would like to know what level of sales would be necessary to generate a February Net Income of $6500 and March of $7000. Use Goal Seek to answer this question.

d. Add a custom header that contains your name and the date left-aligned. Save the workbook file as Lang's Income Statement Revised. Print the workbook.

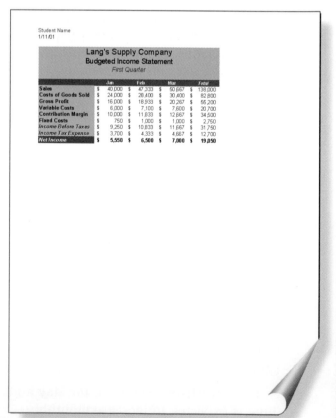

Student Name
1/11/01

**Lang's Supply Company**
Budgeted Income Statement
*First Quarter*

| | Jan | Feb | Mar | Total |
|---|---|---|---|---|
| Sales | $ 40,000 | $ 47,333 | $ 50,667 | $ 138,000 |
| Costs of Goods Sold | $ 24,000 | $ 28,400 | $ 30,400 | $ 82,800 |
| Gross Profit | $ 16,000 | $ 18,933 | $ 20,267 | $ 55,200 |
| Variable Costs | $ 6,000 | $ 7,100 | $ 7,600 | $ 20,700 |
| Contribution Margin | $ 10,000 | $ 11,833 | $ 12,667 | $ 34,500 |
| Fixed Costs | $ 750 | $ 1,000 | $ 1,000 | $ 2,750 |
| *Income Before Taxes* | $ 9,250 | $ 10,833 | $ 11,667 | $ 31,750 |
| *Income Tax Expense* | $ 3,700 | $ 4,333 | $ 4,667 | $ 12,700 |
| **Net Income** | **$ 5,550** | **$ 6,500** | **$ 7,000** | **$ 19,050** |

**3.** Parker Brent works for United Can Corp. He is paid $8.50 per hour plus time and a half for overtime. For example, this past Monday Parker worked 10 hours. He earned $68 (8 hours times $8.50 per hour) for regular time plus $25.50 (2 hours times $8.50 per hour times 1.5) for overtime for a total of $95.50. He has started to create a worksheet to keep track of weekly hours. You are going to complete this worksheet and create another that Parker will use to schedule next week's hours. The completed worksheets are shown here.

**a.** Open the workbook file Time Sheets. Enter a formula in E8 that calculates Monday's total hours by adding Monday's regular and overtime hours. Enter formulas to calculate total hours for the other days by copying the formula in E8 down the column.

**b.** Using an absolute reference to the Hourly Wage in cell C15, enter a formula in cell F8 to calculate Monday's pay. Be sure to include regular and overtime pay in the formula. Enter formulas to calculate pay for the other days by copying the formula in cell F8 down the column. Calculate the total Pay. Format the Pay column to Accounting with two decimal places.

**c.** Parker has received his work schedule for next week and would like to record those times by extending the current worksheet to a second week. Insert a copy of Sheet1 before Sheet2. Rename the Sheet1 tab to First Week and the rename Sheet1(2) tab to Second Week.

**d.** In the Second Week sheet, change the title in cell C2 to Week #2 Time Sheet and enter the following work hours.

|  | Regular Hours | Overtime Hours |
|---|---|---|
| Monday | 8 | 0 |
| Tuesday | 8 | 3 |
| Wednesday | 7 | 0 |
| Thursday | 8 | 4 |
| Friday | 8 | 1 |

1/11/01 — Student Name

**Week #1 Time Sheet**

| | Regular Hours | Overtime Hours | Total Hours | Pay |
|---|---|---|---|---|
| Monday | 8 | 2 | 10 | $ 93.50 |
| Tuesday | 7 | 0 | 7 | $ 59.50 |
| Wednesday | 7 | 0 | 7 | $ 59.50 |
| Thursday | 8 | 1 | 9 | $ 80.75 |
| Friday | 8 | 4 | 12 | $ 119.00 |
| Total | 38 | 7 | 45 | $ 412.25 |

Hourly Wage    $8.50

THRS 10

1/11/01 — Student Name

**Week #2 Time Sheet**

| | Regular Hours | Overtime Hours | Total Hours | Pay |
|---|---|---|---|---|
| Monday | 8 | 0 | 8 | $ 78.43 |
| Tuesday | 8 | 3 | 11 | $ 122.55 |
| Wednesday | 7 | 0 | 7 | $ 68.63 |
| Thursday | 8 | 4 | 12 | $ 137.25 |
| Friday | 8 | 1 | 9 | $ 93.14 |
| Total | 39 | 8 | 47 | $ 500.00 |

Hourly Wage    $9.80

Reg. Pay To-Date: $ 754.90
Overtime To-Date: $ 220.59
Total Pay To-Date: $ 975.49

e.  Enter, bold and right-align the following labels:

**Reg. Pay To-Date:** in cell D17

**Overtime To-Date:** in cell D18

**Total Pay To-Date:** in cell D19

f.  Enter formulas in cell E17 to calculate the regular pay to date by summing cells C14 on both sheets and multiplying by the hourly wage. Enter a similar formula in cell E18 for overtime pay to date. Calculate the total pay to-date in cell E19. Format these values to Accounting with two decimal places.

g.  Parker is thinking about asking for a raise from $8.50 to $9.00 to be effective next week. To evaluate the impact of the raise, change the hourly rate in the Week 2 sheet.

h.  Use Goal Seek to determine the hourly rate required to achieve a weekly total pay of $500 for Week 2.

i.  Add a custom header to both sheets that contains the date centered and your name right-aligned. Preview the workbook. Save the workbook file as Time Sheets Revised. Print the workbook.

4.  Kelly Young works for The Sports Company, a sporting goods retail store. She has nearly completed a six-month forecast for the store. Kelly wants to complete the six-month forecast, extend it for the next six months, and then analyze the forecasts. The completed second half worksheet is shown here.

a.  Open the workbook Sports Company Forecast. Spell-check and correct any errors in the workbook.

b.  Use the Paste Function feature to enter the function to calculate the Average in cell I6. Copy the function down the column.

c.  Profit margin is equal to Income/Total Sales. Enter a formula to calculate January's Profit margin. Format the cell to percent with 2 decimal places. Copy this formula across the row to enter the formulas for February through June's profit margins.

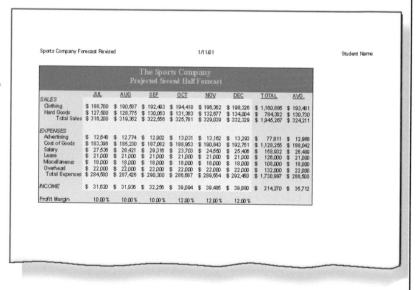

d.  Insert a copy of Sheet1 before Sheet2. Rename the Sheet1 tab to **First Half** and rename Sheet1(2) to **Second Half**.

e.  Use the AutoFill feature to replace the months JAN through JUN with **JUL** through **DEC** on the Second Half sheet. Update the title of the Second Half sheet to **Projected Second Half Forecast.**

**f.** Kelly expects sales of clothing and hard goods for July to increase by 2 percent over June and then to increase 1 percent per month beginning August until the end of the year. Create a formula to calculate the clothing sales for July by taking the clothing sales figure from June in the First Half sheet and multiplying it by 1.02. Copy this formula to hard goods sales for July. Create a formula to calculate August's clothing sales by taking the clothing sales in July and multiplying it by 1.01. Copy this formula down and across to calculate the remaining clothing and hard goods sales.

**g.** The lease will increase to 21000 effective in July and miscellaneous expenses are expected to increase to 18000 for each month. Update the Second Half sheet to reflect these monthly changes.

**h.** Use Goal Seek to achieve a profit margin of 10 percent for July, August, and September and 12 percent in October, November, and December by adjusting Salary.

**i.** Add a custom header that contains the file name left-aligned, the date centered, and your name right-aligned. Preview the workbook. Save the workbook file as Sports Company Forecast Revised. Print the Second Half worksheet using landscape orientation.

☆☆☆

**5.** Alice, a travel analyst for Adventure Travel Tours, is evaluating the profitability of a planned African Safari package. She has researched competing tours and has determined that a price of $4,900 is appropriate. Alice has determined the following costs for the package.

| Item | Cost |
|------|------|
| Air transport | $1,800 per person |
| Ground transportation | $360 per person |
| Lodging | $775 per person |
| Food | $750 per person |
| Tour Guides | $3,000 |
| Administrative | $1,200 |
| Miscellaneous | $4,000 |

Alice has started a worksheet to evaluate the revenues and costs for the African Safari. She wants to know how many travelers are needed to break even (revenues equal costs), how many are needed to make $5,000, and how many are needed to make $10,000. The three worksheets of the completed analysis are shown on this page and next.

**a.** Open the workbook file African Safari. Notice that Alice has already entered the tour price and an estimated number of travelers.

**b.** Spell-check and correct any errors in the workbook.

**c.** Revenue from reservations is calculated by multiplying the tour price times the number of travelers. Enter this formula into C11.

**d.** Based on Alice's cost information, air transportation is $1800 times the number of travelers. Enter this formula into B14. Enter formulas into B15, B16, and B17 for the other expenses (see table above) related to the number of travelers.

e. Enter the remaining expenses into cells B18, B19, and B20.

f. Calculate total costs in cell C21. Net revenue is the difference between revenue from reservations and total costs. Enter this formula into cell C23.

g. Format the currency values in the worksheet to Currency with no decimal places.

h. Use Goal Seek to determine the number of travelers required to just break even (Net revenue equals zero).

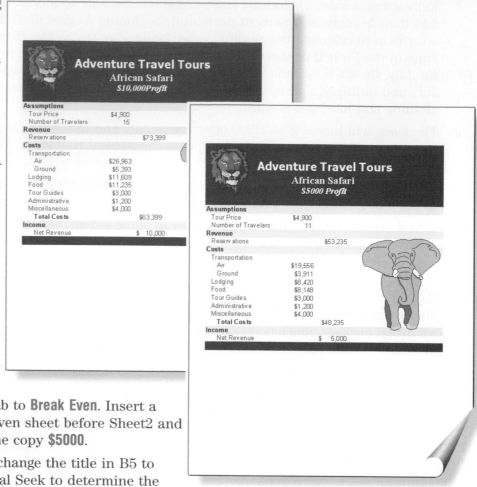

i. Rename the sheet tab to **Break Even**. Insert a copy of the Break Even sheet before Sheet2 and rename the tab of the copy **$5000**.

j. In the $5000 sheet, change the title in B5 to **$5,000 Profit**. Use Goal Seek to determine the number of travelers needed to produce a net revenue of $5,000.

k. Insert a copy of the $5000 sheet before Sheet2 and rename the tab of the copy to **$10,000**. Change the title in B5 to **$10,000 Profit**. Use Goal Seek to determine the number of travelers needed to produce a net revenue of $10,000.

l. Preview the workbook. Add a custom header that contains your name and the date center-aligned to the three sheets. Save the workbook file as African Safari Revised. Print the workbook.

**6.** Amy Marino is a college student who has just completed her first two years of her undergraduate program as a business major. In this exercise, you will calculate semester and cumulative totals and GPA for each semester. The completed worksheet for Spring 2000 is shown here

a. Open the file Grade Report. Look at the four sheets. Rename the sheet tabs **Fall 2000**, **Spring 2001**, **Fall 2001**, and **Spring 2002**.

b. You need to enter the formulas to calculate the Total Points and GPA for the four semesters. You will do this for all four sheets at the same time. Select the four sheets. In the Fall 2000 sheet, multiply the Grade by the Credits Earned to calculate Total Points for Intro to Business. Copy that formula down the column. Sum the Credits Attempted, Credits Earned, and Total Points columns and display the results in the Semester Total row.

c. In cell G13, divide the Semester Total's Total Points by the Semester Total's Credits Earned to calculate the GPA for the semester. Use what-if analysis to see what Amy's GPA would be if she had earned a 3 instead of a 2 in Western Civ. Change the grade back to a 2.

d. Look at each sheet to see that the formulas were entered and the calculations performed.

Student Name
1/11/01

### Spring 2002 Grades

| Course | Course Title | Grade | Credits Attempted | Credits Earned | Total Points | GPA |
|--------|-------------|-------|-------------------|----------------|--------------|-----|
| BIO102 | Biology II | 3 | 3 | 3 | 9 | |
| IST218 | COBOL Prog II | 4 | 3 | 3 | 12 | |
| IST227 | Systems Design | 4 | 3 | 3 | 12 | |
| IST299 | Data Proc. Projects | 4 | 3 | 3 | 12 | |
| PSY101 | Intro to Psychology | 3 | 3 | 3 | 9 | |
| | Semester Total: | | 15 | 15 | 54 | 3.60 |
| | Cumulative Total: | | 60 | 60 | 189 | 3.15 |

e. Go to cell D14 in the Fall 2000 sheet. Enter the reference formula **=D13** to copy the Semester Total Credits Attempted number to the Cumulative Total row. Copy the formula to cells E14 and F14 to calculate Credits Earned and Total Points.

f. Go to the Spring 2001 sheet and calculate a Cumulative Total for Credits Attempted by summing the Spring 2001 Semester Total and the Fall 2000 Cumulative Total. (*Hint:* You can use pointing to enter the Cumulative Totals formula.)

g. Copy that formula to the adjacent cells to calculate Cumulative Totals for Credits Earned and Total Points. Repeat this procedure on the Fall 2001 and Spring 2002 sheets.

h. Go to the Fall 2000 sheet. Select all four sheets. In cell G14, calculate the GPA for the Cumulative Total. Format the Semester Total GPA and the Cumulative Total GPA to display two decimals. Look at each sheet to see the GPA for each semester. (*Hint:* Amy's GPA at the end of the Spring 2002 semester is 3.15.) Display the Sheet tab shortcut menu and ungroup the sheets.

i. Go to the Fall 2000 sheet and preview the workbook. Add a custom header that contains your name and the date center-aligned to the sheets. Save the workbook file as Grade Report Complete. Print the Spring 2000 sheet centered horizontally on the page.

## On Your Own

**7.** In practice exercise 8 of Tutorial 1, you created a workbook for a six-month budget. Extend this workbook by adding two additional sheets. One sheet is to contain a budget for the next six months. The final sheet is to present a full year's summary using 3-D references to the values in the appropriate sheets.

Consider making a special purchase, such as a car, a new computer, or perhaps taking a trip. On a separate line below the total balance in the summary sheet, enter the amount you would need. Subtract this value from the total balance. If this value is negative, reevaluate your expenses and adjust them appropriately. Format the sheets using the features you have learned in the first three tutorials. Include a custom header on all sheets that includes your name. Preview, print, and save the workbook.

**8.** Obtain yearly income and expense data for three major sports at your college or university. In a workbook containing four sheets, record each sport's data in a separate sheet. In a fourth sheet, calculate the total income, total expenses, and net income for each sport. Also in this sheet, calculate the overall totals for income, expense, and net income. Format the sheets using the features you have learned in the first three tutorials. Include a custom header on all sheets that includes your name.

**9.** Select three stocks listed on the New York Stock Exchange. Using the Internet or the library, determine each stock's month-ending price for the past year. In a workbook containing four sheets, record each stock's prices in separate worksheets. In a fourth sheet, calculate the average, standard deviation, and maximum and minimum for each of the three stocks. Also, in the final sheet, chart the average data for the three stocks. Format the sheets using the features you have learned in the first three tutorials. Include a custom header on all sheets that includes your name.

**10.** Owning and managing a small business is a dream of many college students. Visit a local small business that interests you and ask for information showing their quarterly income and expenses over the past year. Enter the information for each quarter in separate worksheets. In a fifth sheet, show the total for the year. Include a year-to-date value in each quarterly sheet. In the last quarter sheet, select one expense and determine what value the expense would have to have been so that the net income for that quarter would have been 10 percent higher than the current level. Format the sheets using the features you have learned in the first three tutorials. Include a custom header on all sheets that include your name.

# Working Together: Linking Excel and Word

Your analysis of sales data for the first quarter has shown a steady increase in total sales. The Café owner has asked you for a copy of the forecast that shows the growth in Internet sales if a strong sales promotion is mounted. You would like to send a memo explaining this information to the owner. In addition, you want to include the worksheet and chart of the sales forecast in the memo.

All Microsoft Office applications have a common user interface such as similar commands and menu structures. In addition to these obvious features, they have been designed to work together, making it easy to share and exchange information between applications. You will learn how to share information between applications while you create the memo. Your completed document will look like that shown below.

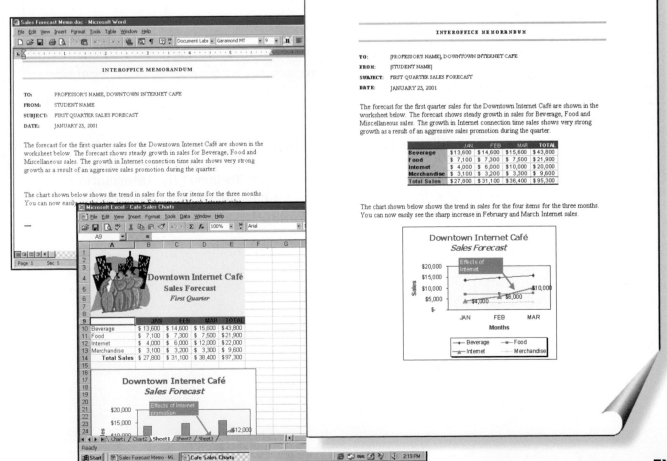

*Note:* This lab assumes that you already know how to use Word 2000 and that you have completed Tutorial 2 of Excel 2000. You will need the data file Café Sales Charts you created in Tutorial 2.

## Copying Between Applications

The memo to the manager about the analysis of the sales data has already been created using Word 2000. However, you still need to add the Excel worksheet data and charts to the memo.

**1** ■ **Start Word and open the file Sales Forecast Memo on your data disk.**

■ **In the memo header, replace [Professor's Name] with** your **instructor's name and [Student Name] with** your name.

Your screen should be similar to Figure 1.

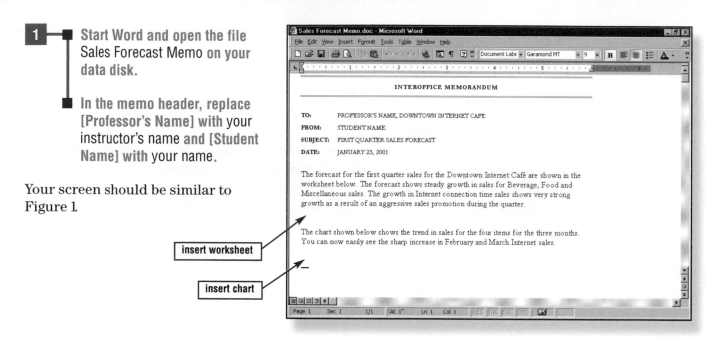

**Figure 1**

You will insert the worksheet data of the first quarter sales forecast below the first paragraph. Below the second paragraph, you will display the combination chart of sales by category. To insert the information from the Excel workbook file into the Word memo, you need to open the worksheet document.

**2** Load Excel and open the workbook file Café Sales Charts on your data disk.

■ If necessary, move to cell A9.

Your screen should be similar to Figure 2.

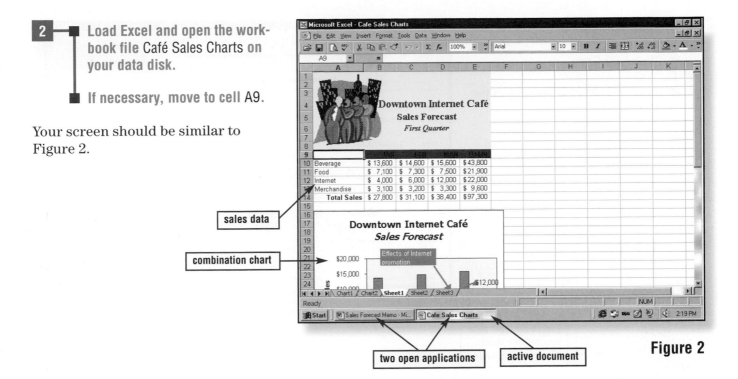

sales data

combination chart

two open applications

active document

**Figure 2**

There are now two open applications, Word and Excel. Word is open in a window behind the Excel application window. Both application buttons are displayed in the taskbar. There are also two open files, Café Sales Charts in Excel and Sales Forecast Memo in Word. Excel is the active application and Café Sales Charts is the active file.

First you will copy the worksheet data into the Word memo. While using the Excel application, you have learned how to use cut, copy, and paste to move or copy information within the same document. You can also perform these operations between documents in the same application and between documents in different applications. For example, you can copy information from a Word document and paste it into an Excel worksheet. The information is pasted in a format that the application can edit, if possible.

You want to copy the worksheet data in cells A9 through E14 into the memo.

**EXCEL 2000**

**3** ■ Select cells A9 through E14.

■ Click 🗈 Copy.

■ Click 📝 Sales Forecast Memo.doc ... in the taskbar.

■ Move to the second blank line below the first paragraph of the memo.

■ Click 📋 Paste to copy the contents of the Clipboard into the memo.

Your screen should be similar to Figure 3.

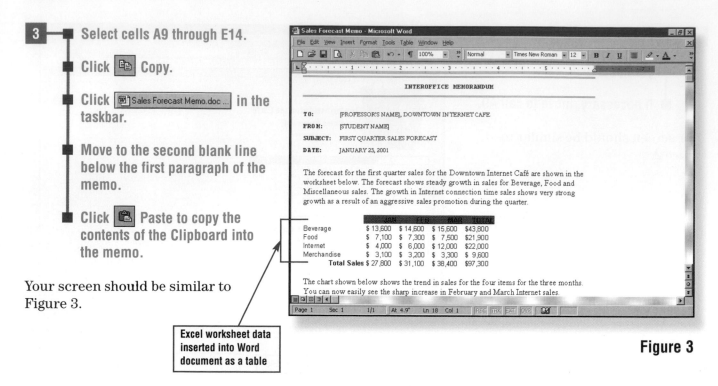

Excel worksheet data inserted into Word document as a table

**Figure 3**

The worksheet data has been copied into the Word document as a table that can be edited and manipulated within Word. Much of the formatting associated with the copied information is also pasted into the document. You think the memo would look better if the table was centered between the margins.

**4** ■ Select the entire table.

■ Click 🖻 Center.

■ Clear the selection.

Your screen should be similar to Figure 4.

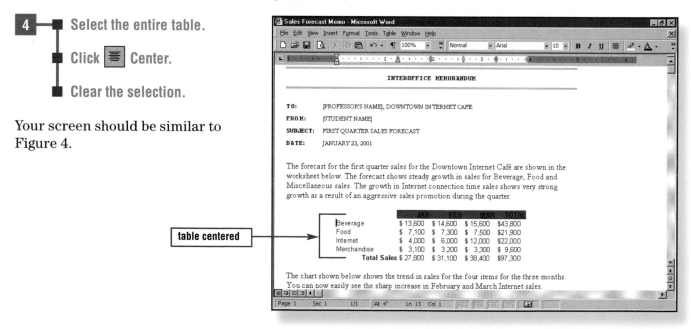

table centered

**Figure 4**

## Linking an Object to Another Application

Next you want to display the combination chart of sales trends for the four categories below the second paragraph in the memo.

**1** ■ **Switch to the Excel application and select the combination chart.**

■ **Click** 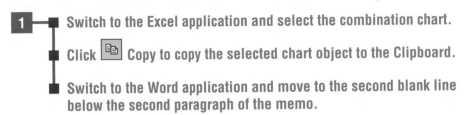 **Copy to copy the selected chart object to the Clipboard.**

■ **Switch to the Word application and move to the second blank line below the second paragraph of the memo.**

You will insert the chart object into the memo as a **linked object**. Information created in one application can also be inserted as a linked object into a document created by another application. When an object is linked, the data is stored in the **source file** (the document it was created in). A graphic representation or picture of the data is displayed in the **destination file** (the document in which the object is inserted). A connection between the information in the destination file to the source file is established by the creation of a link. The link contains references to the location of the source file and the selection within the document that is linked to the destination file.

When changes are made in the source file that affect the linked object, the changes are automatically reflected in the destination file when it is opened. This is called a **live link**. When you create linked objects, the date and time on your machine should be accurate. This is because the program refers to the date of the source file to determine whether updates are needed when you open the destination file.

By making the chart a linked object, it will be automatically updated if the source file is edited. To create a linked object,

**2** ■ **Choose Edit/Paste Special.**

■ **Select Paste Link.**

Your screen should be similar to Figure 5.

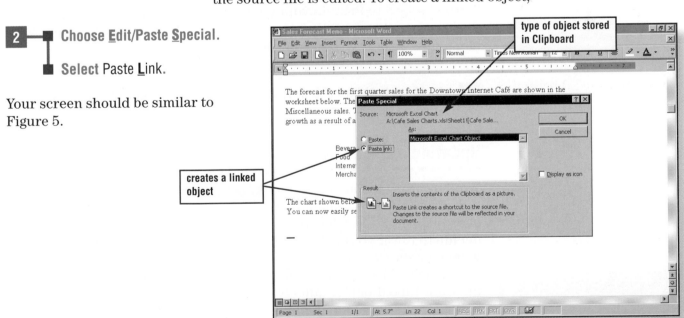

**Figure 5**

**EXCEL 2000**

The Paste Special dialog box displays the type of object contained in the Clipboard and its location in the Source area. From the As list box you select the type of format in which you want the object inserted into the destination file. The only available option for this object is as a Microsoft Excel Chart Object. The Result area describes the effect of your selections. In this case, the object will be inserted as a picture and a link will be created to the chart in the source file. Selecting the Display as Icon option changes the display of the object from a picture to an icon. Double-clicking the icon displays the object picture. The default selections are appropriate.

**3** ■ Click OK .

■ Set the Zoom to 75%.

■ Position the window so you can see both the worksheet and the chart on the page.

Your screen should be similar to Figure 6.

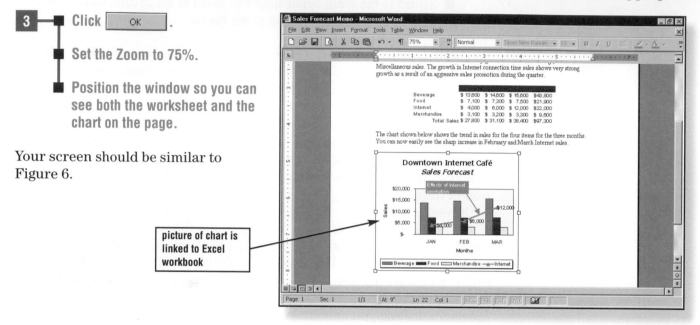

picture of chart is linked to Excel workbook

**Figure 6**

Word changed to Print Layout view and the chart object is displayed at the location of the insertion point aligned with the left margin. The object has been scaled to fit in the document.

**4** ■ Move the chart object so it is centered horizontally on the page.

## Updating a Linked Object

While reading the memo and looking at the chart, you decide to change the chart type from a combination chart to a line chart. You feel a line chart will show the sales trends for all sales items more clearly. You also decide to lower your sales expectation for Internet sales from 12,000 to 10,000 for March.

To make these changes, you need to switch back to Excel. Double-clicking on a linked object quickly switches to the open source file. If the source file is not open, it opens the file for you. If the application is not loaded, it both loads the application and opens the source file.

The menu equivalent is **E**dit/Linked **O**bject/**E**ditLink

1

- Double-click the chart object.

- Click ■ Chart Type.

- Click ■ Line chart.

- Edit the value in cell D12 to **10000**.

- Scroll the window to see both the chart and worksheet data.

Your screen should be similar to Figure 7.

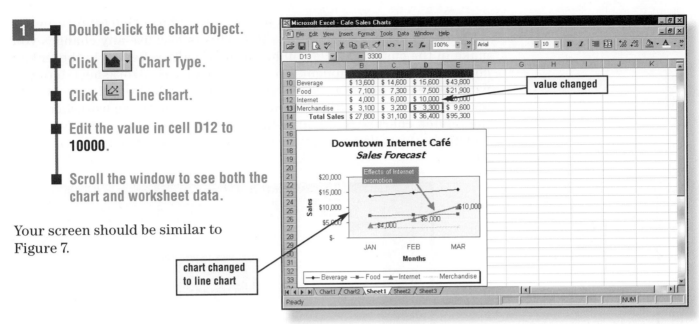

**Figure 7**

The chart type has changed to a line chart and the chart data series has been updated to reflect the change in data. Now you will switch to the memo to see what changes were made to the worksheet and chart.

2

- To see the changes made in the memo, switch to Word.

Your screen should be similar to Figure 8.

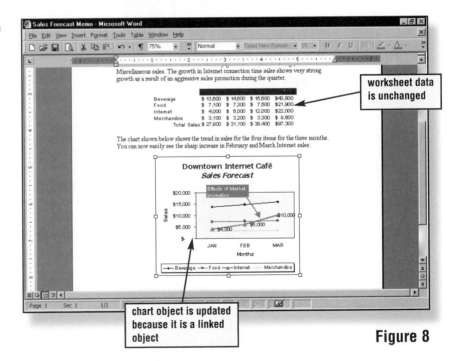

**Figure 8**

The chart in the memo reflects the change in both chart type and the change in data for the Internet sales. This is because any changes you make in the chart in Excel will be automatically reflected in the linked chart in the Word document. However, because the worksheet data is a word table and not a linked object, it does not reflect the change in data made in Excel. Normally you would want to link both the worksheet and the related chart so that both reflect the changes made to the data. You will delete the table and copy the worksheet into the memo as a linked object.

**3** ■ Select the worksheet table.

■ Choose T**a**ble/**D**elete/**T**able

■ Switch to Excel.

■ Select and copy cells A9 through E14.

■ Switch to Word.

■ Choose **E**dit/Paste **S**pecial/Paste **L**ink.

■ Select Microsoft Excel Worksheet Object as the type.

■ Click   OK   .

■ Center the linked worksheet object on the page.

Your screen should be similar to Figure 9.

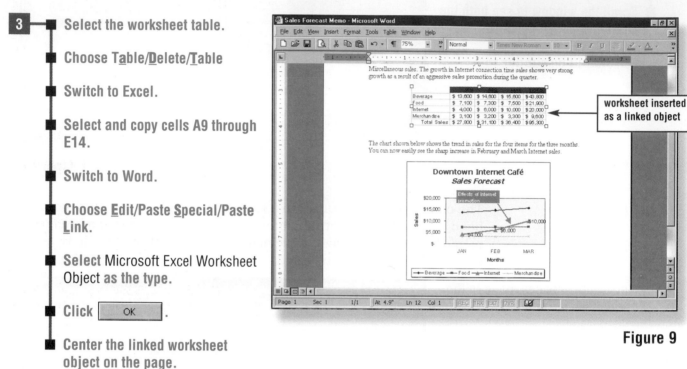

worksheet inserted as a linked object

**Figure 9**

## Applying an Autoformat

The worksheet is inserted into the memo as a linked object. However, you do not like how the formatting of the worksheet looks as a linked object in the memo. To quickly improve the appearance of the worksheet, you will apply an autoformat to the worksheet data.

An **autoformat** is a built-in combination of formats that can be applied to a range of cells. The autoformats consist of a combination of number formats, fonts and attributes, colors, patterns, borders, frames, and alignment settings.

To see both applications on your screen at the same time and watch the changes as they are made to both documents,

**1** ▪ **Right-click on a blank area of the taskbar to open the shortcut menu.**

▪ **Select** Tile **V**ertically.

Your screen should be similar to Figure 10.

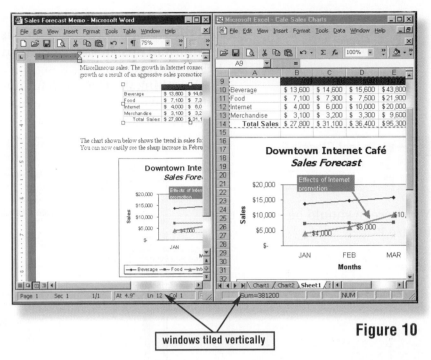

windows tiled vertically

**Figure 10**

To use an autoformat, you first specify the range you want affected by the formatting. In this case, you want to apply an autoformat to cells A9 through E14. You can select the range or you can let Excel select the range for you. To have Excel automatically select the range, the cell selector must be on any cell in the range. Excel determines that the range you want to autoformat is the range of cells that includes the active cell and is surrounded by blank cells.

**2** ▪ **Click on the Excel window to make it active.**

▪ **Move to any cell in the worksheet data.**

▪ **Choose F**o**rmat/A**utoformat

Your screen should be similar to Figure 11.

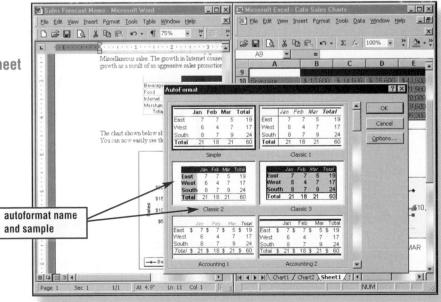

autoformat name and sample

**Figure 11**

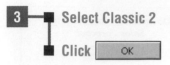

Use the None autoformat design to remove an existing autoformat.

The range A9 through E14 is correctly selected as the range to autoformat, and the AutoFormat dialog box is displayed. Samples of the 16 different autoformat designs are displayed with the names assigned to the design below the sample.

You think the Classic 2 autoformat would be appropriate for the Sales data. To format the worksheet using this layout,

**3** ■ **Select Classic 2**

■ **Click** OK

Your screen should be similar to Figure 12.

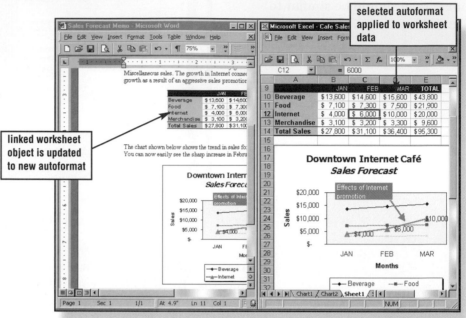

**Figure 12**

The Classic 2 autoformat has been applied to the worksheet range and the linked worksheet object in the memo has been updated. This format includes border lines of different weights, color, accounting number format with no decimal places, and adjustment of column widths to fit the entries in the selected range.

**4** ■ **Save the revised worksheet as Café Sales Linked.**

■ **Make the memo the active window.**

■ **Select Undo Tile from the taskbar shortcut menu.**

## Editing Links

Whenever a document is opened that contains links, the application looks for the source file and automatically updates the linked objects. If there are many links, updating can take a lot of time. Additionally, if you move the source file to another location, or perform other operations that may interfere with the link, your link will not work. To help with situations like these, you can edit the settings associated with links. To see how you do this,

**1** ▪ **Select the worksheet object.**

▪ **Choose Edit/Links.**

Your screen should be similar to Figure 13.

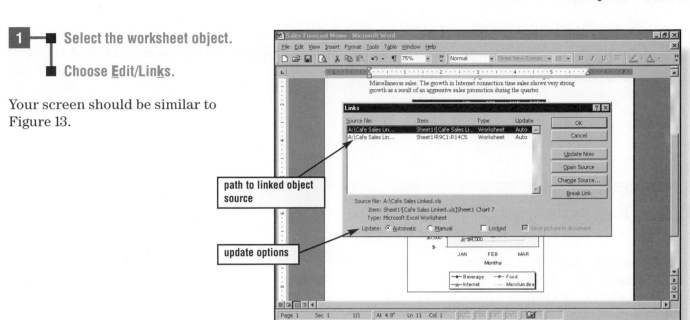

**Figure 13**

The Links dialog box displays the object path for all links in the document in the list box. The field code specifies the path and name of the source file, the range of linked cells or object name, the type of file, and the update status. Below the list box, the details for the selected link are displayed. The other options in this dialog box are described in the table below.

| Option | Effect |
|---|---|
| Automatic | Updates the linked object whenever the destination document is opened or the source file changes. This is the default. |
| Manual | The destination document is not automatically updated and you must use the Update Now command button to update the link. |
| Locked | Prevents a linked object from being updated. |
| Open Source | Opens the source document for the selected link. |
| Change Source | Used to modify the path to the source document. |
| Break Link | Breaks the connection between the source document and the active document. |

**2** ▪ Click   Cancel   .

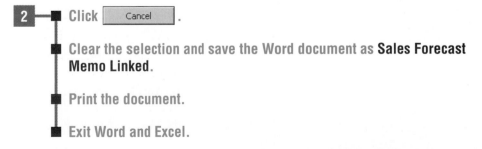

▪ **Clear the selection and save the Word document as Sales Forecast Memo Linked.**

▪ **Print the document.**

▪ **Exit Word and Excel.**

Linking documents is a very handy feature particularly in documents whose information is updated frequently. If you include a linked object in a document that you are giving to another person, make sure the user has access to the source file and application. Otherwise the links will not operate correctly.

# Key Terms

- - - - - - - - - - - - - - - - - - - - - - - - - - - - - - - - - - - - - - - - - - -

autoformat    EXW-9
destination file    EXW-5
linked object    EXW-5
live link    EXW-5
source file    EXW-5

# Command Summary

- - - - - - - - - - - - - - - - - - - - - - - - - - - - - - - - - - - - - - - - - - -

| Command | Action |
|---|---|
| Edit/Paste Special/Paste Link | Creates a link to the source document |
| Edit/Links | Modifies selected link |
| Edit/Linked Object/Edit Link | Modifies selected linked object |
| Format/Autoformat | Applies one of 16 built-in table formats to the worksheet range. |

# Hands-On Practice Exercises

- - - - - - - - - - - - - - - - - - - - - - - - - - - - - - - - - - - - - - - - -

**Step by Step**

**Rating System**
☆ Easy
☆ ☆ Moderate
☆ ☆ ☆ Difficult

**1.** Adventure Travel Tours travel agency sends a monthly status report to all subsidiary offices showing the bookings for the specialty tours offered by the company. Previously the worksheet data was printed separately from the memo. Now you want to include the worksheet in the same document as the memo.

   **a.** Load Word and open the Tour Status Report file on your data disk. Replace Student Name with **your name** on the From line in the heading.

   **b.** Load Excel and open the Adventure Travel Monthly worksheet on your data disk.

   **c.** Copy the worksheet as a linked object into the memo below the paragraph.

   **d.** Insert a new column for March in the worksheet and enter the following data for the month's bookings.

| Tour | March Data |
|------|------------|
| Tuolumne Clavey Falls | 20 |
| Costa Rica Rainforest | 4 |
| Kilimanjaro | 4 |
| Machu Picchu | 3 |
| Himalayas | 6 |
| Tanzania Safari | 6 |

   **e.** Save the worksheet as Adventure Travel Monthly March. Exit Excel.

   **f.** Center the worksheet object in the word document

   **g.** Save the Word document as March Status Report. Print the memo.

---

INTEROFFICE MEMORANDUM

TO:     ADVENTURE TRAVEL EMPLOYEES

FROM:  STUDENT NAME

SUBJECT:  TOUR STATUS REPORT

DATE:   4/1/01

The bookings to date for our upcoming specialty tours are displayed in the following table. As you can see the new white water rafting tour to below the Tuolumne Clavey Falls in California is almost full to capacity and we are considering offering a second week. Because several others are also close to capacity you may want to advise any clients who are considering one of these tours to make reservations as soon as possible.

**Adventure Travel Tours**
**Speciality Tours Status Report**

| Tour | Jan | Feb | Mar | Total | Tour Capacity |
|------|-----|-----|-----|-------|---------------|
| Tuolumne Clavey Falls | 8 | 14 | 20 | 22 | 46 |
| Costa Rica Rainforests | 5 | 9 | 4 | 14 | 36 |
| Kilimanjaro | 2 | 2 | 4 | 4 | 15 |
| Machu Picchu | 4 | 8 | 3 | 12 | 30 |
| Himalayas | 0 | 0 | 6 | 0 | 18 |
| Tanzania Safari | 4 | 3 | 6 | 7 | 21 |

**EXCEL 2000**

**2.** Karen works for a large hotel chain in the marketing department. She has recently researched hotel occupancy rates for the Phoenix area and has created a worksheet and stacked-column chart of the data. Now Karen wants to send a memo containing the chart to her supervisor.

**a.** Load Word and open the document Hotel Memo on your data disk.

**b.** In the header, replace the place-holder information in brackets with the following:

| | |
|---|---|
| TO: | **Brad Wise** |
| FROM: | **Karen Howard** |
| CC: | **[your name]** |
| RE: | **Hotel Occupancy** |

**c.** Load Excel and open the workbook file Hotel Occupancy Data. Link the column chart to below the paragraph in the Word memo. Center the chart in the memo.

**d.** You decide you need to clarify that the data for 2000 and 2001 is projected. Add a second title line **(2001 - 2002 projected)** to the chart in 12 point, italic.

**e.** Save the Word document as Hotel Occupancy. Preview and print the document. Exit Word.

**f.** Save the Excel workbook as Hotel Data Linked. Close the Excel file.

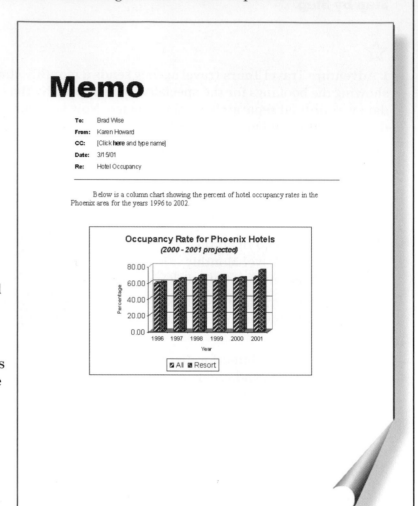

**3.** To complete this problem, you must have created the worksheet in exercise 3 of Tutorial 2. Tyler Johnson works for Books Online. He has compiled a list of the 10 best-selling children's books and created a chart comparing their price to the list price for each book. He wants to send a memo showing this information to management.

**a.** Load Word and open the Children's Book Memo file on your data disk. Enter your name on the To line in the heading.

**b.** Load Excel and open the Book List Chart worksheet on your data disk.

**c.** Copy the worksheet range B5 through D15 as a linked object into the memo below the first paragraph. Center it on the page.

**d.** Copy the chart into the memo as a linked object below the second paragraph. Reduce the chart size and move it so it fits on a single page with the worksheet. Center it on the page.

**e.** Apply an autoformat of your choice to the worksheet range B5 through D15.

**f.** Save the worksheet as Book List Linked. Exit Excel.

**g.** Save the Word document as Children's Book Memo Linked. Print the memo.

# Memo

| | |
|---|---|
| **To:** | [Click here and type name] |
| **From:** | Tyler Johnson |
| **Date:** | 1/31/99 |
| **Re:** | Top Children's Book Price Comparison |

The following table lists the top 10 best selling children's books. To increase sales in this area, we have discounted the prices of these books considerably.

| Ranking | Title | Our Price | List Price |
|---|---|---|---|
| 1 | Today I Feel Silly | $11.17 | $15.95 |
| 2 | Green Eggs & Ham | $5.59 | $7.99 |
| 3 | Chicken Soup for the Kid's Soul | $10.36 | $12.95 |
| 4 | The Suspicion, Animorphs #24 | $3.99 | $4.99 |
| 5 | The 20th Century Children's Book Treasury | $26.00 | $40.00 |
| 6 | Teletubbies Play Hide-And-Seek | $4.19 | $5.99 |
| 7 | The Hork-Bajir Chronicles | $9.07 | $12.95 |
| 8 | Cheerios Play Book | $3.49 | $4.99 |
| 9 | The Diary of Margaret Ann Brady | $6.97 | $9.95 |
| 10 | NewWay Things Work | $24.50 | $35.00 |

The chart shown below compares our discounted price to the list price for these books.

# Glossary of Key Terms

**3-D reference:** A reference to the same cell or range on multiple sheets in the same workbook.

**Absolute reference:** A cell or range reference in a formula whose location remains the same (absolute) when copied. Indicated by a $ character entered before the column letter or row number or both.

**Active cell:** The cell displaying the cell selector that will be affected by the next entry or procedure.

**Active pane:** The pane that contains the cell selector.

**Active sheet:** A sheet that contains the cell selector and that will be affected by the next action.

**Adjacent range:** A rectangular block of adjoining cells.

**Alignment:** The vertical or horizontal placement and orientation of an entry in a cell.

**Area chart:** A chart that shows trends by emphasizing the area under the curve.

**Argument:** The data used in a function on which the calculation is performed.

**Autofill:** Feature that logically repeats and extends a series.

**Autoformat:** A built-in combination of formats that can be applied to a range.

**Automatic recalculation:** The recalculation of a formula within the worksheet whenever a value in a referenced cell in the formula changes.

**Category-axis title:** A label that describes the X axis.

**Category name:** Labels displayed along the X axis in a chart to identify the data being plotted.

**Cell:** The space created by the intersection of a vertical column and a horizontal row.

**Cell selector:** The heavy border surrounding a cell in the worksheet that identifies the active cell.

**Chart:** A visual representation of data in a worksheet.

**Chart gridlines:** Lines extending from the axis lines across the plot area that make it easier to read and evaluate the chart data.

**Chart object:** One type of graphic object that is created using charting features included in Excel 2000. A chart object can be inserted into a worksheet or into a special chart sheet.

**Chart title:** Appears at the top of a chart and is used to describe the contents of the chart.

**ClipArt:** A collection of graphics that is usually bundled with a software application.

**Column:** A vertical block of cells one cell wide in the worksheet.

**Column chart:** A chart that displays data as vertical columns.

**Column letters:** The border of letters across the top of the worksheet that identifies the columns in the worksheet.

**Combination chart:** A chart type that includes mixed data markers, such as both columns and lines.

**Constant:** A value that does not change unless you change it directly by typing in another entry.

**Copy area:** The cell or cells containing the data to be copied.

**Custom dictionary:** An additional dictionary you create to supplement the main dictionary.

**Data labels:** Labels for data points or bars that show the values being plotted on a chart.

**Data marker:** Represents a data series on a chart. It can be a symbol, color, or pattern, depending upon the type of chart.

**Data series:** The numbers to be charted.

**Date numbers:** The integers assigned to the days from January 1, 1900, through December 31, 2099, that allow dates to be used in calculations.

**Destination:** The cell or range of cells that receives the data from the copy area or source.

**Destination file:** A document in which a linked object is inserted.

**Drawing object:** Object consisting of shapes such as lines and boxes that can be created using features on the Drawing toolbar.

**Embedded chart:** A chart that is inserted into another file.

**Embedded object:** Information inserted into a destination file of another application that becomes part of this file but can be edited within the destination file using the server application.

**Explode:** To separate a wedge of a pie chart slightly from the other wedges in the pie.

**Fill handle:** A small black square located in the lower-right corner of the selection that is used to create a series or copy to adjacent cells with a mouse.

**Font:** The typeface, type size, and style associated with a worksheet entry that can be selected to improve the appearance of the worksheet.

**Footer:** A line (or several lines) of text that appears at the bottom of each page just above the bottom margin.

**Format:** Formats are settings that affect the display of entries in a worksheet.

**Formatting toolbar:** A toolbar that contains buttons used to change the format of a worksheet.

**Formula:** An entry that performs a calculation.

**Formula bar:** The bar near the top of the Excel window that displays the cell contents.

**Freeze:** To fix in place on the screen specified rows or columns or both when scrolling.

**Function:** A prewritten formula that performs certain types of calculations automatically.

**Goal Seek:** Tool used to find the value needed in one cell to attain a result you want in another cell.

**Graphic:** A non-text element or object, such as a drawing or picture that can be added to a document

**Group:** An object that contains other objects.

**Header:** A line (or several lines) of text that appears at the top of each page just below the top margin.

**Heading:** Row and column entries that are used to create the structure of the worksheet and describe other worksheet entries.

**Landscape:** The orientation of the printed document so that it prints sideways across the length of the page.

**Legend:** A brief description of the symbols used in a chart that represent the data ranges.

**Line chart:** A chart that represents data as a set of points along a line.

**Linked object:** Information created in a source file from one application and inserted into a destination file of another application while maintaining a link between files.

**Live link:** A linked object that automatically reflects in the destination document any changes made in the source document when the destination document is opened.

**Main dictionary:** The dictionary included with Office 2000.

**Merged cell:** A cell made up of several selected cells combined into one.

**Minimal recalculation:** The recalculation of only the formulas in a worksheet that are affected by a change of data.

**Mixed reference:** A cell address that is part absolute and part relative.

**Name box:** The area located on the left side of the formula bar that provides information about the selected item such as the reference of the active cell.

**Nonadjacent range:** Cells or ranges that are not adjacent but are included in the same selection.

**Number:** A cell entry that contains any of the digits 0 to 9 and any of the special characters + = ( ) , . / $ % E e.

**Number formats:** Affect how numbers look onscreen and when printed.

**Object:** An element such as a text box that can be added to a workbook and that can be selected, sized, and moved.

**Operand:** A value on which a numeric formula performs a calculation.

**Order of precedence:** Order in which calculations are preformed and can be overridden by the use of parentheses.

**Pane:** A division of the worksheet window, either horizontal or vertical, through which different areas of the worksheet can be viewed at the same time.

**Paste area:** The cells or range of cells that receive the data from the copy area or source.

**Picture:** An illustration such as a scanned photograph.

**Pie chart:** A chart that compares parts to the whole. Each value in the data range is a wedge of the pie (circle).

**Plot area:** The area of the chart bounded by the axes.

**Portrait:** The orientation of the printed document so that it prints across the width of the page.

**Range:** A selection consisting of two or more cells in a worksheet.

**Reference:** The column letter and row number of a cell.

**Relative reference:** A cell or range reference that automatically adjusts to the new location in the worksheet when the formula is copied.

**Row:** A horizontal block of cells one cell high in the worksheet.

**Row numbers:** The border of numbers along the left side of the worksheet that identifies the rows in the worksheet.

**Sans serif font:** A font, such as Arial or Helvetica, that does not have a flair at the base of each letter.

**Selection handles:** Small boxes surrounding a selected object that are used to size the object.

**Selection rectangle:** Border around selected object indicating it can be sized or moved.

**Series formula:** A formula that links a chart object to the source worksheet.

**Serif font:** A font, such as Times New Roman, that has a flair at the base of each letter.

**Sheet reference:** Used in references to other worksheets and consists of the name of the sheet enclosed in quotes and is separated from the cell reference by an exclamation point.

**Sheet tab:** On the bottom of the workbook window, the tabs where the sheet names appear.

**Sizing handle:** Box used to size a selected object.

**Source:** The cell or range of cells containing the data you want to copy.

**Source file:** The document that stores the data for the linked object.

**Spell-checking:** Feature that locates misspelled words and proposes correction.

**Spreadsheet:** A rectangular grid of rows and columns used to enter data.

**Stack:** The order in which objects are added in layers to the worksheet.

**Stacked-column chart:** A chart that displays the data values as columns stacked upon each other.

**Standard toolbar:** A toolbar that contains buttons used to complete the most frequently used menu commands.

**Style:** A named combination of formats that can be applied to a selection.

**Syntax:** Rules of structure for entering all functions.

**Tab scroll buttons:** Located to the left of the sheet tabs, they are used to scroll sheet tabs right or left.

**Text:** A cell entry that contains text, numbers, or any other special characters.

**Text box:** A rectangular object in which you type text.

**Title:** In a chart, descriptive text that explains the contents of the chart.

**Typeface:** The appearance and shape of characters. Some common typefaces are Roman and Courier.

**Value axis:** Y axis of a chart that usually contains numerical values.

**Value axis title:** A label that describes the values on the Y axis.

**Variable:** The resulting value of a formula that changes if the data it depends on changes.

**What-if analysis:** A technique used to evaluate what effect changing one or more values in formulas has on other values in the worksheet.

**Word wrap:** Feature that automatically determines when to begin the next line of text.

**Workbook:** The file in which you work and store sheets created in Excel 2000.

**Workbook window:** A window that displays an open workbook file.

**Worksheet:** Similar to a financial spreadsheet in that it is a rectangular grid of rows and columns used to enter data.

**Workspace:** The area of the Excel 2000 application window where workbook windows are displayed.

**X axis:** The bottom boundary line of a chart.

**Y axis:** The left boundary line of a chart.

**Z axis:** The left boundary line of a 3-D chart.

# Command Summary

| Command | Shortcut | Toolbar | Action |
|---|---|---|---|
| **F**ile/**O**pen <file name> | Ctrl + O | | Opens an existing workbook file |
| **F**ile/**C**lose | | X | Closes open workbook file |
| **F**ile/**S**ave <file name> | Ctrl + S | | Saves current file on disk using same file name |
| **F**ile/Save **A**s <file name> | | | Saves current file on disk using a new file name |
| **F**ile/Page Set**u**p/Header/Footer | | | Adds header and/or footer |
| **F**ile/Print Pre**v**iew | | | Displays worksheet as it will appear when printed |
| **F**ile/**P**rint | Ctrl + P | | Prints a worksheet |
| **F**ile/**P**rint/**E**ntire Workbook | | | Prints all the sheets in a workbook |
| **F**ile/Propert**i**es | | | Displays information about a file |
| **F**ile/E**x**it | | X | Exits Excel 2000 |
| **E**dit/**U**ndo | Ctrl + Z | | Undoes last editing or formatting change |
| **E**dit/**R**edo | Ctrl + Y | | Restores changes after using Undo |
| **E**dit/**C**opy | Ctrl + C | | Copies selected data to Clipboard |
| **E**dit/**P**aste | Ctrl + V | | Pastes selections stored in Clipboard |
| **E**dit/Paste **S**pecial/Paste **L**ink | | | Creates a link to the source document |
| **E**dit/Edit Lin**k**s | | | Modifies selected link |
| **E**dit/Linked **O**bject/**E**dit Link | | | Modifies selected linked object |
| **E**dit/F**i**ll | | | Fills selected cells with contents of source cell |
| **E**dit/Cle**a**r/**C**ontents | Delete | | Clears cell contents |
| **E**dit/**D**elete/Entire **R**ow | | | Deletes selected rows |
| **E**dit/**D**elete/Entire **C**olumn | | | Deletes selected columns |
| **E**dit/**M**ove or Copy Sheet | | | Moves or copies selected sheet |
| **V**iew/**T**oolbars | | | Displays or hides selected toolbar |
| **V**iew/**Z**oom | | 100% | Changes magnification of window |

| Command | Shortcut | Toolbar | Action |
|---|---|---|---|
| **I**nsert/Copied C**e**lls | | | Inserts row and copies text from Clipboard |
| **I**nsert/**R**ows | | | Inserts a blank row |
| **I**nsert/**C**olumns | | | Inserts a blank column |
| **I**nsert/C**h**art | | 📊 | Inserts chart into worksheet |
| **I**nsert/**F**unction | ⇧Shift + F3 | *f*ₓ | Inserts a function |
| **I**nsert/**P**icture/**F**rom File | | | Inserts picture at insertion point from disk |
| F**o**rmat/Cells/Number/Currency | | $ | Applies Currency format to selection |
| F**o**rmat/C**e**lls/Number/Accounting | | | Applies Accounting format to selection |
| F**o**rmat/C**e**lls/Number/Date | | | Applies Date format to selection |
| F**o**rmat/C**e**lls/Number/Percent | | | Applies Percent format to selection |
| F**o**rmat/C**e**lls/Number/Decimal places | | ←.0 .0→ | Increases or decreases the number of decimal places associated with a number value |
| F**o**rmat/C**e**lls/Alignment/**H**orizontal/Left (Indent) | | ≣ | Left-aligns entry in cell space |
| F**o**rmat/C**e**lls/Alignment/**H**orizontal/Center | | ≣ | Center-aligns entry in cell space |
| F**o**rmat/C**e**lls/Alignment/**H**orizontal/Right | | ≣ | Right-aligns entry in cell space |
| F**o**rmat/C**e**lls/Alignment/**H**orizontal/Left (Indent)/1 | | 讀 | Left-aligns and indents cell entry one space |
| F**o**rmat/C**e**lls/Alignment/**H**orizontal/Center Across Selection | | 讀 | Centers cell contents across selected cells |
| F**o**rmat/C**e**lls/**F**ont | | | Changes font and attributes of cell contents |
| F**o**rmat/C**e**lls/Font/F**o**nt Style/Bold | Ctrl + B | **B** | Bolds selected text |
| F**o**rmat/C**e**lls/Font/F**o**nt Style/Italic | Ctrl + I | *I* | Italicizes selected text |
| F**o**rmat/C**e**lls/Font/**U**nderline/Single | Ctrl + U | U | Underlines selected text |
| F**o**rmat/C**e**lls/Font/**C**olor | | **A** ▾ | Adds color to text |
| F**o**rmat/C**e**lls/Patterns/**C**olor | | ✎ ▾ | Adds color to cell background |
| F**o**rmat/**R**ow/He**i**ght | | | Changes height of selected row |
| F**o**rmat/**C**olumn/**W**idth | | | Changes width of columns |
| F**o**rmat/**C**olumn/**A**utofit Selection | | | Changes column width to match widest cell entry |
| F**o**rmat/S**h**eet/**R**ename | | | Renames sheet |
| F**o**rmat/**A**utoformat | | | Applies one of 16 built-in table formats to the worksheet range |
| F**o**rmat/**S**tyle/**S**tyle name/Currency | | $ | Applies currency style to selection |

| Command | Shortcut | Toolbar | Action |
|---|---|---|---|
| Fo**r**mat/**S**tyle/**St**yle name/Percent | | % | Changes cell style to display percentage |
| Fo**r**mat/**Se**lected Data Series/Data Labels | Ctrl + 1 | | Inserts data labels into chart |
| Fo**r**mat/**Se**lected Legend | Ctrl + 1 | | Changes legend |
| Fo**r**mat/**Se**lected Chart Title | Ctrl + 1 | | Changes format of selected chart title |
| Fo**r**mat/**Se**lected Data Series | Ctrl + 1 | | Changes format of selected data series |
| Fo**r**mat/**Se**lected Object | | | Changes format of embedded objects |
| **C**hart/Chart **T**ype | | | Changes type of chart |
| **C**hart/Chart **O**ptions | | | Adds options to chart |
| **C**hart/**L**ocation | | | Moves chart from worksheet to chart sheet |
| **T**ools/**S**pelling | F7 | | Spell-checks worksheet |
| **T**ools/**G**oal Seek | | | Adjusts value in specified cell until a formula dependent on that cell reaches specified result |
| **W**indow/Un**f**reeze | | | Unfreezes window panes |
| **W**indow/**F**reeze Panes | | | Freezes top and/or leftmost panes |
| **W**indow/**S**plit | | | Divides window into four panes at active cell |
| **W**indow/Remove **S**plit | | | Removes split bar from active worksheet |

# Index

# Notes